THE INFORMATION-BASED CORPORATION
STAKEHOLDER ECONOMICS AND THE TECHNOLOGY INVESTMENT

THE
INFORMATION-BASED
CORPORATION
STAKEHOLDER ECONOMICS AND
THE TECHNOLOGY INVESTMENT

David R. Vincent
The Information Group, Inc.
Santa Clara, California

Dow Jones-Irwin
Homewood, Illinois 60430

This publication is designed to provide accurate and
authoritative information in regard to the subject matter
covered. It is sold with the understanding that the
publisher is not engaged in rendering legal, accounting, or
other professional service. If legal advice or other expert
assistance is required, the services of a competent
professional person should be sought.

*From a Declaration of Principles jointly adopted by a Committee
of the American Bar Association and a Committee of Publishers.*

Project editor: Joan A. Hopkins
Production manager: Ann Cassady
Jacket design: Image House
Compositor: Carlisle Communications, Ltd.
Typeface: 11/13 Century Schoolbook
Printer: Arcata Graphics/Kingsport

Library of Congress Cataloging-in-Publication Data

Vincent, David R.
    The information-based corporation : stakeholder economics and the
technology investment / David R. Vincent.
        p.   cm.
    Bibliography: p.
    Includes index.
    ISBN 0-87094-684-6
    1. Information resources management.   I. Title.
T58.64.V46   1990
658.4'038—dc20   89–11964
                                                                          CIP

Printed in the United States of America
  2 3 4 5 6 7 8 9 0 KP 6 5 4 3 2 1 0

CONTENTS

PART 2 DETERMINING ORGANIZATIONAL AND TECHNOLOGY INVESTMENT ACTIONS

PREFACE

This book is targeted at senior executives who are rebuilding their corporations so that they can survive in a global economy. The demand for survival is embodied in relationships with people and organizations that have a vested interest in a corporation's success. Simplified organizations and creative uses of information technology are the keys to corporate survival and will be illustrated in the book based on examples from The Information Group's consulting experience.

You've read about and experienced the effects of a globalized economy, whether you're doing business in North America or internationally. In addition to the everyday market pressures from domestic competition, foreign competitors are vying for your share of the North American market. In overseas markets, you're finding that international competition can identify and react to market needs faster than ever. If you think the heat's on now, you haven't seen anything yet. Things are going to get hotter in ways that you can't even imagine now. The changes in the economy are real; they're here to stay.

There are other forces impacting your company as well. Paramount among these is the increased demand for information in your business. Whether you're in banking, manufacturing, fast foods, distribution, or some other arena, information will differentiate your product or service from your competitor's. Information will also contribute to your competitive posture on the supply side of your business. This book will help you understand how information and information technology can contribute to your company's survival in a new business era.

The performance of your company depends on how well you utilize the three resources of any business: its capital, people, and information. This book will show you how information technology can leverage these three resources to greater advantage.

As always, the success of your business depends on how well you satisfy the needs of your customers while increasing the wealth of your investors. But long-term business success goes beyond satisfying just your customers and investors. Long-term success depends on dealing fairly with the needs of all the people who have a vested interest in the success of your business. These people include, in addition to your investors and customers, your employees, suppliers, regulators, community, management, and even your competitors.

This book will show you ways that information technology can enhance these essential corporate relationships to bring about improved financial performance for the corporation.

The book has three parts that show you

- How to discover the leverage points for your business.
- How to determine organizational and technology investment actions.
- How to plan for the transition from where you are now to where you need to be.

The book's format is based on a well-established and straightforward approach to business planning. You will be able to apply the concepts to your company's planning process, even though some of the terminology may be slightly different.

ACKNOWLEDGMENTS

First, many thanks to two trusted friends and colleagues in The Information Group: Dr. Jack A. Hamilton, who helped me immeasurably with many of the concepts and ideas in this book; and C. H. "Hutch" Hutchinson, who gave me the opportunity early in my business career to experience the unfolding global economy.

Thanks also to the hundreds of executives with whom we've worked to build their new, information-based organizations. It's these executives who have provided us with the opportunity to discover how corporations and information technology really can work together to build the corporation of the future.

And finally, deepest appreciation to my wife, Judy, and my daughter, Amber, for their constant support and for keeping the home fires burning.

PART 1

DISCOVERING THE CORPORATION'S LEVERAGE POINTS

CHAPTER 1

INTRODUCTION: The New Management Challenge

The new challenge to American management comes from a global economy where every producer could potentially be competing in a pure commodity market that will see little or no growth in the next decade.

Such electronic technology products as televisions, video cassette recorders, calculators, and even personal computers have become virtual commodities with little product differentiation or manufacturing added value built into the product. To the consumer, one is quite like another. Thus consumers will make their buys based on price and quality.

The companies that produce these electronic goods compete for market share and strive for advantage based on economies of scale for low cost and a reputation for quality. Not many companies will survive in the long run under these conditions.

While America remains the largest single market for these products, they are no longer manufactured here. Production facilities have moved from America to Japan, to Taiwan, Korea, Hong Kong, and on to Southeast Asia. If this trend continues, these products will ultimately be manufactured in China with its huge, untapped human resource, and, because of these consumer products, America will never be able to reverse its trading deficit.

To overcome the exodus of commodity production facilities, American industry must find ways to create regional advantages. For example, in the chemical and detergents industry, regional advantages exist because of the cost of shipping water.

The water content of these commodities is so high that the cost of transportation almost dictates regional production. Likewise, in the electric utility business, there's a physical limit to how far power can be transmitted.

Even Japanese automakers found limitations on what they can export into a market without creating regional production, assembly, and service facilities. In the case of North America, the United States and Canada have erected nonmarket barriers such as government regulation and national pride ("buy American"). As a result, Japanese automobile manufacturers are building manufacturing facilities here to support the continued expansion of their business in our market.

There's also a limit to how far commodity goods can serve the needs of a particular economy. For example, value-added retailers, who add value to the basic product through their special relationship with buyers, are becoming an integral part of the distribution and sales for computing products.

Thus, the ability to rise above pure commodity competition is based largely on focusing corporate energies on strengthening and enhancing corporate relationships. To do this, companies need to simplify their organizational structures for greater effectiveness. In our work with our clients, The Information Group has found that proper use of information technology is the key to simplifying organizations, building consensus and corporate focus, and integrating the activities of the various business functions. As a result, our view of the American management challenge centers on how we can create value and advantage with the information-based organization supported by the effective use of technology.

CORPORATE RELATIONSHIPS

Corporate relationships provide the context in which information technology can improve corporate performance, add value, and realize advantages. This book focuses first and foremost on corporate relationships. These are the corporate leverage points. Information technology is the lever. Just as a lever and a fulcrum can magnify the strength of human muscle, information technology can amplify corporate influence on its relationships.

For example, integrating the supplier-customer relationship provides an opportunity for competitive advantage. The best known examples of this are American Hospital Supply (AHS) and American Airlines (AA), which forged special relationships using creative applications of information technology. AHS and AA understood the needs and potential of a special corporate relationship: the relationship with the customer. They used information technology in innovative ways to satisfy the need and to build on the potential of this relationship.

AHS captured increased market share when it put its customers online with its order entry system. This allowed the hospitals served by AHS to order all their supplies through the AHS system. Because of the special relationship AHS enjoyed with its customer hospitals, it realized an advantageous bargaining position with the companies whose supplies AHS distributed.

AA's famous Sabre reservations system let travel agents schedule all airlines through the AA system. The Sabre system generated a great deal of controversy because it listed AA's scheduled flights first. Other airlines blamed AA for discriminating against them. Braniff Airlines contended that their bankruptcy was a result of the Sabre system.

AA's superior Sabre system has become the preferred travel agent system. Its cost effectiveness and accuracy enable travel agents to serve their customers well and to make profits in a tough business. Because of this special relationship with travel agents, AA has become a preferred, and highly profitable, airline.

AA's advantage through Sabre of being the preferred carrier has long since passed. But, it almost gained a $650 million advantage through allowing other airlines to buy a 50 percent share in Sabre.

THE IMPACT OF INFORMATION TECHNOLOGY

You can use information technology to improve your corporation's financial performance by

1. Replacing people who perform repetitive tasks.
2. Amplifying people's mental capabilities.
3. Building new organizational and economic corporate structures.

In all three cases, the potential result is greater productivity, lower costs, and increased value.

During the past 30 years, information technology has been synonymous with cost reduction. However, in the 1980s more and more companies have increased employee and management productivity by providing the right information in the right time frame for making decisions.

Now, information technology is having a different impact. It is changing social and economic systems. It is flattening the corporate organization and bringing new focus to entrepreneurial teams. This book shows how information technology enables people at low levels of the organization to make key decisions, thus eliminating the need for large numbers of middle managers. Furthermore, it shows how information technology provides people from disparate corporate functions with the information they need to form teams for achieving strategic business goals.

In this book, you will see how clearly defined corporate strategy supported by information technology will enable your company to achieve unity of both purpose and action. You will see how information technology can be used to form internal partnerships between disparate corporate functions that focus on the company's relationships with external entities such as customers, investors, and suppliers. These partnerships result in improved corporate performance.

INFORMATION AS A CORPORATE ASSET

This book demonstrates why management today must focus on value as well as cost. Information is a commodity that can add value to your business, or it can remain buried in your expenses and add nothing. Your information investment is comprised of both labor and information technology, labor being of greater magnitude in terms of cost. This means that your company needs to rethink how people are used and how information technology can improve their productivity.

Adam Smith, in his book, *The Wealth of Nations,* described two kinds of capital: fixed and circulating. Circulating capital, such as money, precious metals, commodities, and inventories, is shown on balance sheets as current assets. Fixed capital, such as land, buildings, and equipment, is shown on balance sheets as fixed assets.

Today's business leaders are expanding Smith's economic views to include a new commodity: information. Information is a special kind of circulating capital. Economists today are less likely to view the value of a corporation in terms of its traditional assets and liabilities. With the emerging view that information has value, we need new management paradigms for the use of information and information technology to create corporate value.

THE CHANGING USE OF LABOR

Table 1–1 gives an estimate of labor distribution in our economy over time.[1] This table reflects the massive shift that took place when we moved from an agrarian to an industrial economy. Note the spectacular transformation of agricultural work that allows only 3 percent of the 1988 work force to feed the other 96 percent. In addition to feeding ourselves, our agricultural sector produces surpluses and exports sufficient to feed other countries.

A similar transformation is taking place in the industrial sector. Industrial blue-collar jobs are declining in the industrial sector while information-based jobs are increasing. By the end of the next decade, two-thirds of the people employed will be working with information.

TABLE 1–1
Labor Utilization

	1700	1800	1900	1988	1995
Agriculture	70%	65%	40%	3%	3%
Manufacturing	10	15	40	26	15
Service	15	15	15	15	15
Information	5	5	5	56	67
Total	100%	100%	100%	100%	100%

INFORMATION: A PART OF DURABLE GOODS

Labor usage is no longer directly linked with the production of automobiles or basic materials. In his recent book *Megatrends,* John Naisbitt portrayed manufacturing and basic metal industries as sunset, or low-growth, industries as compared to the information-driven industries that will experience high growth.[2] The implication is that future U.S. industries will produce more information-based products than traditional durable goods. Naisbitt stretches his point a bit too far. For example, automobile manufacturers such as Ford, Chrysler, and General Motors are designing automobiles that have more information content. Electronic maps, built-in computers, and a greater degree of automation for drivers are ways that manufacturers are building more and more information into today's automobiles.

Nevertheless, our economy depends on the production of basic durable goods. We can't hope to eliminate our trade deficit unless we both produce more of the durable goods we consume and also favorably compete in international durable goods markets. To accomplish this, we need to develop a reputation for quality as the Japanese and the Germans have.

The greatest deficiency in American manufacturing today is that of product quality. Quality and the value-added use of information are, in many cases, synonymous. By investing in information technology that enables workers and managers to focus on product quality, corporations are demonstrating that world-class quality is achievable.

Frost, Inc., a Michigan manufacturer of conveyer rollers, has 60 percent of the world market for its product. It is the price leader in Japan. Chad Frost, the CEO of the company, invested in information technology to the point that every employee has a terminal with access to statistical information on production and quality. This has enabled workers to monitor their own production and quality. The result is a high-quality, cost-effective product. An investment in quality includes a significant investment in information and information technology.

A larger issue regarding today's labor market is the fact that it now requires fewer blue-collar workers to produce an automobile. With greater emphasis on the information content of an automobile, information-based jobs are replacing semi-skilled positions. As a result, the direct-labor component is becoming a much smaller percentage of the total cost of production. On a direct-labor basis, this will allow us to compete with countries with lower labor costs.

At the same time, we need to better understand the nature of information-based jobs. Most information work is conveniently lumped into overhead. This book takes a look at information work and the new rules required to achieve a competitive added value. U.S. products will contain a larger element of information technology and will be built by automated processes driven by information transfer.

This phenomenon is not just happening in the automobile industry. For that matter, it is not just happening in the manufacturing sector. Financial service industries are paring their head counts to be more competitive. Banks are merging and consolidating to offer a greater variety of services in a more geographically dispersed market. At the same time, they are making greater investments in information technology, thus eliminating significant numbers of clerical and middle-management jobs.

The same is true in the communications industry. The divestiture of the Regional Bell operating companies by AT&T has resulted in personnel reductions at all the surviving companies.

As this shift in labor usage occurs, what happens to displaced workers?

Ideally, the shift in the use of labor would be matched by the redeployment of an adequately trained labor force. In the short run, this is wishful thinking. Much of what we are experiencing is indeed the loss of jobs as a result of technology. Our economy is providing an increasing number of jobs. But, they are different jobs. The current mismatch between the products of our educational system and these different jobs is a threat to our national productivity. Filling these jobs requires more appropriate education for those being displaced as well as for those who will enter the job market for the first time.

THE SHIFT TO AN INFORMATION-BASED ECONOMY

The shift from an industrial economy to an information-based economy will have a major impact on the way our businesses value labor. It will also have a major impact on the way that information-oriented output is valued. In the manufacturing environment, labor is traditionally viewed as a part of the cost of goods sold. Thus, labor is carried as an asset in the inventory account. The inventory process then matches current and future revenue (cash flow) to cost of goods sold (the manufactured goods distributed and sold in the market). This method of accounting reinforces the management emphasis on reducing the labor component in goods manufactured in the United States so that U.S. exports can compete in the world market.

On the other hand, accountants treat the increasing investment in information workers (and equipment, facilities, etc.) as a routine expense item. Information investment is neither inventoried nor capitalized as is labor in the manufacturing environment. Consequently, the benefits realized from the information investment may or may not be matched with revenue. This causes management to make decisions based on the current profit squeeze. It discourages management from investing in proper, top-down, decision-oriented, information-based systems that will favorably impact the return on investment over a longer period of time.

INFORMATION AS A TRANSFORMING RESOURCE

Walter B. Wriston, former chairman of Citicorp, addressed a March 1987 conference in New York sponsored by the Financial Executives Institute's Committee on Information Management. His comments focused on a central theme:

> In the Industrial Age, we used electrical and fossil fuel energy to transform natural resources into goods and services. In the Information Age, information is the transforming resource.

The information contained in today's products outweighs the natural resource content in value. An $8.00 microchip contains less than $.50 of natural resources. The value of the design, engineering, logistics, and automation of an automobile has displaced much of the material value. Even the total cost of an automobile is now less than 20 percent direct labor.

To harness the potential of information as a transforming resource, we need to better understand how to measure its value to a business, its customers, and its investors. To achieve this understanding, we must go back to economic basics and develop new measures of the impact of information technology.

ENDNOTES

1. This approximation is based on data from *Employment and Earnings,* U.S. Bureau of Labor Statistics, Adam Smith's *The Wealth of Nations,* and John E. Pfeiffer's *The Emergence of Society.*

   The January 1989 issue of *Employment and Earnings* published by the U.S. Department of Labor, Bureau of Labor Statistics, includes the base data. The labor categories are shown on page 36. The categories of the table may be correlated to the categories in the *E & E* report as follows:

Table	E & E Report
Agricultural	Farming, forestry, and fishing
Manufacturing	Precision production, craft and repair
	Operators, fabricators, and laborers
Service	Service occupations
Information	Managerial and professional specialty
	Technical, sales, and administrative support

2. John Naisbitt, *Megatrends* (New York: Warner Books, 1982).

CHAPTER 2

BACK TO BASICS:
New Ways to Measure
the Economic Impact
of Information Technology

Is management's fascination with the promise of information technology (IT) over? Recent studies show dwindling or, in some cases, negative returns on IT investments made in the late 1970s and early 1980s. A recent working paper from MIT's Management in the 1990's Program reports that corporations would have earned a better return by investing the same money in non-IT capital such as production equipment.[1] A Morgan Stanley economist claims that in the service industry, many large investments in IT have resulted in decreased productivity.[2]

Many senior executives feel let down by their IT organizations. And well they should. They were often led to believe that throwing technology at problems would guarantee results. It hasn't.

Nevertheless, while some companies disparage their investments in information technology, others foresee that information technology still has enormous potential for financial return. Some corporations are realizing significant performance gains by adroitly balancing the mix of strategy, management skill, and information technology.

During the next decade, business corporations will be the crucible of change in industrialized countries. Global competition requires corporations to replace obsolete, top-heavy management structures with lean, energetic, and flexible organizations, and IT will play a major role in that change. To achieve this, forward-thinking corporations are simplifying their capital structures and decentralizing decision making. Information technology makes new forms of capital and organizational management possible.

THE ENTREPRENEURIAL ORGANIZATION

During the industrial revolution, centralization and specialization produced economies of scale. Hundreds, and sometimes thousands, of people were gathered into assembly-line or specialized functions. The corporation added layers upon layers of management to oversee mountains of detail.

In the information age, computers are making middle managers obsolete. In the corporate hierarchy that is the legacy of the industrial age, there are three levels of activity:[3]

1. Executive management—possibilities-oriented activities including new forms of corporate relationships, strategic direction, the driving force, and corporate beliefs and philosophy.
2. Middle management—action-oriented activities that interpret executive management directions and strategies and build action plans.
3. Workers—response-to-request activities that result in specific tasks.

In megacorporations such as AT&T, middle management served the role of interpreting strategy, building plans of action, and communicating tasks downward in the organization. This required many layers of management. The low productivity of this extensively hierarchical organization became apparent at AT&T after it was ordered to divest itself of its regional operating companies. One third of AT&T employees—100,000 people—was fired. Most of these people were administrators or middle managers.

Information technology enables executive management to communicate down into the organization, eliminating some of the need for extensive interpretation of policies. IT also enables employees at the bottom of the organization to assume more responsibility. Business analysts refer to this phenomenon as the *flattening* of the organization.

The industrial age required large numbers of middle managers to interpret and relay information. Today, they are being squeezed out of the organization. Senior management is pushing accountability and authority down the organizational ladder. The result is smaller, highly responsive, and flexible entrepreneurial units.

The corporation that uses information technology to leverage the efforts of these small entrepreneurial units will position itself to survive in today's global economy. Corporations that don't take advantage of this leverage will die.

Ironically, new management models reflect a very old form of organization: that of the hunter-gatherer tribe. The optimal number for members of a hunter-gatherer tribe was about 30 people. More people caused the tribe to split. A tribe was a highly communications-efficient, highly mobile group. More than 30 people produced a serious breakdown in efficiency and mobility.

The same principle applies to today's organizations. Corporations that have structured themselves along the lines of small, tribe-like entrepreneurial units have found new efficiencies and mobility. At the same time, large corporations cannot operate simply as a collection of independent tribes. The tribal-sized groups require a corporate infrastructure to integrate and align team efforts with the overall direction of the corporation. Information technology makes this integration possible.

These tribal-sized groups represent the front line of today's streamlined business organization. For example, Jan Carlzon, president of Scandinavian Airlines, refers to pilots, flight and ground crews, baggage handlers, ticketing agents, and other publicly visible employees as making up the *front line* of his company. These people work as teams (or tribes, if you will) at each airport. The front line has the opportunity to excel every day in the eyes of the customer.

In airline companies, the front line can't operate effectively without an extensive information technology investment. Carlzon feels strongly that top and middle management must support the front line by enabling them to make decisions at the lowest level. At Scandinavian Airlines, this means giving the front line the necessary information and discretion to take whatever action a situation requires.[4]

General Bill Creech has achieved worldwide recognition for his radical ideas on decentralized management. In 1978, General Creech took over command of the Tactical Air Command (TAC) of the U.S. Air Force. At that time, TAC was a huge bureaucracy of 115,000 people. The performance was marginal. Fifty percent of the aircraft couldn't fly. There was one death per 1,300 flying hours. The sortie rate had been declining at a 7.8 percent compounded annual rate for the past 10 years. It took an average of four hours to get a part to an inoperable aircraft.

In 1984, when General Creech left TAC, 80 percent of the aircraft could fly. The rate of deaths had declined to one per 6,000 hours of flying. The sortie rate between 1978 and 1983 rose at an 11.2 percent compounded annual rate. It took an average of only eight minutes to get a part to an inoperable aircraft.

The key to Creech's success at TAC was the creation of tribal-sized work units. When he arrived, there were three huge pools of workers: mechanics, pilots, and ground support personnel. TAC assigned crews from these pools; crew members returned to the pools after they completed their assignments. There were no permanent teams.

Creech broke up the pools. He assigned workers to teams dedicated to a specific aircraft. Each aircraft represented a small business, or tribe, with its own pilots, maintenance crew, and ground-support personnel. Each team was identified with its aircraft. Under Creech's system, TAC rewarded each team based on its performance. With each team focused on its own business unit, the overall performance of TAC changed dramatically.

NEW MANAGEMENT MODELS

Information technology provides the infrastructure for new management models such as the one Creech created at TAC. To make the models work, information is needed at all levels within the organization. Concepts such as electronic data interchange (EDI) and world class manufacturing (WCM) are changing the way manufacturing organizations are managed.

EDI integrates the purchasing, distribution, and accounting processes of buyer and seller. Parties in the external value chain are better informed. This results in smaller inventories, higher quality, and reduced overall costs. WCM includes just-in-time, statistical–process-control, total–quality-control, and total–preventive-maintenance manufacturing techniques. WCM works well when accountability, authority, and the corresponding information exist at the lowest level in the organization.

NEW FINANCIAL MODELS: VALUE ADDED

American corporations are having tremendous difficulty in flattening and thinning out their organizations to prepare for global competition. They usually do so only when threatened by takeover or after a leveraged buyout.

One reason for this is that in the case of takeover or buyout, stock prices and interest payments determine the amounts that the corporation can spend on overhead. Without the occasion of takeover or leveraged buyout, these same corporations are unable to place a value on intangible assets, including information, and overhead work.

In their recent book, *Relevance Lost,* Johnson and Kaplan deplored the fixation of corporate executives on short-term performance of their companies.[5] They felt that the short-term view prevented management from understanding the long-term benefits of intangibles. The authors attributed this attitude to the inappropriate use of information technology in corporations—that is, using IT solely for production tasks and not using it to measure the value and contribution of intangibles and information work.

Computers offer substantial possibilities for assisting management in analyzing the largest element of cost—overhead. Typically, corporate accounting practices lump overhead elements such as management and administration into a huge overhead bucket for reporting in financial statements. A good example is the automobile business. Direct labor now represents less than 20 percent of the cost of an automobile. Another 30 percent is raw materials and components. The remaining 50 percent is considered overhead. Today, new computer-based costing systems can identify total product cost, including intangibles and corporate overhead. With today's information technology, detailed accounting for corporate and divisional overheads, earlier considered economically impractical, is now entirely possible.

Understanding overhead, or information work, requires a step-by-step approach. The first step is to study information work. The second step is to set goals for improvement. The third step is to measure actual performance against goals. The final step is to reward performance that results in achieving goals and penalize performance that results in falling short.

A new, long-range approach to determining corporate performance is needed. Assessing the economic value added by a company provides an appealing alternative. Value-added measures assess the company's ability to meet stakeholder expectations.

VALUE-ADDED CASE STUDY

Let's take, for example, the results of two companies whose names are changed but represent real cases. Both companies make extensive use of information technology for supporting basic operations, for providing information to use in decision making, and for minimizing the number of middle managers required to run the business. Table 2–1 gives statistics representing one year for each company.

ABC Computer's 1987 sales were about $2.7 billion. The company accomplished this with 7,228 employees for a whop-

TABLE 2–1
Comparison of Two Companies Using Information Technology

	ABC Computer	Smith's
Net Sales $(000)	$2,661,068	$597,420
Number of Employees	7,228	2,500
Sales per Employee	$ 368,161	$238,968

ping $368,161 sales per employee. In the same year, Smith's Pharmaceutical Company sold about $597 million with 2500 employees for $238,968 per employee. The sales-per-employee method to assess corporate performance shows that ABC employees outperformed Smith's by 154 percent.

Why is there a difference in sales per employee?

At first glance, the difference in sales-per-employee performance may be attributed to the companies being very different. ABC produces and markets computers; Smith's produces and markets pharmaceuticals.

Upon closer analysis, however, these companies appear more alike than dissimilar. Both deal in high-technology products that are very dependent on R&D investment. Both sales and marketing organizations rely heavily on wholesalers, distributors, and retailers. Both are highly information driven.

Further analysis reveals that sales per employee is not the same measure as economic value added per employee. Table 2–2 shows the calculation of an estimated valued added per employee for ABC and Smith's.

At ABC, sales per employee includes materials and parts contracted out to other manufacturers. The subcontracted material and parts become part of a value-added chain. The company then incorporates them in higher-level assemblies.

TABLE 2–2
Estimated Value Added per Employee for ABC and Smith's

	ABC Computer	Smith's
Net Sales $(000)	$2,661,068	$597,420
Number of Employees	7,228	2,500
Sales per Employee	$ 368,161	$238,968
Value-Added Basis		
Cost of Goods Sold $(000)	1,296,220	140,000
% Purchased	90	60
Purchase Passthrough $(000)*	1,166,598	84,000
Corporate Value Added $(000)	$1,494,470	$513,420
Value Added per Employee	$ 206,761	$205,368

To calculate the value added per ABC employee, subtract such passthrough purchases from sales. In 1987, ABC had a cost of sales of $1.3 billion. ABC is a highly leveraged manufacturing company. Since it subcontracts most of its manufacturing, we can estimate passthrough purchases of components and subassemblies as high as 90 percent of its cost of sales.

Likewise, in 1987 Smith's had a cost of sales of $140 million. Smith's is less leveraged than ABC. The company purchases raw materials and formulations and then passes them on as ingredients in their ethical drugs. An estimate of Smith's passthrough purchases is around 60 percent of the cost of sales.

On a value-added basis, the results are almost equal. Why is this?

One possibility is the similar corporate cultures and market-driven infrastructures of the two companies. Both organizations place a high value on people, invest heavily in training and professional development, invest heavily in personal information technology, and reward team and individual performance. Both have very human-oriented policies and beliefs. Both have very successful profit-based reward systems. As a result, both companies have a reputation for highly cooperative corporate environments. The aggressive use of information technology enhances the achievement of high value added per employee in both environments.

Economic value added provides a new perspective on corporate performance. Value-added analysis is crucial to assessing and improving corporate productivity. It clarifies an important issue.

The key to improving productivity is understanding when to make and when to buy. Could ABC improve its value added per employee by bringing subcontracted work in-house? What would the impact be on value added per employee?

If the subcontracted work has less valued added per employee than the overall corporate rate has, bringing subcontracted work in-house will reduce the overall value added per employee. In particular, it will dilute the value added by management. To maintain a high value added per employee, ABC should continue giving the work to a subcontractor who specializes in lower value-added work.

Value-added analysis is causing automobile manufacturers to rethink vertical integration. General Motors once drew strength from a high degree of vertical integration. Now, vertical integration is diluting GM's management talent, talent that is needed to refocus on the market and the timeliness of new products.

CREATING VALUE BY SHORTENING THE BUSINESS CYCLE

The Ford Motor Company reported record earnings for 1987, exceeding previous performance for Ford as well as for any other automobile manufacturer. Much of Ford's success can be attributed to its being the first American company to bring out the design of the 90s, with advanced IT and an entirely new aerodynamic body. The Taurus and Sable models are each a smashing success.

General Motors, Ford's major U.S. competitor, actually had similarly designed models on the drawing boards before Ford. The major difference in performance between the two auto manufacturers is the length of the business cycle for each.

Ford management aggressively tackled the issue of management overhead in the late 1970s and early 1980s. In addition to reducing the overall numbers of middle managers, Ford also invested in improving quality and automating manual design and engineering functions. Management carried out their quality program at all levels of the organization using computer-integrated manufacturing (CIM) as the foundation. The result was

- Lower overhead costs.
- A more capable direct work force.
- Lower direct costs per auto.
- Reduced lead times for implementing changes.

The last result, reducing lead times, turned out to be the key to beating GM to the market. While GM's business cycle from initial design to deliverable product is four to five years, Ford's is three to four years.

When you are last with new models in the market by a year, you will lose more than a year's revenue. The latecomer must win back the loyalty of lost customers, a process that can take several years.

Japanese automobile manufacturers already had business cycles that equaled Ford's 1987 turnaround. As a result, Ford didn't take market share from the Japanese. Rather, Ford gained its increased market share from GM.

HOW INFORMATION TECHNOLOGY CAN IMPROVE BUSINESS CYCLES

Information technology played a key role in reducing the business cycle of the Ford Motor Company. Ford made IT investments that satisfied customer needs by daring to break with its conservative tradition. Because Ford automated the design-to-manufacture process, management accepted larger design risks. Computer-aided designs (CAD) were transferable to computer-aided manufacturing machines (CAM). The computer-aided operations resulted in improved overall lead time, quality, consistency, and cost. The result was record profits.

General Motors likewise made a significant investment in CAD/CAM. Nevertheless, the focus was on producing lower-cost automobiles rather than on satisfying customer needs for distinctive models. The various GM divisions used a standard body type for their Chevrolet, Pontiac, Oldsmobile, Buick, and Cadillac models. The luxury models suffered the most because there was very little design difference between an expensive Cadillac and a much cheaper Chevrolet. So most of the 10 percent market-share loss over the past two years came from the more profitable luxury line. The results were sagging profits.

THE IMPORTANCE OF VALUE-ADDED SERVICE

American businesses are trying to create win-win solutions through innovative applications of information technology. Higher quality and reliability mean more value delivered. More value delivered and lower costs result in increased shareholder wealth. In a service-conscious economy, the corporation, its customers, its shareholders, and all other parties with a stake in the enterprise can realize benefits. These parties with a vested interest in the success of the company, the company's *stakeholders,* are a key ingredient in creating value-added service and long-term corporate financial success.

CASE STUDY: WELLS FARGO & COMPANY

Wells Fargo & Company, a western American bank, gained a preeminent position in the financial services industry in the 1980s by combining strategy, management skill, and information technology to integrate key management functions, innovate new product offerings, and satisfy stakeholder needs. Chairman Carl E. Reichardt led the executive team in creating a new strategic direction for the bank. With the strategy in place, he then made the necessary organizational and executive changes that paved the way for Wells Fargo to use today's information technology more effectively than its competitors do.

Table 2–3, constructed from data contained in *The Quarterly Bank Monitor,* shows that in the five-year period between 1982 and 1987 Wells Fargo's capitalized market value increased 263 percent, from $634.4 million in 1982 to $2.3 billion in 1987! This outstanding equity performance was due in large part to the five-year increase in Wells Fargo's net value added of 184 percent (excluding the effect of loan losses). Furthermore, the net value-added performance per employee improved 140 percent,[6] and assets managed per employee improved 53 percent.

Wells Fargo's product and marketing strategy is, in part, reflected in the increased investment in information technology per employee. According to *The Quarterly Bank Monitor,* the 1982 investment per employee was $4,202. By 1987, the IT investment per employee had grown to $6,299. Accompanying Wells Fargo's product and marketing strategy, Reichardt made broad organizational and executive changes to reduce the bank's costs and to place concentrated energy on those activities that added the most value to the bank and its customers.

TABLE 2–3
Value-Added/Expense Trends, Wells Fargo & Company

	1982	1983	1984	1985	1986*	1987*
			$(000,000)			
Spread income†	$ 875	965	$ 1,124	$ 1,269	$ 1,697	$ 1,999
Non-Interest Income	294	276	271	396	460	470
Total Value Added	$ 1,169	$ 1,241	$ 1,395	$ 1,664	$ 2,156	$ 2,470
Non-Interest Expense	835	840	887	944	1,315	1,521
Net Value Added	$ 334	$ 401	$ 508	$ 721	$ 841	$ 949
Average # of Employees	17,800	16,650	15,800	14,700	17,750	21,100
Value Added/Employee	$65,685	$74,511	$88,291	$113,218	$121,487	$117,047
Expense/ Employee	46,910	50,450	56,114	64,204	74,096	72,062
Net Value Added/ Employee	$18,775	$24,060	$32,177	$49,014	$ 47,392	$ 44,986
Net Assets $(000,000)	$24,818	$25,438	$27,233	$ 28,569	$ 37,374	$ 44,854
Assets/Employee $(000)	$ 1,394	$ 1,528	$ 1,724	$ 1,943	$ 2,106	$ 2,126
Equipment Exp. $(000)	$74,800	$68,300	$74,200	$ 75,900	$108,000	$132,900
Equip exp.$/Employee	$ 4,202	$ 4,102	$ 4,696	$ 5,163	$ 6,085	$ 6,299

*Includes the Crocker merger.
†Excluding provision for loan losses.

RESTRUCTURING WELLS FARGO
FOR SUCCESS

When Wells Fargo chairman Carl Reichardt came to the bank in 1983, the bank was engaged in almost every kind of banking venture from retail to commercial banking and from home mortgages to international banking. Soon after his arrival, Reichardt's management team evolved a new strategy that redefined Wells Fargo as a regional bank serving the seventh largest economy in the world, the economy of California.

Wells Fargo shocked its bank examiners by doing away with their cumbersome five-year plan. In its place, the bank substituted a 22-page strategic document that presented a much clearer statement of the bank's direction. When Wells Fargo bought Crocker National Bank in 1985, the strategy remained intact. The negotiating process was already laid out. Because of the clearly defined strategy, Wells Fargo was able to use IT to support the merger team. Computer models of the 613 branches, 1,190 automatic teller machines, and 26,000 employees of the two banks demonstrated how they could best be combined. As a result, the success of the merger exceeded expectations.

One of Reichardt's most creative moves was to combine strategic planning, personnel, and information systems into an integrated unit. As executive vice president for systems and strategy, Jack Hancock led the restructuring of Wells Fargo that resulted in decentralizing information systems, personnel administration, and strategic planning.

At the same time, the systems and strategy unit retained centralized direction for IT systems standards, personnel reward systems standards, and the consolidation and dissemination of the strategic plan.

As a result, Wells Fargo transformed information from a computer by-product into a resource for creating strategic alternatives. For example, the personnel, information systems, and strategic planning departments jointly created a business model that is used by line supervisors to determine the appropriate salary for a job.

Until 1984, Wells Fargo used a point-based job evaluation system and annual merit reviews. In the restructuring, management did away with both outmoded compensation methods. In their place, they developed a computerized model that calculates the value of employees based on their fulfillment of corporate and division objectives. This empowers line supervisors to better manage their staff without costly intervention by middle managers.

Instead of budgeting the old merit system's expense, management established a bonus pool. The bank now awards bonuses based on the performance of the bank, the division, the department, and the individual. The result is a win-win situation. Wells Fargo serves both its employees and its shareholders better.

Wells Fargo made a substantial investment in information technology to create a customer information file (CIF). The executive team used the CIF data together with demographic data to create geographic banking relationship characteristics. This cross-referencing of information led to the discovery that within the California region there were at least 185 subregions, each with its own market characteristics. Based on overall market characteristics, Wells Fargo developed a menu of products that could be offered in each market area. Each branch manager, whose performance was measured by branch performance, decided which products to offer in the branch area. The result has been strong branch management with outstanding branch performance.

The restructuring of Wells Fargo demonstrated the bank's commitment to its stakeholders—the parties who have a vested interest in the success of Wells Fargo. The new management team endeavored to meet the needs of today's customers while at the same time meeting employee and shareholder needs. IT enabled the bank's strategy to be implemented. It also helped management to improve the bank's financial performance.

CITICORP'S COMPARABLE FIVE-YEAR PERFORMANCE

Like Wells Fargo, Citicorp has experienced substantial improvements in financial performance over the past several years.

Table 2–4, based on data reported in *The Quarterly Book Monitor,* indicates that during the comparable five-year period, Citicorp's capitalized market value increased 44 percent, from $4.1 billion to $5.9 billion. Their net added value increased 219 percent (excluding the effect of loan losses). The net value-added performance of $48,291 per employee in 1987 was slightly higher than that of a Wells Fargo employee. Their assets managed per employee, like those of Wells Fargo, exceeded $2 million.

Citicorp's exceptional growth rate reflects their long-term strategy for growth through the aggressive use of information technology and product innovation. *The Quarterly Bank Monitor*'s statistics substantiate Citicorp's large information technology expense per employee, which increased from $4,832 in 1982 to $8,504 in 1987. This emphasis on technology was a continuation of a program established in the 1970s by Walter B. Wriston and implemented by John Reed, Citicorp's current chairman.

Citicorp's IT investment program often led to short-term decreases in productivity but substantial competitive gains over time. The corporate treasurer's terminal program was a key Citicorp product that changed the nature of commercial banking in the late 1970s. The corporate treasurer's terminal program placed an online terminal on the desk of the treasurer of each commercial customer. From this terminal, the treasurer could draw down deposit balances each evening and put them to work in the money market overnight.

The short-term results were negative. The investment in IT actually reduced the bank's interest income. Nevertheless, the long-term impact was phenomenal. The new relationship established between the bank and customer treasurers gave Citicorp new leverage in providing additional services to their commercial accounts. At the same time, it forced other banks to provide the same service to their commercial accounts or lose business to Citicorp. By taking the initiative, Citicorp assumed a leadership position in commercial banking that it still enjoys today.

TABLE 2–4
Value-Added/Expense Trends, CITICORP

	1982	1983	1984	1985	1986	1987
			$(000,000)			
Spread Income*	$ 3,628	$ 4,123	$ 4,484	$ 5,599	$ 6,337	$ 6,606
Non-Interest Income	1,595	1,840	2,300	3,030	4,272	5,994
Total Value Added	$ 5,233	$ 5,963	$ 6,784	$ 8,629	$ 10,609	$ 12,600
Non-Interest Expense	3,871	3,757	4,456	5,517	6,875	8,290
Net Value Added	$ 1,352	$ 2,206	$ 2,328	$ 3,112	$ 3,734	$ 4,310
Average # of employees	59,400	62,150	67,350	76,150	84,900	89,250
Value Added/Employee	$ 87,929	$ 95,945	$100,728	$113,316	$124,959	$141,176
Expense/Employee	65,168	60,451	66,162	72,449	80,978	92,885
Net Value Added/Employee	$ 22,761	$ 35,495	$ 34,566	$ 40,367	$ 43,981	$ 48,291
Net Assets $(000,000)	$121,482	$127,931	$142,631	$160,502	$184,013	$198,683
Assets/Employee $(000)	$ 2,045	$ 2,058	$ 2,118	$ 2,108	$ 2,167	$ 2,226
Equipment Exp. $(000)	$287,000	$331,000	$376,000	$481,000	$630,300	$759,000
Equip. exp. $/Employee	$ 4,832	$ 5,326	$ 5,583	$ 6,316	$ 7,424	$ 8,504

*Excluding provision for loan losses.

BANKAMERICA CORPORATION'S COMPARABLE FIVE-YEAR PERFORMANCE

BankAmerica invested vast sums in IT during the same five-year period. But because it lacked the needed strategy and management skill, the IT investment plan didn't achieve management's hoped-for results.

Instead of improving, as Table 2–5 figures from *The Quarterly Bank Monitor* show, BankAmerica's capitalized market value dropped 63 percent, from $3 billion to $1.1 billion. Its net value added dropped 10 percent (excluding the effect of loan losses). Its net value-added performance per employee improved a mere 21 percent over the five-year period, while the assets managed per employee were essentially flat. The dollar figures for employee productivity were mediocre.

Table 2–5 reveals that BankAmerica increased the information technology expense per employee over the five-year period by 123 percent. Much of this increase was attributable to the bank's attempt to catch up from a prior lack of investment. BankAmerica didn't invest in IT in the 1970s as did Citicorp. Many observers, including former Citicorp chairman Walter B. Wriston, attribute BankAmerica's decline to the belated use of information technology. In 1982, the IT expense per employee trailed Wells Fargo's and Citicorp's by over 40 percent, and even in 1987, BankAmerica's mix of people and technology still lagged the other two banks.

The strain on BankAmerica's chief information executives was apparent as first Max Hopper of American Airlines and then Lou Mertes of SeaFirst attempted to put the BankAmerica IT investment on course. Max Hopper, unable to overcome BankAmerica's huge corporate bureaucracy, returned to American Airlines in 1985 to resume his very successful executive career there. Lou Mertes, along with the bank's senior trust executive, left in 1987 when the IT organization repeatedly failed to deliver a crucial trust application.[7] As a result of the failed delivery, BankAmerica set aside $60 million in 1987 as special reserves for correcting the system's problems, including making up any trust fund losses suffered by its customers.[8]

TABLE 2–5
Value Added/Expense Trends, BankAmerica Corporation

	1982	1983	1984	1985	1986	1987
			$(000,000)			
Spread Income*	$ 3,075	$ 3,508	$ 4,044	$ 4,118	$ 3,850	$ 3,256
Non-Interest Income	1,185	1,347	1,603	2,145	2,352	2,023
Total Value Added	$ 4,260	$ 4,855	$ 5,647	$ 6,263	$ 6,202	$ 5,279
Non-Interest Expense	3,057	3,537	4,208	4,434	4,491	4,200
Net Value Added	$ 1,203	$ 1,317	$ 1,439	$ 1,829	$ 1,711	$ 1,079
Number of Employees	86,387	88,167	89,192	85,308	73,282	64,000
Value Added/Employee	$ 49,308	$ 55,063	$ 63,313	$ 73,416	$ 84,632	$ 82,484
Expense/Employee	35,385	40,120	47,179	51,976	61,284	65,625
Net Value Added/Employee	$ 13,923	$ 14,942	$ 16,134	$ 21,440	$ 23,348	$ 16,859
Net Assets $(000,000)	$119,989	$123,045	$120,187	$118,574	$113,869	$ 92,833
Assets/Employee $(000)	$ 1,389	$ 1,396	$ 1,348	$ 1,395	$ 1,554	$ 1,451
Equipment Exp. $(000)	$219,200	$265,500	$342,000	$388,000	$385,000	$363,000
Equip. Exp. $/Employee	$ 2,537	$ 3,011	$ 3,834	$ 4,548	$ 5,254	$ 5,672

*Excluding provision for loan losses.

Bank chairman Tom Clausen hired key executives from Wells Fargo and announced a substantial reduction of employees in 1988. These actions are helping the bank to significantly improve its operating performance. The outlook will be even better if the bank's strategy makes better use of the information technology investment as well.

A step in this new direction is BankAmerica's Alpha product, an integrated offering that uses IT to combine the bank's retail offerings as a package for its retail customers. This relationship-banking approach has been used successfully by most major banks to increase revenue from existing customers. The product is supported by a customer information file (CIF) similar to that used by Wells Fargo to expand its net value added.

In the last half of 1987 and in 1988, BankAmerica announced six consecutive quarters of improved earnings based on improvements in operational performance.

USING INFORMATION TECHNOLOGY TO LEVERAGE PERFORMANCE

These banking examples indicate the positive potential for IT when it is combined with strategy and management skill and negative potential when it's not. During the next decade, financial service corporations will be at the center of change in industrialized countries. Global competition is already requiring them to replace obsolete, top-heavy management structures with lean, energetic, and flexible organizations. Accordingly, major banks are simplifying their capital structures and decentralizing decision making. With sound strategy and management skill, they can use information technology to make new forms of stakeholder, capital, and organizational leadership possible.

INFORMATION WORK AND VALUE ADDED

In 1985, information work represented about 55 percent of the work force. All industry segments have information jobs. That information work is replacing direct population work is key to the new business era. By 1995, information work will represent 67 percent of the work force. The key to managing information work is understanding its relationship to creating value for the company's stakeholders.

During the industrial age, economic studies focused on the use of labor and material in producing goods and services. Charles Babbage and Frederick Taylor pioneered scientific management. Using scientific management, industrial enterprises discovered efficiencies in the use of labor and material.

In the information age, information is the transforming resource, and we need to measure the impact and value of information work as it relates to value. For example, quality provides economic value for the company's customers. Information work that improves quality and the value of the product is valid work. Information work that produces no perceivable value to the company's stakeholders should cease.

Using information technology to create and measure the value added per employee, team, department, and division will lead to realizing the company's economic potential.

END NOTES

1. Gary Loveman, "An Assessment of the Impact of Information Technologies," (Management in the 1990's, Working Paper 88-054, Sloan School of Management, MIT, Cambridge, Mass., July 1988).
2. Stephen Roach, *The BusinessWeek Newsletter for Information Executives*, May 27, 1988.
3. Terry Winograd and Fernando Flores, *Understanding Computers and Cognition* (Reading, Mass.: Addison-Wesley, 1987).
4. Jan Carlzon, *Moments of Truth* (Cambridge, Mass.: Ballinger, 1987).
5. H. Thomas Johnson and Robert S. Kaplan, *Relevance Lost* (Boston: Harvard Business, 1987).
6. Goods purchased and included in the final delivered product "pass through" the company and are at a basic value entering the organization. Deduct their cost from sales to derive the net value added by the organization to the goods and commodities that pass through.
7. Wall Street Journal, October 22, 1988.
8. Wall Street Journal, January 22, 1988.

CHAPTER 3

ASSESSING THE ENTERPRISE:
A Stakeholder Approach

Today's businesses are characterized by increased accessibility of information, even faster information transfer, and the resultant collapse of management hierarchies. Corporate executives in these streamlined organizations are beginning to realize that to be successful in the long term, they must focus outward on the needs of the corporation's stakeholders, including its customers, employees, investors, and all other parties with a stake in the success of the corporation.

Few senior executives today fully understand the nature of the information technology investment and how it influences corporate performance. This is because they must first understand the potential of corporate relationships with both internal and external stakeholders. Analysis of these relationships will uncover leverage points where investment in information technology will improve corporate performance.

THE ORGANIZING PRINCIPLE

The organizing principle governs a corporation's relationships with its stakeholders. Some stakeholders are more important than others in determining the success of the business. There may even be conflicting interests between some of them. It is the founders of an organization who originally define its stakeholders and their relative importance to the survival of the corporation.

Time and circumstances change. So do stakeholder relationships and their importance to the survival of the corporation. It is senior management's responsibility to constantly assess the corporate organizing principle and manage stakeholder relationships. To manage these relationships effectively, the corporation needs appropriate measures of performance and feedback systems.

Figure 3–1 illustrates that the entire planning process revolves around the organizing principle and the relationships that make up the company.

Any organization, whether it is a nation, city, or private business, receives explicit or implied assent from the individuals

FIGURE 3–1
Maximizing the Information Technology Investment

and groups affected by its existence. In forming a business corporation, a diverse aggregation of people—including investors, customers, suppliers, regulatory bodies, management, employees, unions, competitors, and the community—gives assent to the new enterprise.

Assent can be expected to be in only a rudimentary form at the beginning of a business; it develops over time. The corporate purpose statement, which is intentionally expressed in very broad terms to encompass all the possible dimensions that may unfold in the future, contains the ingredients of an organizing principle. However, it is important not to leave the relationships among those giving assent to the organization vague and ambiguous.

As a business becomes more involved with its stakeholders over time, a clearer sense of its organizing principle emerges. However, few senior executives adequately express their corporation's organizing principle. Fewer understand that a change in one stakeholder's relationship with the corporation affects all the rest. And, even fewer measure corporate performance against stakeholders' expectations.

By combining, extending, and enhancing stakeholder relationships, senior management can leverage corporate performance. Today, their main tool is information technology, which can link business entities in a cooperative chain focused on accomplishing specific results.

The purpose of this book is to explain the process shown in Figure 3–2. The organizing principle provides the foundation for the beliefs that form corporate imperatives used to drive the business. It also provides for the policies that are used to manage the corporation's three basic resources: people, capital, and information.

CASE STUDY: A FREIGHT-FORWARDING COMPANY

Take, for example, the case of a freight-forwarding company and its success in combining two separate categories of customer

FIGURE 3–2
An Overview of the Business Planning Process

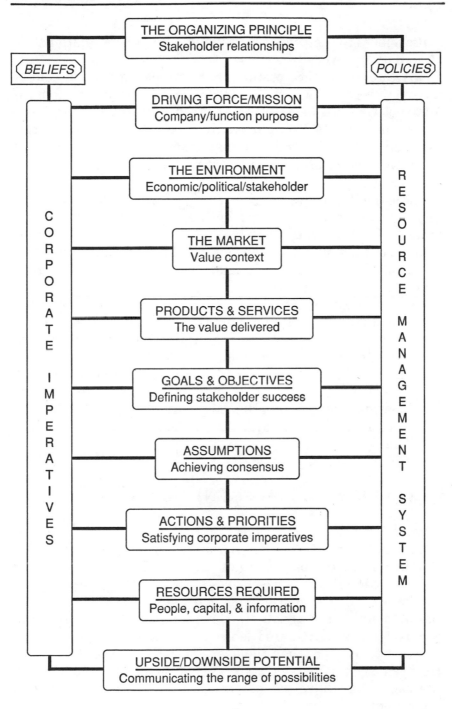

stakeholders in a process that strengthened these relationships as well as the overall business.

According to U.S. customs regulations, importing companies may receive import duty credit for goods later exported. Many electronics firms build electronic assemblies from imported components. These firms then export some of the larger assemblies. Customs regulations entitle exporting firms to a refund for the duties paid on the imported components included in the exported assemblies.

The freight-forwarding company decided to look at its import and export customers together. They found that many of them had overlapping interests; many export customers were also import customers, and vice versa. The company integrated its import and export departments through the use of information technology. This resulted in integrated systems that allowed exporting companies to track the quantities of imported components built into larger assemblies and then exported. The exporting companies realized significant reductions in duties paid. Furthermore, they were able to view their business relationship with the freight forwarder in a new, value-added way.

This is an example of combining disparate stakeholders and creating new, strengthened relationships that have a substantial business reward. Information technology made it possible.

THE CURRENT MANAGEMENT MINDSET

Typically, senior management issues a long list of policies and beliefs that, in some cases, may conflict with an implied understanding of the company's organizing principle.

For example, many executives state that their corporation's employees are their most important asset, and therefore they claim to hire only the best. However, many of these same companies use point-based job-rating systems to be sure that they don't pay more than the average wage for a particular job. How can a company have a strategy of hiring top people and at the same time have a mediocre pay policy that is bound to attract only mediocre people?

More and more corporations are installing just-in-time (JIT) manufacturing systems that call for a very close relationship with suppliers. Yet some of these companies still reward their purchasing staffs based on the size of the favorable purchase price variances that result from lower prices exacted from suppliers. Purchase price variance measures how well purchasing agents and buyers perform in hammering down the vendors' prices. It doesn't measure the quality of the product or if it was properly packaged for use. How can a company develop a quality relationship with a supplier when the only measures of success are low prices?

The challenge to senior management is to develop strategies that will achieve mutual advantage among the company's stakeholders. This requires an understanding of the relationships that compose a business and of how enhancing them will yield benefits for all concerned.

The key to realizing strategic advantage lies in balancing the relationships of the organizing principle so that all parties benefit.

ALLEGIS: A CASE STUDY

Allegis, the much-publicized company previously known as UAL, Inc., is an example of stakeholders in conflict. They finally achieved unity in the removal of Richard J. Ferris, chairman and CEO of Allegis, and the renaming of Allegis back to UAL, Inc.

The history of United Airlines also reveals periods of stakeholder conflict, followed by resolution.[1] United Airlines, the free world's largest airline, is the result of several airline mergers over the years. The company began in the late 1920s. By 1931, it was a holding company consisting of several companies, including the Boeing Company and Pratt & Whitney. These two firms were split off following a 1934 congressional decision that airlines and airplane manufacturers had to be separate entities.

W. A. "Pat" Patterson was chosen to head the new company. Patterson had come from Wells Fargo Bank where he had financed the early operations that later became United Airlines. During Patterson's tenure from 1934 to 1965, United became a nationally prominent airline. United's code of ethics included Patterson's "Rule of Five": safety, passenger comfort, dependability, honesty, and sincerity. Patterson's view of the United Airlines organizing principle during his tenure was described by Gardner Cowles, a director, as one that

1. Placed the safety of the passenger first, regardless of the cost or effect on airline earnings.
2. Attended to the welfare of the employees, from whom no complaint was too trivial to merit attention.
3. Was always alert to the interests of the shareholders.
4. Recognized that the interests of the shareholders could not be disassociated from that of the public it served or the employees who were its blood and bone.

In 1966, Patterson was succeeded by George Keck, who formed UAL, Inc., a holding company, with United Airlines as a subsidiary. Western International Hotels was acquired as another subsidiary. With the Western International acquisition, Richard J. Ferris arrived on the scene. He was then appointed president of UAL's food service division.

In the first four years of Keck's term as president, United experienced tremendous growth. In the fourth year, UAL, Inc., recorded a net profit of $47.7 million, $44.7 million of which came from United Airlines. In the fifth year, UAL, Inc., sustained a loss of $41 million, with a $46 million loss recorded by United Airlines. Not surprisingly, Keck was ousted from his job. A combination of factors led up to Keck's demise, but the most influential was a progressive deterioration of communication between top management and outside directors. That revealed a blatant disregard for the organizing principle.

In 1971, the UAL Board chose one of its outside directors, Edward E. Carlson, to succeed Keck as CEO. Under Carlson's leadership, UAL prospered. Carlson strengthened the relationship between management and the outside directors. He formed a senior management committee to evolve policy as well as solve major problems. The senior management committee cut across the various functions and provided focus on the major issues confronting UAL. Carlson also instituted profit centers and accountability. His view of the organizing principle emphasized three key relationships for management: "Management must deal fairly with the interests of three groups of partners— customers, employees, and shareholders."[2]

In 1979, Richard Ferris was named CEO, and in 1982 he was named chairman and president. Ferris had a vision of a diversified travel service empire—a vision that was not generally shared by the other parties to the organizing principle. Ferris's policy meant taking cash generated by profitable operations such as the airlines and the reservation systems companies and reinvesting it in diversified services such as the Hertz unit purchased in 1985 and the Hilton International subsidiary acquired in 1986.

Ferris tried to wield power by pitting one set of relationships against another and, often, one subsidiary against the other. He handled the pilots', machinists', and flight attendants' unions as though they were involved in adversarial relationships not only between themselves and UAL management but also between one another. For example, the airline pilots' union maintained that when Ferris negotiated budgets with the United Airlines subsidiary, he threatened to divert reinvestment to other subsidiaries if profit and return on investment (ROI) targets weren't accepted. The pilots felt that this could cause safety and passenger comfort to be sacrificed.

In addition, under Ferris, financial analysts and institutional investors were not treated with customary care and became very critical of Allegis management. The souring of this relationship may have been the straw that broke the camel's back.

In the final analysis, Ferris had no supporters for his dream. UAL, renamed Allegis, became a bedlam of factions seeking the overthrow of management. The Allegis board lost confidence in Ferris's ability to lead. Ferris was later ousted, and Frank Olson, the former CEO of Hertz, was named the CEO of United Airlines, the new name for Allegis. Edward Carlson was once again brought back as a board member. The Hertz and hotel subsidiaries were sold. The company turned down the airline pilots' offer for buyout but said it would consider an employee stock-ownership plan.

In early 1988, the board of directors brought in Flying Tiger's Stephen Wolfe to be the CEO of Allegis. Wolfe brought with him a reputation for being a person who could unite the Allegis stakeholders, in particular the unions. By mid-1988, Wolfe had reinstated the name of UAL, Inc. In a letter to UAL's customers, Wolfe reaffirmed Pat Patterson's commitment to the customers, employees, and shareholders.

The Allegis/United Airlines story is rife with both good and bad examples of management's ability to understand the organizing principle. Patterson and Carlson demonstrated a relatively good understanding, and the company flourished under their leadership. The actions of Keck and Ferris showed a lack of understanding. The results were disastrous, and in the end they were both ousted.

THE IMPORTANCE OF CREATING AND ENHANCING RELATIONSHIPS

There are many more stakeholders in a corporation than just its customers, shareholders, and employees. Also included as stakeholders are the management, suppliers, vendors, community, regulators, legislators, and competitors. The corporation must keep its organizing principle up-to-date so that it continues to unify the many relationships with stakeholders. In a new business era, information technology will play a key role in monitoring, finding new stakeholder relationship opportunities, and implementing new stakeholder relationships and economic alliances.

Understanding the corporation's organizing principle and how it changes over time is a fundamental requirement for business leadership. The organizing principle establishes the linkage between the enterprise's stakeholders—all parties who have a vested or implied interest in the enterprise. The stakeholders have different roles to play, different reasons for participating, and differing expectations for reward. Nevertheless, they are inextricably linked in a common entity, and it is management's duty to ensure that the expectations of the stakeholders are either met or renegotiated. The board of directors and the chief executive officer (CEO) share the key responsibility for guiding the evolution of the corporation's organizing principle.

The organizing principles of corporations are characterized by dynamic relationships that continually interact with one another. For example, if a company is focused solely on its relationship with its investors or if it is preoccupied with destroying a competitor, this will adversely affect its relationships with the remaining stakeholders.

The challenge for chief executives is to lead the evolution of the organizing principle by

1. Consciously and deliberately enhancing the relationships of the parties essential to the organizing principle.
2. Nurturing new and viable relationships for the benefit of all.
3. Sustaining harmony and balance among the various relationships.

CREATING STAKEHOLDER VALUE

It can be argued that corporations that pay close attention to the needs of their stakeholders financially outperform those who don't. In a study commissioned by a major firm, it was reported that companies with a codified set of principles for serving the public and a record of implementing these ideas for at least a generation showed a 10.3 percent growth in profits compounded over 30 years.[3]

Corporations that were innovative and responsive in their treatment of people outperformed the nonresponsive companies over a 20-year period on several financial measures:[4]

- Return on equity.
- Return on total capital.
- Net profit.
- Growth in sales.
- Growth in earnings per share.

How, then, may corporate leaders establish a method for understanding and advancing the organizing principle of their enterprise?

There is a four-phase method executives can follow for understanding and advancing the organizing principles of their companies:

1. Understanding the process of change in organizations and in society at large.
2. Understanding the original organizing principle of the enterprise and its evolution over time.
3. Understanding the complexities of the stakeholder relationships included in the organizing principle.
4. Understanding that stakeholder relationships are enhanced by focusing on common interests and pooling of resources.

By understanding the original organizing principle, its evolution over time, and the process of change, executives gain perspective. Changes occur because needs change. Appropriate behavior at one time becomes inappropriate in another. The old rules no longer explain current behavior. By understanding the complexities of stakeholder relationships, executives can begin to find leverage points where the corporation can invest. By focusing on common interests and resource pooling, executives can add value to stakeholder relationships.

At Allegis, Ferris might have unified the various unions by emphasizing that they have a common stake in the organization. Like Iococca at Chrysler, Ferris could have combined the union relationship with that of the shareholders by having union leadership participate in the Allegis board of directors. Ferris could have embraced the employee stock-ownership program (ESOP), a program put forth by the pilots' union. Instead, Ferris kept the stakeholders apart and played them one against the other.

The most serious mistake Ferris made was to force the dream of the complete travel empire down the throats of Allegis's stakeholders. He didn't adequately communicate his dream to Allegis's stakeholders or ask for their support. So, they rebelled. Allegis had the potential to integrate the hotel, car rental, and airline businesses. An information systems subsidiary had extensively developed relationships with travel agents and had a service to offer that had the potential of being unique. Not even American Airline's Sabre system had that potential because, unlike the Allegis system, it wasn't yet tied into hotels and car rentals.

Ferris chose to divide rather than integrate. He paid a big price for that mistake. So did Allegis's stakeholders.

INTERNAL ALIGNMENT

To advance the concept of the organizing principle, senior executives must find ways to internally align the various functions within the business so that they can address external issues in unison. They need to promote cooperative instead of adversarial roles. Cooperation is the key to overcoming the fractionalization endemic in most large organizations and, in addition, to synthesizing business processes. The sharing of technology-based systems and information provides the opportunity to integrate disparate corporate functions.

CORPORATE LEADERSHIP DIVIDED

The CEO can achieve internal alignment by removing artificial barriers that exist within the corporate structure. These barriers were originally erected to protect division turf—each department strives to maintain its own dynasty. The accounting department has the exclusive right to keep corporate financial records. The personnel department has the exclusive right to establish pay grades. The MIS (Management Information System) department has the exclusive right to deal with information technology. And so it goes.

These barriers, including departments that have become so specialized and so esoteric that they have often lost touch with their stakeholders, have existed for many years. The industrial revolution brought with it the notion of dividing labor (specialization). In his famous movie, *Hard Times,* Charlie Chaplin created a lasting visual image as he worked on an assembly line, turning a nut over and over one-half turn. This specialization, as caricatured by Chaplin, was carried up through the management ranks to create the various divisions in a business.

Notable among these divisions in a company were the finance, human resources, information systems, and strategic planning departments:

> The finance department, being primarily concerned with its relationship to senior management and the board, has viewed the world as return on investment and earnings per share.
>
> The human resources department, being concerned with its relationship with employees and management, has viewed the world as salary grades, pay quartiles, health benefits, and litigation.
>
> The information systems department, being concerned about its ability to cope with technology, has viewed the world as users of I/S resources, complex systems, networks, and computer applications.
>
> The strategic planning department, being focused exclusively on its relationship with management, has viewed the world as a five-year plan.

Because of a limited vision, the executives heading these functional departments have not been able to understand their collective mission as part of a higher-order corporate organizing principle. They have typically given short shrift to the two most important external relationships: customers and shareholders.

Even though a personnel department may have changed its name to "Human Resources" (as many have), much more is needed than a new name. The personnel department will undergo substantial change in the next few years, resulting in a line department staffed with line people. The major contributing factor is technology and its impact on work. Neither factory nor office automation will be achieved with current personnel methods. To effect the change, there must be changes in job design, in the organization and flow of work, and in organizational relationships.

The information systems department will undergo significant change. Just as with the personnel department, it will be far more concerned about improving job design, the organization and flow of work, and organizational relationships. Information systems are the foundation for making such improvements. The culture of the information systems group will change from having an introverted, technical mindset to having a proactive, relationship-oriented one.

Many corporations have found that their corporate strategic planning department has been unable to deliver a strategic plan in accord with the plans of the operating groups. For example, General Motors disbanded its corporate strategic planning department, keeping only a small staff to consolidate plans created by the operating divisions. The role of the corporate executive in charge of strategic planning changed from preparing the strategic plan to coordinating the strategic planning process in the various operating groups. The result is strategic plans synchronized with the operating plans.

The corporate financial executive has wielded a great deal of power in a corporation because of close alignment with two of the parties to the organizing principle: management and investors. Under pressure from these stakeholders, the financial executive has built strategies that focus on minimizing costs and has not been able to support strategies for adding value to the business.

CORPORATE LEADERSHIP UNITED

Senior corporate executives can take the lead to enhance relationships that benefit all stakeholders. This is not possible when they are preoccupied with controlling or manipulating stakeholders. Leadership by wielding power and exercising brute force does not enhance relationships.

Today, the power available to corporate executives stems from a new set of ethics that guides the evolution of the organizing principle. The new set of ethics involves nurturing an organization's relationships in a candid and positive environment. Adhering to these standards, executives will develop the wisdom and interaction necessary for aligning internal functions so as to regain corporations' competitive strength.

STRATEGY, CULTURE, AND INFRASTRUCTURE

The organizing principle and stakeholder management are the first steps in creating a corporate strategy and culture. These, in turn, provide a new, unified focus for internal corporate functions. They also provide the basis for the information technology investment by identifying points of leverage for corporate performance. These leverage points can be found at each and every relationship with each and every stakeholder.

Corporate strategy reflects the relationship that management desires with the corporation's stakeholders. Information technology can be used to promote the new or extended relationship. For example, banks initially invested in automatic teller machines (ATM's) to reduce the costs of maintaining employees in their branches. As a vehicle for reducing costs, ATM's failed to deliver. Nevertheless, the ATM's resulted in an unexpected benefit—a new and expanded relationship with the bank's customers. Now ATM's are a competitive necessity to keep market share.

The culture reflects the value placed on stakeholder relationships. In most businesses, the sales and marketing department has a great deal of clout. This is because of their special relationship with the customers, a highly valued stakeholder. Sales people have a uniquely simple reward system based on their relationship with the customer—a percentage of sales.

A corporation's infrastructure includes the systems that deliver value to its stakeholders. Systems that strengthen, combine, and communicate stakeholder relationships and strategy add value to the corporation and provide the basis for reward systems.

SUMMARY

A corporation exists only if it has assent from the various stakeholders that have a vested interest in its success. If corporate management wants to improve a business, it must start with improving stakeholder relationships.

Today's information technology allows new and better ways of enhancing stakeholder relationships, but management will never realize the IT potential if they haven't fathomed their stakeholder interests and potential.

ENDNOTES

1. Robert E. Johnson, *Airway Inc.* (Chicago: Lakeside Press, R. R. Donnelly & Sons, 1974) Many thanks to Captain James T. Davis of United Airlines for providing this and other source material for the Allegis case study.
2. Ibid.
3. Rosabeth M. Kanter, "Creating Stakeholder Value," pamphlet, NCR Corporation (1988).
4. Rosabeth M. Kanter, "Change Masters and the Intricate Architecture of Corporate Culture Change," *Management Review,* October 1983, pp. 18–28.

CHAPTER 4

STRATEGY, CULTURE, AND THE INFRASTRUCTURE: Forming the New Organization

The organizing principle explains the way in which a corporation's relationships are unified. Most companies have a fairly standard set of stakeholder relationships included in their organizing principle. Nevertheless, it's the unique strategy and culture of an organization that puts the spotlight on certain relationships and prioritizes them. This priority-setting process gives a company its distinctive traits. The specific relationships that a company intends to develop and enhance over time stem from its strategy and culture.

FUNCTIONAL SPECIALIZATION

Corporations have specialized internal business functions that are set up to deal with each and every set of stakeholders. Table 4–1 matches each stakeholder with its respective business function.

The way a company's business functions relate to the stakeholders determines the organization's culture. Unfortunately, most companies allow each business function to operate as a separate, independent business unit. Thus, business functions tend to become isolated, each speaking its own business dialect.

TABLE 4-1
Business Functions and Stakeholders

Stakeholder	Business Function
Customer	Sales, Marketing
Investor	Finance, Management
Vendors, Suppliers	Purchasing, Manufacturing
Employees	Personnel, Management
Management	Finance
Competitors	Sales, Marketing, Management
Regulators	Legal, Management
Community	Public Relations

Let's take, for example, the personnel department. This department has exclusive jurisdiction over pay systems, recruiting, firing, promotions, employee benefits, and so forth. Over the years, the personnel department has become overly structured, litigation oriented, and highly protective of its role in determining what a job should pay. At the same time, line managers have surrendered their line responsibilities for leadership.

All too often, the results of this corporate schism are rigid pay systems that establish cultures rewarding mediocrity. Line managers, trapped by the point-based pay systems, blame the systems when the real culprit is their own lack of leadership. The result is a culture that stifles creativity and performance.

This is particularly severe in companies that have personnel departments so removed from the stakeholders that they have created and subscribed to reward systems that operate independently from corporate performance. The point-based job evaluation system is one such reward system.

The Point-Based Job Evaluation System

To give an idea of how many companies have personnel departments that are too far removed from their stakeholders, let's note how many use point-based job systems instead of paying directly for performance.

Over 95 percent of major American corporations use point-based pay systems.[1]

Point-based pay systems were developed for bureaucratic environments where relative job worth is difficult to measure (e.g., the corporation considers information work too hard to measure for determining individual and group performance).

Point-based systems attempt to fairly estimate the worth of a job based on several factors. Typically, these are

1. Size of staff managed.
2. Size of budget.
3. Risk associated with decision making.

The larger the staff and budget and the riskier the decisions, the more a job is worth. Under this system, employees are rewarded for having larger staffs, bigger budgets, and more risk associated with decisions.

These rewards run contrary to the needs of today's environments. We need smaller staffs, smaller budgets, and less risk. For example, information technology permits information sharing. Separate staffs to create similar information don't make any sense.

Point-based evaluation systems are tied into the annual merit increase. The emphasis is on salary maintenance rather than paying for performance. Again, this runs contrary to today's understanding of stakeholder needs.

With today's information technology capability, we have the opportunity to measure performance at all levels in the organization. By measuring performance, we can tie reward systems to achievement of company, divisional, departmental, team, and individual objectives. This can be done on an hourly, weekly, or daily basis according to the frequency of performance rewards necessary to spark productivity increases. This was the secret of Creech's success at the Tactical Air Command and why TAC was able to improve its performance in the eyes of its stakeholders.

STAKEHOLDERS, BUSINESS FUNCTIONS, AND SYSTEMS

Figure 4–1 illustrates the need for your business systems to reflect the company's strategy and reward systems (its culture)

FIGURE 4–1

Stakeholders, Business Functions, and Systems: Integrating the Strategy and Culture

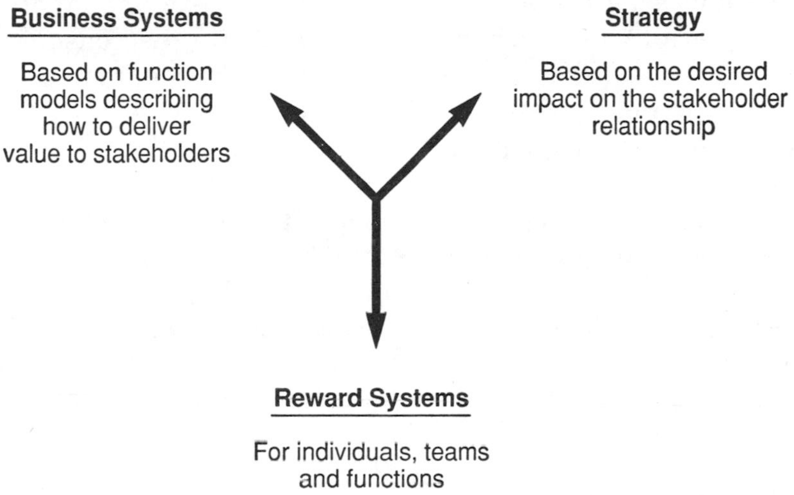

Business Systems	Strategy
Based on function models describing how to deliver value to stakeholders	Based on the desired impact on the stakeholder relationship

Reward Systems

For individuals, teams
and functions

and for reward systems to be based on your business strategy and systems. When you don't consider these three areas as integral parts of the company's infrastructure, your business systems won't reflect your strategy, and reward systems will work independently of business systems and company strategy. Such is the case with the point-based job-rating system described above. It's tied to neither the company's business systems nor its strategy.

Is it any wonder that it's so hard to get productivity improvements in your company? As you can see in this simple illustration, this is a key leverage point for your company. By tying together these three critical areas, you can achieve immediate benefit by focusing on your firm's organizing principle and purpose.

Unity of Purpose

By having a well-articulated organizing principle, your company can help the separate business functions recognize that together they all have a unity of purpose. Each has a role to play in enhancing stakeholder value. Figure 4–2 shows the first step in declaring a unity of purpose. The circle containing the various business functions represents the corporation, with linkages to each of the various stakeholders. Take sales, for example. While it specializes in the customer relationship, all other business functions have a vested interest in that relationship, too.

The Customer Relationship

Let's examine the customer relationship. The assessment of the customer relationship depends on the business function performing the assessment. For example, the sales function's assessment of a customer is that the customer can do no wrong. Customers are all-important. There can be no sale without a customer. Sales persons seek help from the rest of the organiza-

FIGURE 4–2
The Organizing Principle: Defining Simple Relationships

tion to make the sales process easier through better products, lower prices, faster delivery, and so forth.

The finance department considers whether the customer will pay the invoice on time or whether the customer will pay at all. The finance department tries to get the sales department to avoid selling to doubtful accounts. Furthermore, the finance department will turn to other organizations, such as Dun & Bradstreet, for help in evaluating the creditworthiness of customers.

The distribution function often sees the customer in a different way—as an adversary demanding unreasonable delivery terms. The legal function sees the customer simply as a business risk. Thus, the sales contract must cover every potential liability—and, of course, from the company's point of view.

All these views of a customer are valid. Nevertheless, the corporation and the customer suffer when each business function treats the customer stakeholder's needs differently. The customer needs not only the company's product or service but also financing, delivery, and an understanding of risk. These are all an integral part of the long-term customer relationship.

If unity of purpose is so important, how does a company integrate its internal and external relationships? The answer lies in understanding its strategy, culture, and infrastructure.

Businesses can gain significant competitive advantage by aligning internal functions and stakeholders with a well-articulated strategy, culture, and infrastructure. As illustrated in Figure 4–1, business systems, strategy, and reward systems are inseparable. The human resource, information systems, and financial executives play key integrating roles for defining and implementing corporate strategy, culture, and business systems. In addition, there are the executives with prime responsibility for managing the corporation's key strategic resources: people, information, and capital.

STRATEGY

The business strategy sets forth the processes for achieving competitive advantage in the marketplace and improving corporate performance. It gives direction and substance to the corporate objectives for relationships with stakeholders. Strategy integrates and aligns the business functions and stakeholders of the company through establishing the objectives for each stakeholder relationship. In so doing, strategy embodies the mutual interests of the stakeholders in the company's organizing principle.

Until now, an acceptable corporate strategic plan consisted of correct balance sheets, ratios such as return on investment and return on assets, and static organizational charts. This simplistic approach is unacceptable for the new business era because it overlooks the investment in information technology and the value of information to the business.

For example, the Allegis strategy, with its total travel concept, had the potential for creating value for the participating and interconnected airline, hotel, and car rental businesses. This was a potentially valid business strategy, one that we might well see come to fruition in the travel business in the next decade. However, Ferris' strategic plan lacked an essential component to make it happen—stakeholder assent. For a strategy to be valid, the company's various stakeholders need to buy into the concept and be willing to take short-term sacrifices for long-term gain.

The United pilots hadn't bought into the total travel strategy. Consequently, they were unwilling to make sacrifices in the airline to support the growth of nonairline businesses. Had Ferris taken a different tack with the pilots as stakeholders, they may have bought into the total travel concept. Had the pilots bought in, we might have a very different Allegis story today. But, they didn't, nor did other stakeholders. In the end, Ferris' plan received no stakeholder consideration, and the empire was dismantled.

Strategy Case Study: Wells Fargo & Company

Until 1983, Wells Fargo & Company had a five-year plan, as did all other banks. This five-year plan was the long-range planning document. It contained business plans and financial forecasts. Management updated the five-year plan each year. The revised version went back on the shelf where it gathered dust for another year.

One of the primary reasons for making the five-year plan was to satisfy the bank examiners. The examiner's checklist of things to go over included being sure that the bank had a five-year plan.

In 1983, Wells Fargo underwent a thorough self-examination and, as a result, scrapped its five-year plan. In its place, senior management built a 22-page strategic document. This strategy is the basis for Wells Fargo's current success. The bank changed from an international organization to a regional organization doing business in California. As a result of the regional focus, the bank began to view its region not as a state but as a collection of 185 geographical markets, each having its own needs.

The bank found that people in Weed, California, didn't have a strong need for converting foreign currency. Therefore, the rural Weed branch doesn't offer this service. However, the Christmas Club is popular, so the local branches offer it. In Palm Springs, the Christmas Club isn't a big seller; not surprisingly, the Palm Springs branches don't offer it.

The bank dropped unprofitable lines of service and created a menu of standard products. Branch managers, who are rewarded for branch financial performance, decided which products to offer in their local markets.

Wells Fargo sold or wrote off those high-risk loans tied to land speculation. They closed most of their international branches because few California customers used them. In their place, the bank made correspondence agreements with foreign local banks.

The bank changed its structure by utilizing technology in a new way. It decentralized the information systems organization and gave operating divisions the responsibility for their own applications.

As the bank made more and more use of information technology, it began to realize it had too many people—a handover from the now-obsolete banking structure. Looking forward, bank management realized that they needed to restructure the organization and remove at least one layer of middle management to enable greater productivity in the bank's branches and operating groups. Thus, Wells made the appropriate restructuring adjustments before a deteriorating financial position of the bank forced such adjustments. This made for an orderly transition conducted over time as opposed to panic actions after the bank began to report declining performance.

CULTURE

Culture describes the internal factors that are important to management, employees, and the company at large, such as systems for reward and performance. It includes the system of values that supports the carrying out of the strategy. Culture is the personality of the organization, including its shared beliefs and the symbols or artifacts that embody those beliefs.

The effect of information on the corporate culture is governed by two basic concepts:

1. Personal and organizational behavior is a direct result of accumulated knowledge.
2. Knowledge is a result of transferred information.

The information transfer is necessary to create corporate cultures. The way your corporation's employees and executives behave is a result of the knowledge created by information brought into and transferred within the corporation. This is where the information technology investment today differs from its use in the past.

You should view today's systems as vehicles for creating behavior that will fulfill corporate strategy. Information and knowledge contained in information systems complement human behavior and are essential to the information-based corporation.

Data, Information, and Knowledge

More and more, corporations are realizing the value of information and information technology. In understanding the relative value of different forms of information, it is important to distinguish between data, information, and knowledge:

1. Data is an accumulation of facts, measurements and observations. Data, in and of itself, does not point to the need for any kind of action or modification of behavior. Moreover, it is not self-interpreting.
2. Information is data converted so that intelligent animals (e.g., people) or machines can take action. Information answers the question "So what?" Information suggests the need for specific actions.
3. Knowledge combines information with experience to understand what types of action are possible and recommended. People or programmable machines have knowledge. Flight simulators program (teach) an airline pilot to fly an airplane. The information comes from flight instruments or a ground controller. An artificial intelligence system is knowledgeable when it successfully combines information sources with logical action paths.

Information and knowledge are inevitably intertwined with culture. Culture is a result of information-based programming of people or machines to take a predetermined action on new information received. The proper management of the corporate culture means establishing information-transfer mechanisms, including information systems.

Information management, covered later in this book, has as its focus assuring that executives and employees will send and receive quality information for translation into quality action. Companies that ignore this aspect of information management will miss out on the productivity potential for information technology.

Information and cultural management are key issues in corporate mergers and acquisitions. If you don't plan and manage both the cultural and information aspects when combining companies, real losses may occur. Mergers and acquisitions result in the meshing of different cultures. Few survive intact. Many don't survive at all.

The Case of the Merger

Let's examine a small, successful firm in the business of automated factory data collection. A large computer mainframe and terminal manufacturer acquired this smaller firm. The acquired company's success came from its management's in-depth understanding of the complexities of the manufacturing environment. The small firm's culture was very service oriented. Its business processes and information systems focused on service response time, customer site coverage, and its support for field-service technicians.

The new parent company emphasized leading-edge technology products with little after-sales support. The larger company's culture was product rather than service driven. Its information systems focused on product differentiation for pricing, sales, and market penetration.

The larger organization forced the acquired company to abandon its former culture. In its place, the parent installed a culture based on high-technology products and minimum service. It modified executive reward systems accordingly. As a result, the acquired company's management had to conduct business in a way that was strange to both them and their customers.

The acquired company no longer focused on service and its supporting information systems. As a result of converting to a product-driven environment, the acquired company now needed systems supporting sales, market penetration, and product differentiation for pricing. These systems were not available at the outset. The stakeholder result was confused executives, employees, and customers. The financial result was a significant loss of market share, revenue, and profitability.

Suffice it to say, attempting to instill the larger organization's culture in the new subsidiary was ineffective and killed any positive effects of the merger. The smaller organization hadn't yet built the infrastructure for a new way of running the business. The net result was that the new parent company's return on investment from the acquisition dwindled to nil and even to negative.

From the stakeholders' point of view, it would have been better for both companies if the acquisition had never taken place. The only winners were the major stockholders of the acquired company who sold out at an inflated price. Such is the saga of most acquisitions—grabbing the brass ring without a thought given to the merging of unlike corporate cultures. Most mergers fail for this reason alone.

Cultural Pathologies That Prevent Effective Use of IT

There are several identifiable illnesses that can negate any possible return on the information technology investment. They are vestiges of the industrial age and need removal in order to allow you to maximize your technology investment. They are

- The fortress mentality.
- Pecking-order systems.
- Outpostitis and corporatitis.

The Fortress Mentality

The observer can find a universal phenomenon in all corporate cultures—the fortress mentality. This mentality comes from the animal behavioral characteristic called the *territorial imperative*. Most animals live in geographic areas over which they feel they have the exclusive rights to occupancy and control. When other animals invade their territory, animals are ready to defend to their death such territorial rights. This has been a major factor for the survival of a species.

This behavior is also a major obstacle to information sharing and realizing the potential of the IT investment.

Pecking-Order Systems

This same territorial imperative exists within corporations. It usually arises when it comes to the issue of who owns corporate assets (especially information). Top management implements lines of demarcation with official corporate pecking-order schemes. Does your company allocate office space as follows?

1. Clerical workers are entitled to 100 square feet of workspace.
2. Supervisors are entitled to 150 square feet.
3. Managers are entitled to a partitioned work space and a telephone with two extension numbers.

4. Directors are entitled to a larger partitioned work space with a larger desk, two side armchairs, and a work table.
5. Assistant vice presidents are entitled to a table, sofa, large desk, credenza, and a potted plant.
6. Finally, executives of the inner circle have offices designed to reflect corporate image to influential outsiders.

Such pecking-order systems are further strengthened by point-based salary administration packages that reward compliance with corporate structure. They focus on the number of people supervised, the size of the budget, and the impact level of decision making. Such salary administration systems would have been ideal for Professor C. Northcote Parkinson's days at the Royal British Admiralty. The Hay point system of ranking job pay structures for professionals is one such system. Its use is falling out of favor with executive management because it perpetuates the belief that pay is based on the position and not on performance.

Senior management divides organizations into functional departments (e.g., marketing, financial, operations, and development divisions). There are also informal demarcations formed between car poolers and joggers as well as the company baseball and volleyball teams.

Today, divisive organizations are no longer appropriate. A cooperative ethic has set the scene for a new kind of corporation. Internal data and information sharing gives the new corporation power over its competitors. Internal partnerships create value for a corporation's stakeholders. The net result is improved quality, productivity, and financial performance.

Outpostitis and Corporatitis

Another corporate phenomenon is the demarcation created by the geographical separation of divisions from centralized corporate staffs, with two corporate illnesses resulting:

1. *Outpostitis.* "Those corporate types are only out to use us. They issue idiotic directives and find every opportunity to keep us in the dark and unrecognized by upper management."

2. *Corporatitis:* "We have to tell those clowns in the field over and over how to do things. All they care about is their myopic effort of bringing in orders for things we don't sell or making things that won't sell. They constantly request funds that they don't need. They are chronic complainers about every little real or imagined problem, especially when we try to assist them to meet our corporate objectives. In fact, they are downright nasty and resist any attempt for corporate assistance."

Both of these corporate illnesses are treatable and curable. But, it takes a concerted effort on the part of the entire executive team. Chief information executives who are thrown into this environment without support from the executive team need to keep their resumes up-to-date.

Cultures and Information

In their book, *Corporate Cultures,* Terrence E. Deal of Harvard and Allan E. Kennedy of McKinsey & Co. analyzed four basic kinds of corporate cultures:

1. The Tough Guy, Macho Culture.
2. The Bet-Your-Company Culture.
3. The Process Culture.
4. The Work Hard/Play Hard Culture.

Each culture is different. Each is the result of a certain kind of information structure. And each values information and the technology investment differently.

Tough Guy, Macho cultures breed managers of the major organizational components who emulate the top Tough Guy, Macho, or Tough Gal, Macha. In this environment, the lines of demarcation are clear. The Toughies will seek the heads of transgressors as vehemently as a fierce animal who is protecting its territory. The Toughies consider that they have exclusive ownership rights to their information. It is a sign of weakness to share it with any other part of the organization. In fact, a request for information sharing will result in intense reactive behavior. In this setting, corporate executives grab for the information resource and make it their exclusive property.

The *Bet-Your-Company* culture may be receptive to information sharing in general. Nevertheless, due to the very specialized nature of its divisions, it's difficult to reach consensus on common terminology or data definitions. Such groups as sales will often take the initiative to work with these variables for common customers. For example, American Hospital Supply and McKesson separately found competitive advantage when they shared their information with their customers.

Executives in the Bet-Your-Company environment are betting their company on a few key decisions with little or no feedback expected for years. A good example is an oil exploration company. Decision making focuses on doing it right the first time. Long deliberations follow. A mistake in oil exploration could result in a dry hole that cost $100 million to drill. In order to reduce the dry hole exposure, oil companies invest heavily in computer resources to perform geological analyses.

In a pharmaceutical company, a faulty medication could produce catastrophic results. Pharmaceutical companies' high-priority information needs deal with product research or exploration and legal requirements. Marketing information has the next priority. Other information, which is for doing such routine things as payroll and other accounting applications, is tertiary.

In the Bet-Your-Company environment, the chief information executive will experience a slow, methodological approach to doing business. Hence, the implementation of information management methodologies will be laborious. The basic business cycle is like a flywheel that forces all other corporate activity to revolve at the same speed. If the Bet-Your-Company cycle is six to eight years, the implementation time for information resource management must take into account the same six-to-eight-year flywheel.

On the other hand, the *Process* (or bureaucratic) environment pays meticulous attention to detail. It produces more alleged information than does any other culture. In fact, there is an outright information (data) glut. It's difficult to understand why the information is being created in the first place, much less how to use it. The government investment in information is huge. It dwarfs the corresponding investment in automated information-handling systems.

The *Work Hard/Play Hard* culture is the predominant culture in the high-technology industries. Emphasis is on growth. The sales organization drives the rest of the organization to provide product that will blow away the competition. The corporate heroes are those who produce results. Information exists in this environment, but it is dispersed, personalized, and informal. The bulk of the information generated in this environment identifies sales prospects and aids in closing sales. Quota plans, competitive moves, and sales results receive high attention. Yet any attempt to centralize information bases in this environment falls short of expectations. People are just too busy to provide the proper information for a centralized system. The folks at the central site are too busy putting out fires to install a quality, usable, and effective information base.

The cultural pressure in this environment is to show short-term results. Long-range information management plans simply don't fit the corporate scheme of things. These involve too much expense in the current period. So, this culture keeps running hard and working hard by the seat of its pants.

Understanding Your Culture

The foregoing discussion about various cultures is meant as a guide to help you decide what is possible and what may be difficult to accomplish in your company. If your company is divided into fiefdoms, information technology projects to be shared by the fiefdoms are likely to be expensive and less effective. If your company is very hierarchical and heavily dependent on the point-based job pay system, you have severe limitations to the return investments in information technology can bring you.

The key is to understand your culture and its limitations. The limitations should be removed through organizational restructuring and new rewards systems—not through building technology solutions designed to make the limitations go away. If your development backlog has projects with expectations for correcting basic organizational and rewards deficiencies, it would be better to shelve them until the organization is ready.

Paving the Way for Technology: An I/S—HR Partnership

One of the key functions of senior corporate executives is to identify changes needed in the company's culture. Line managers, in turn, put these new values or beliefs into action. Human resources (HR) and information systems (I/S) executives support the line managers in carrying out their responsibilities. The human resources department designs and carries out educational programs aimed at changing the appropriate attitudes and behavior of employees. I/S executives develop and implement the systems that reflect and deliver the changes.

For example, Wells Fargo Bank changed its culture by instituting a new pay system. It completely abolished merit increases. It put the funds normally drawn upon to award merit increases into a pool. The size of this pool varied with the overall financial performance of the bank. At the end of the year, line managers used the pool to award bonuses to those employees who contributed to the success of the business.

Another example is AT&T, which instituted changes in its reward systems for middle managers to change the corporate culture vis-à-vis teamwork. Top management established bonuses to go to the middle managers who did the most to support team efforts. In 1986, one such manager had 8 percent of his compensation tied to this structure, with 30 percent based on overall corporate performance and 70 percent based on his team's performance.

When the company changes its reward systems to coincide with desired behavior, you have a golden opportunity for leveraged information technology investment.

Combining Cultures: Unisys

In 1986, Burroughs Corporation acquired the Sperry Corporation. Wall Street observers gave the merger only a slight chance of success. Looking from the outside, the two cultures were very different. (See Table 4–2.)

Burroughs, for the most part, engaged in selling medium-range business and accounting systems. Their primary customer

TABLE 4-2
Burroughs Corporation Compared with Sperry Corporation, 1986

	Burroughs	Sperry
Industry Culture	Financial	Engineering
I/S Positioning	Part of finance	Technical service
Market View	Accounting	High technology
Market Base	Medium-sized businesses	Government/research
Product	Medium-range systems	Large systems

sources were financial institutions and small- to medium-sized businesses. There were sales of high-technology systems to the military, but this was a secondary business. Because of Burroughs's business orientation, sales, financial, and marketing executives drove the corporation.

Sperry, on the other hand, built large systems for government and research customers. It was a technology-driven company. The research and development functions drove the company.

Considering that Burroughs acquired Sperry, combining the two cultures meant only one thing: the death of Sperry. To avoid this, Michael Blumenthal, chairman of Burroughs, decided on a different course of action.

Blumenthal declared that Burroughs was not *acquiring* Sperry; it was a *merger* of equals. Secondly, he declared that he would replace both the Burroughs and Sperry cultures with a new culture. A systems engineer won a contest for naming the new, integrated company. He received $5,000 for his winning entry, Unisys.

Now Blumenthal began to build the new culture. When asked whether he would use Burroughs or Sperry management, he replied, "Neither." The new company, Unisys, selected the Burroughs or Sperry person best qualified for the job. Management selected the best person for each opening, regardless of past affiliation with Burroughs or Sperry.

Alan Jones, Staff Vice President of Information Systems & Communications, led the effort to interconnect the various Burroughs and Sperry systems. Once this was accomplished, he received the task of building the new Unisys system's infra-structure.

INFRASTRUCTURE

The infrastructure is the arrangement of people, systems, and facilities. It serves as the delivery vehicle to carry out the company strategy and culture. In the industrial age, the basic infrastructure consisted of plants, workers, machinery, and railroads. It was visible and tangible. Senior management could easily see the nature of these long-term investments.

Today's corporate infrastructure is far less tangible. The word *soft* even describes a key part of the infrastructure in the information age: software. Information systems are complex, interdependent, and ever-evolving webs of relationships that link all aspects of the organization. In the industrial age, infrastruc-ture meant bricks and mortar. In the information age, it means systems and networks.

Figure 4–3 gives an illustration of how systems are related to stakeholders. This particular example comes from a restau-rant. By relating each system to its stakeholder impact, you can begin to appreciate the value of the system to the company. For example, if you didn't have a reservation system, you wouldn't be able to reserve tables for guests. By not having the ability to meet your guest stakeholder's needs, financial results would suffer. This would impact yet two other stakeholders, manage-ment and investors.[2] Senior management is beginning to under-stand the value of systems and networks as a part of the corporate infrastructure. But what is the best guide to help management decide when to invest in information technology?

Value-Added IT Investments in the Infrastructure

To gain the greatest value added for the corporation, informa-tion technology investments should be linked to the corpora-

FIGURE 4–3
Stakeholder Relationships: Systems Used by Stakeholders

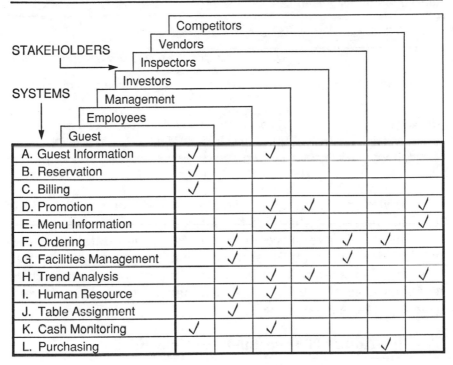

SYSTEMS \ STAKEHOLDERS	Guest	Employees	Management	Investors	Inspectors	Vendors	Competitors
A. Guest Information	✓		✓				
B. Reservation	✓						
C. Billing	✓						
D. Promotion			✓	✓			✓
E. Menu Information			✓				✓
F. Ordering		✓			✓	✓	
G. Facilities Management		✓			✓		
H. Trend Analysis			✓	✓			✓
I. Human Resource		✓	✓				
J. Table Assignment		✓					
K. Cash Monitoring	✓		✓				
L. Purchasing						✓	

tion's primary resources: people, information, and capital. (See Table 4–3.)

One of our clients made a value-added information-technology investment in people. Working together, the information systems and personnel functions built a system for establishing base pay. This system reflected the degree to which a job contributed to the organization's goals and objectives. Line managers, not the personnel department, used the system. The result was improved job design with full participation of the line manager and the job holder.

Just-in-time applications are an example of an information technology investment that has leveraged capital. Many companies have experienced a dramatic reduction in inventories as a result of converting to a pull-oriented manufacturing system.

TABLE 4–3
Value-Added Information Technology Investments
Linked to Primary Resources

Primary Resource	Value-Added Investment
People	Systems changing the nature of work and providing leverage on relationships
Information	Systems facilitating access to and speeding the transmission of information resulting in enhanced relationships.
Capital	Systems providing new sources of capital, leveraging investors and other relationships

The inventory reductions provide a new source of working capital and reduce the need for outside capital sources.

Information resource investments include databases, networks, decision support systems, and executive information systems. For example, an executive information system (EIS) changed executive behavior and enhanced the employee relationship at Comshare, Inc.

A Value-Added IT Investment at Comshare

In 1988, Rick Crandall, president of Comshare, talked to the Financial Executives Institute about Comshare's Commander executive information system (EIS) product. As president, he receives his executive briefing report from the Commander EIS. One section of the briefing reports on employees leaving the company. Rick asked that the report also show whether an exiting employee had received an excellent performance rating. This additional information helped Rick keep track of employees with excellent ratings who were leaving the company.

Comshare senior executives soon caught on to the significance of the new report. They went to personnel to get a list of employees in their functions who had excellent ratings. They then met with each employee with an excellent rating to find out how they were getting on in the company. The result was greater retention of excellent employees.

Redefining the Organization

The infrastructure will be most effective in delivering an organization's strategy and culture if the organization takes three steps.

First, it must integrate information technology into its strategic business plan.

Second, it needs to make significant organizational changes to take advantage of information technology.

And third, it must dovolop offective structures to deliver information technology benefits.

Wells Fargo & Company recognized this when it underwent reorganization in 1983. The new organization had to be far more adaptive to customer needs. The various business units (e.g., retail, commercial, trust, and real estate) needed direct involvement in the information systems supporting their business processes. For this reason, Jack Hancock, executive vice president of Systems and Strategy, dismantled the large, centralized information systems organization.

Hancock turned business and operations systems over to proponents in the operating business divisions. Proponents are executives charged with the responsibility for developing, running, and maintaining the systems part of the infrastructure in each division. For example, the systems proponent in the trust division had the responsibility for overseeing the development, running, and maintenance of the trust division's systems.

When Wells Fargo acquired the Crocker National Bank in 1985, the proponent network was already in place. Wells Fargo and Crocker National offered similar products in the same regional markets. The primary benefit of the Crocker acquisition for Wells Fargo was an immediate expansion of its customer base. The benefit for the British bank, Midland, of selling Crocker was to cut its losses short.

Because Wells Fargo had just undergone a major reorganization of its own infrastructure, it didn't want Crocker's. In the acquisition negotiations, Wells Fargo put two non-negotiables on the table:

1. The new infrastructure of the two merged banks would use Wells Fargo systems. There would be no discussion of which Crocker systems were better than their Wells Fargo equivalents.
2. Crocker management would leave. Wells Fargo management would manage the infrastructure of the combined banks.

Crocker National investors accepted these two conditions and the banks merged. The Wells Fargo systems accepted Crocker customers. Crocker management left. The merger, notwithstanding the human toll, was a financial success.

The Industrial Age Organization

Figure 4–4 shows the classic industrial, hierarchical organization for delivering the corporate strategy and culture. The vertical structure was useful: it facilitated distributing information, interpreting policy, and controlling business activities. Middle management served as information brokers. Senior management focused on business possibilities. This resulted in strategy and direction. Top functional executives focused on action plans for carrying out the strategy in their areas of responsibility. Further layers of managers and supervisors provided more and more detailed information for the carrying out of lower- and lower-level tasks. Finally, the lowest-level worker simply responded to requests for specific chores.

The hierarchical organization was designed for controlling capital, direct labor, and material resources. Information flowed down the functional hierarchies until someone took action. The lateral flow of information was minimal. The information flow back up the hierarchy was a virtual trickle.

The Information Age Organization

Figure 4–5 represents an organization designed for the delivery of strategy and culture in today's corporation. The cross-functional executive committee focuses on strategy and establishing a culture that will carry out the strategy. The front line,

FIGURE 4–4
The Old Corporate Model

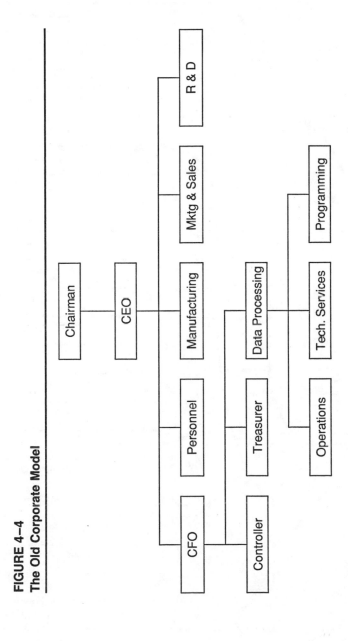

FIGURE 4–5
The New Corporate Model

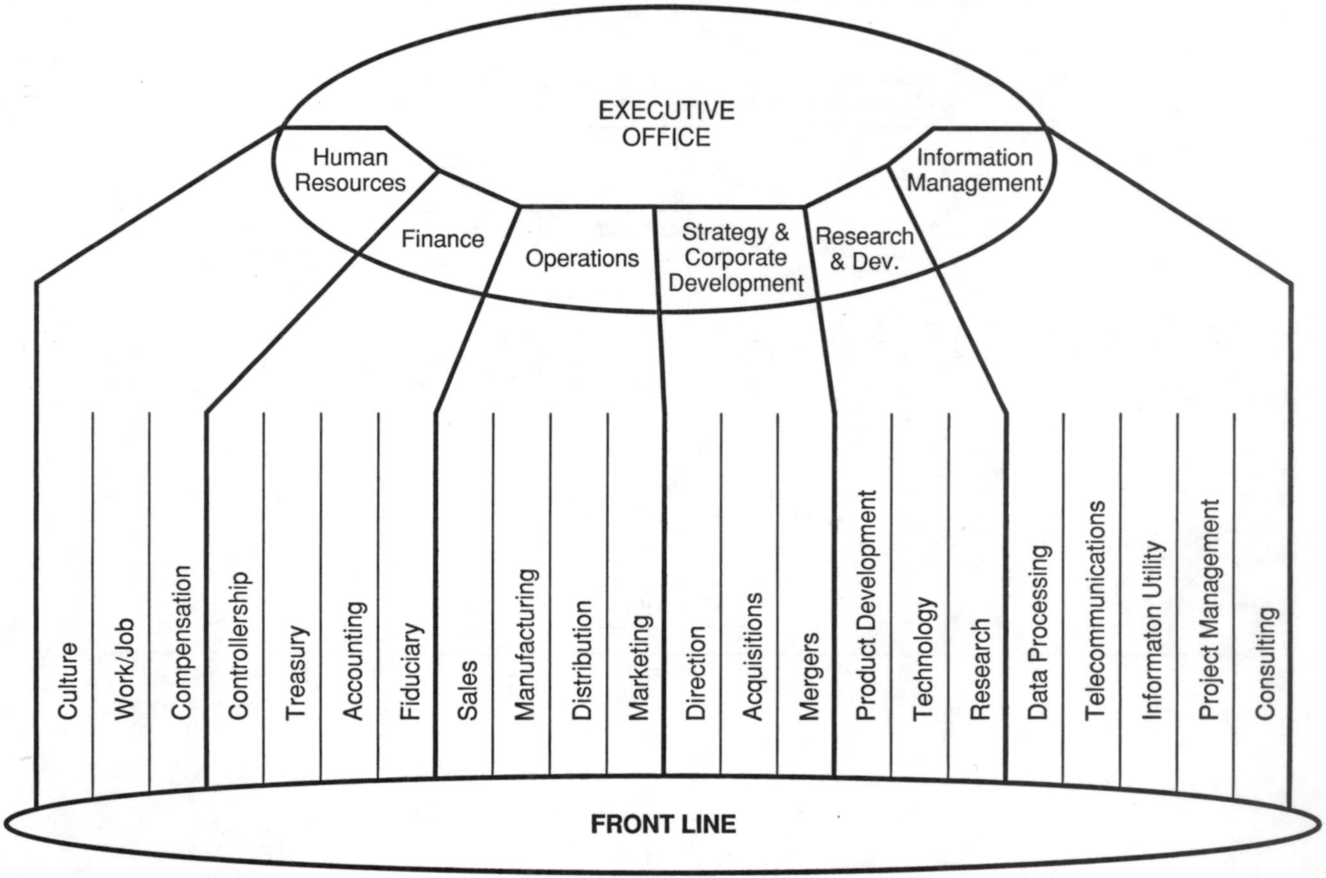

EXECUTIVE OFFICE

Human Resources
Finance
Operations
Strategy & Corporate Development
Research & Dev.
Information Management

Culture
Work/Job
Compensation
Controllership
Treasury
Accounting
Fiduciary
Sales
Manufacturing
Distribution
Marketing
Direction
Acquisitions
Mergers
Product Development
Technology
Research
Data Processing
Telecommunications
Information Utility
Project Management
Consulting

FRONT LINE

supported and coordinated by middle management, deals directly with stakeholders.

The network represented by this new organization is only possible with extensive information-technology investment. Rapid access to information and data drive the new business partnerships between functional executives and business units. The backbone of the new organization is its communications systems that enable access to information throughout the enterprise.

By moving to the new information-based organization, you can reduce overhead costs by simplifying the management structure. You can improve the performance on the front line by enabling decision making at the lowest organizational level. You will be more competitive with highly responsive and high-quality products and services. The strategy, culture, and infrastructure supported by information technology provide a foundation for growth and achievement at all organizational levels.

ENDNOTES

1. Edward E. Lawler III, "Job Evaluation: A Critique." University of Southern California School of Business Administration (1985).
2. Thanks to Richard K. Davis, Chairman, Performance Development Corporation, for this example.

CHAPTER 5

THE DRIVING FORCE AND
THE FUNCTIONAL MISSION:
Unity of Action

The organizing principle provides the unity of purpose to integrate the company's stakeholders. The corporate strategy and culture provide the direction and reward systems for prioritizing the needs of various stakeholders. The corporation's infrastructure furnishes the mechanism for communicating the strategy and culture and delivering value to the stakeholders.

Albeit that unity of purpose is essential, the business must have more than that. It must also have unity of action. An enterprise gains competitive strength when it focuses its actions on the strategic area that provides the most stakeholder leverage.

The organizing principle, through its stakeholder relationships, reveals the locations of the corporation's external leverage points. For example, shareholders have a need to increase their wealth through their participation in the corporation. Customers want a product or service that satisfies their need. Employees want to attain personal security from a fair wage, good working conditions, and a chance to benefit from their association with the company. And so on.

Through the same stakeholder relationships, the driving force identifies the internal leverage points and relative priority among them. By being totally clear about the corporation's driving force, senior executives can align the corporation's internal relationships and functions so that they will act in harmony in satisfying stakeholder needs.

THE DRIVING FORCE

In their book, *Top Management Strategy,* Tregoe and Zimmerman identified nine basic strategic areas of endeavor in a corporation. These nine basic areas are divided into three groups:

> *Products/Market*
> > Products offered
> > Market needs
>
> *Capabilities*
> > Technology
> > Production capability
> > Method of sale
> > Method of distribution
> > Natural resources
>
> *Results*
> > Size/growth
> > Return/profit

All strategic areas are important for an enterprise to succeed. Only one can be its driving force. This means that the leaders of the various functions within an organization must agree on which strategic area is most important. Once consensus is achieved, functional leaders are better able to act in concert.

The three strategic groups—products/market, capabilities, and results—are differentiated by the stakeholder relationship that is key to the success of the particular business. Each group also provides special insight into where the information technology investment will leverage the financial performance of the organization.

The Products/Market-Driven Enterprise

The products/market-driven enterprise has its success or failure determined in the marketplace. It must produce the right products and meet the right market needs to grow and prosper. This means that the customer relationship is paramount. The chief executive officers of products/market-driven companies generally come from the sales and marketing functions.

Products Offered as a Driving Force

A products-offered driven company uses a basic technology to produce a line of products for diverse customers. For example, pharmaceutical manufacturing and marketing companies are typically products-offered companies. They develop, produce, and market ethical and over-the-counter pharmaceutical products. Their speed in introducing and promoting new products directly determines financial results. In particular, Merrell Dow Pharmaceuticals, Inc., has a best-selling nonsedative antihistamine. Merck has a best-selling cholesterol reducing drug. Syntex is the market leader in selling birth control medications.

The customer relationships of a products-offered company can be very complex. For example, it's difficult to decide who's the customer in a pharmaceutical company. Figure 5–1 illustrates the different stakeholders involved in distributing, marketing, selling, prescribing, dispensing, and consuming medications. All of the stakeholders shown are, in a sense, customers. To succeed in the market, the pharmaceutical company leverages the flow of its product into the marketplace with these stakeholders.

The first recommendation concerning strengthening customer relationships that we make to marketing information systems organizations is to get rid of the word *customer*. By doing this, the company can better understand the complex web of relationships external to the company. For example, doctors have a special relationship with patients, another with pharmacists, and yet another with pharmaceutical companies. Patients have a special relationship with health maintenance organizations (HMO's), another with their personal physicians, another with pharmacists, and yet another with hospitals. And so on.

By understanding the nature of the company's relationship with each stakeholder in its market and the special relationships that exist between stakeholders, the pharmaceutical company in this example can position itself to add greater value to all relationships. If the pharmaceutical company considers all

FIGURE 5–1
CUSTOMER RELATIONSHIPS

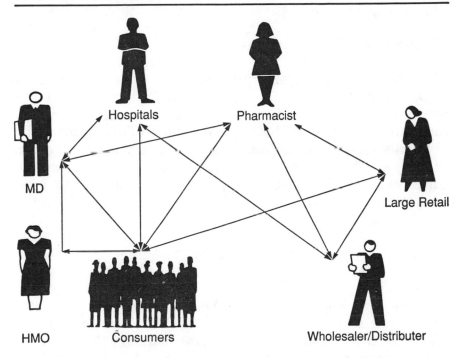

these stakeholders merely as customers, it will lose the insight needed to create competitive advantages.

Market Needs as a Driving Force

The company whose driving force is market needs has identified a different way to create value for its stakeholders. Rather than relying on a basic technology to create products for a diverse market, it provides diverse products and/or services for a particular market. How well an organization satisfies the needs of a particular market segment determines its success.

The American Association for Retired Persons deals exclusively with a market segment characterized by the needs of people who are aged 50 years or more. It provides diverse services ranging from insurance to travel. Christian Dior satisfies its customers' needs for style and elegance. Its customers are young, urban professionals—yuppies. It provides everything from cologne to ties to suits.

Capabilities-Driven Enterprises

The capability-driven enterprise has the same assortment of stakeholders as do those enterprises that are products/market driven. The difference is the focus on a capability. There is normally an established market for the products provided by capability-driven companies. Customers and market needs are important. But the most important element is the capability that produces the product or service. This means that the stakeholders involved in providing the capability are of primary importance.

A Technology-Driven Case Study:
Ampex Corporation

Alexander M. Poniatoff founded Ampex Corporation right after World War II to develop audio and video recording technology. He attracted investors, one of whom was Bing Crosby, and a brilliant group of engineers to pioneer this industry. Poniatoff established high rewards for the young engineers: high salaries, stock, and stock options. The driving force was clearly Ampex's technology capability. The result was an outstanding business that captured the studio video-recording market.

Ampex hired additional engineers after the original group, but the rewards to individuals diminished as time went on. By the 1970s, Ampex treated new engineers as any other employee. Ampex was no longer technology driven. In fact, Ampex management viewed technology as a marketable commodity and helped a future Japanese competitor, Sony, to enter the video-recording business by licensing Ampex technology.

Over the years, Ampex's stock grew in value. By 1980, most of the original group of engineers had reached retirement age. They wanted to cash in their chips and start new chapters in their lives. Signal Corporation bought Ampex and paid off the engineers. The new owners invested less and less in technology.

At the same time, Sony's commitment to being the technology leader in video recording was bearing fruit. The result: Sony, Ampex's chief competitor today, now leads in the video-recording business.

This example points out the importance of the driving force. It's not the story of a Japanese company simply doing a better job of manufacturing a product than does a U.S. company. It's the story of one company that has abandoned, versus another company that has retained, its successful driving force.

Since Ampex's original engineers won financial independence, other stakeholders' value has declined. Could the original group of engineers have achieved financial independence while the other stakeholders' value increased as well? We will explore the answer to this question with results-driven companies.

A Production- Capability Case Study: Champion International

Champion International is a large paper company. It produces a variety of commercial paper for use in other industries. Its products are sold as commodities to newspapers, publishers, and manufacturers of paper products.

At first blush, you might consider Champion to be a products-offered company. If this were the case, however, we would expect to find a former sales or marketing executive in the chief executive officer's position.

Champion's chief executive officer came up through the ranks in its capital- intensive mills. So did his predecessors. This gives a clear message. The most important part of Champion International is its mills, which represent its production capability. Champion's driving force is clearly its production capability of various commodity paper products.

On the other hand, Appleton Papers, Inc., is a product-driven company. Its top executives are marketing oriented. Appleton Paper's primary product, its famous NCR (no carbon required) paper forms, is a specialty paper product. Appleton Paper is heavily involved with its customers, whereas commodity paper producers are minimally involved.

It's interesting to note here that, as is true at Champion (a commodity, capability-oriented company), chief executive officers of data processing service companies usually come from the operations or development divisions. Operations and development executives understand the investment in information technology represented by hardware and software. The services offered must present a substantial price advantage to the customer. Otherwise, it makes no sense for companies to go outside for their data processing needs. In this environment, data processing operations executives understand how to optimize equipment usage for low unit prices.

Method of Sale: Avon, Inc.

Avon, Inc., is the company most often associated with the strategic method-of-sale area. This company has developed a reputation for house-to-house selling. "Avon calling" is a familiar phrase to many people.

At first, Avon concentrated on cosmetics. As time went on, they found that they could sell other products by this method. The house-to-house salesperson is a key stakeholder in this setting.

Method of Distribution: Wendy's International

Wendy's International has over 3,500 fast food outlets. Wendy's major product has been its top-quality hamburger. The hamburger is still its premier product, although Wendy's has introduced other products to appeal to an aging and health-conscious United States.

To determine the driving force at Wendy's, one only has to identify the key stakeholders in the Wendy's culture: the store manager and the franchisee. These stakeholders manage the distribution channel. Information systems and corporate support are focused on making every store manager and franchisee successful.

Up to now, the hamburger has satisfied the customer's need for a quick and inexpensive meal. The motive for purchase is simple: hunger. The primary customer is teenagers.

Now, an aging market is looking for ways to satisfy hunger with less fattening food. In response, Wendy's is installing the Super Bar with selections from Mexican, Italian, and Chinese cuisine. The Super Bar also has a full selection of salads. In the future, we can expect other quick, low-priced meals from this method-of-distribution–driven company.

Natural-Resource–Driven Companies

The category of natural-resource–driven companies includes organizations involved in developing sources, refining, and distribution of natural resources. Commercial examples include oil and gas companies. Governmental examples include the U.S. Department of Agriculture and its Division of Forestry.

An interesting example of a company in the business of developing sources of natural resources is Freeport-MacMoRan, Inc. Headquartered in New Orleans, Freeport-MacMoRan is a company that manages an investment fund for exploring for oil, gold, and other precious commodities. It has no extensive sales or marketing functions. The results of exploration, if successful, yield commodities that have a ready market.

At Freeport-MacMoRan, the shareholder is the real customer. Freeport-MacMoRan's shareholder is a stakeholder who wishes to invest in the exploration for precious commodities. The company's expertise is in managing a natural resource exploration business. Their performance has been excellent.

Results-Driven Corporations

Results-driven corporations generally fall into three categories:

1. Portfolio-managed organizations.
2. Organizations recovering from a disaster.
3. Corporations fending off a takeover attempt.

These companies are managed for their growth in size or earnings. The shareholder is the most important stakeholder, although there are some exceptions. The focus on results is for the short term. In the longer term, corporations have to return their focus to the entire group of stakeholders to continue to prosper.

Portfolio-Managed Companies: ROI as a Driving Force

Portfolio management became an important management concept in the 1950s. Its proponents included firms like McKinsey & Company; the Boston Consulting Group; and Booz, Allen & Hamilton. Portfolio management is the buying and selling of companies based on their potential for return on investment to the parent company.

Figure 5–2 depicts a concept developed in the 1960s by The Boston Consulting Group, a concept used extensively in portfolio management. A holding company manages its investment in subsidiary companies. The subsidiaries are judged on their current return or near-term potential for return. The company adjudged a *star* is a company that provides a good return now and for which the outlook is for continued revenue and earnings growth. The holding company uses the cash generated by a star to continue the star's expansion.

A *problem child* is a company that probably should be a star. It is doing business in a growing market, but for some reason is

FIGURE 5–2
PORTFOLIO MANAGEMENT

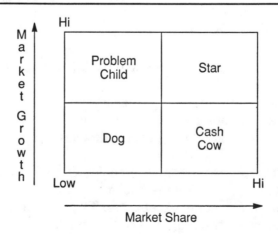

losing market share. The holding company must either turn a problem child around or sell it.

A *cash cow* is a company that is presently generating excess cash but has limited potential for future growth. The typical pattern is for the holding company to take cash from the cash cow and reinvest it in a star or a problem child.

The *dog* is a loser with no prospects for turnaround and growth. Portfolio-managed companies sell dogs as quickly as possible.

The weakness of the portfolio-management concept is the same as its perceived strength—its narrow focus. A few years ago, Allied Corporation, a portfolio-managed company, bought Signal Corporation, another portfolio-managed company. The new Allied-Signal Corporation consolidated its holdings and spun off a number of dogs that were formed into The Henley Group. Surprisingly, The Henley Group has outperformed the new Allied-Signal Corporation ever since. The message is that in a global economy, dogs are in the eye of the beholder.

A Portfolio Case Study: Ampex Corporation, Continued

Ampex's original group of engineers and Ampex's management arranged the sale of Ampex to Signal Corporation. Under Signal's aegis, Ampex conducted business as usual. The understaffed engineering group was left as it was, and Ampex generated profits for a while.

By the time Allied bought Signal in 1982, Ampex was having difficulties. Under a severe cost-cutting program, Ampex's profitability returned and generated cash. Allied-Signal made no significant investment in Ampex R&D, even though many of Ampex's patents were to expire in the 1980s.

In 1987, Allied-Signal sold Ampex to Hillside Capital Corporation. Hillside has a reputation for buying companies that have potential but need capital to become healthy and growing. Hillside's successful Congoleum Corporation is an example. With a new source of capital, Ampex again has a possibility for recovering some of its former vitality.

Chrysler: A Phoenix That Arose from the Ashes

When Lee Iococca took over Chrysler, it was in shambles. Chrysler had a long history of being an engineering-driven company. Its technical success had led it into other businesses such as building tanks for the defense industry.

Chrysler's main business was under attack from both the Japanese, with their emphasis on quality and design, and from Ford's marketing-driven efforts. Its financial performance and investor credibility were at rock bottom—so much so that it took the government to provide the necessary funds for Chrysler to survive.

For the first few years after the government bailout loan, Chrysler's driving force was clearly profit growth. Drastic cost-cutting, excellent marketing, and premier showmanship on Iacocca's part permitted Chrysler to repay its loans early. Iacocca thus regained the necessary investor confidence sorely needed for a robust, long-term recovery. But this was not without the help of another very important stakeholder—the unions.

Iococca demonstrated his genius at getting stakeholders to pull together when he gave the United Auto Workers (UAW) president a seat on Chrysler's board of directors. Prior to this, the relationship between Chrysler and the UAW was adversarial, if not downright militant. By making the unions a part of the recovery, their vested interest in the success of Chrysler matched that of other stakeholders.

When Chrysler had recovered financially and had restored investor confidence, Iococca changed the driving force from results-driven to market-driven. The company we see today is a premier marketing organization, supported with effective stakeholder partnerships that drive other strategic areas of the business.

Growth for Survival: The Story of American Banks

The financial services industry is consolidating. Bigger banks are swallowing up smaller banks. Today it's only a matter of time before a small bank faces being taken over. As a result, small and medium-sized banks must adopt a growth/results driving force for a period of time.

Many small and medium-sized American banks have adopted two strategies, one growth-oriented and one results-oriented. With these temporary strategies as driving forces, the bank's stakeholders will receive better value.

> The *growth-related* driving force dictates a strategy of increasing the market value of the bank by acquiring smaller banks to increase the asset base.
>
> The *results-related* driving force dictates a strategy of producing excellent short-term financial results, thereby increasing the market value of the bank's stock.

Both strategies are aimed at improving the short-term perception of the bank's worth. The higher the price to acquire the bank, the more difficult it is to acquire.

For example, Sovran Bank began with the merger of two equals, Virginia National Bancshares and First & Merchants Bank. The combined assets were about $13 billion. Since then, Sovran has acquired other banks so their asset base is now over $25 billion. The result has been that they remain an independent bank producing excellent results for their stakeholders.

THE FUNCTIONAL MISSION

A function's mission is based on the company's organizing principle, its policies and beliefs, and driving force. The mission statement is brief with broad scope. It defines the function's role in creating value for the stakeholders.

The following are examples of mission statements for the financial, corporate development, human resource, and information systems functions. The actual mission statements must consider the nature of the business, the strengths and weaknesses of the executive team, and the organization's ability to assimilate change.

Finance

The finance division supports senior management in increasing the value of the shareholders' investment. It does this through

- Controlling costs.
- Protecting the corporation's assets.
- Giving advice on capital investments.
- Finding low-cost sources of corporate capital.
- Meeting regulatory and tax requirements.
- Participating in the executive management of the corporation.

Corporate Development

The corporate development division supports senior management in its assessment of the current business and its ability to satisfy stakeholder needs as well as its assessment of new business opportunities. It does this through

- Assisting senior management in developing the corporate strategy.
- Assessing business and organizational performance.
- Finding opportunities for expanding the basic business.
- Finding new business opportunities that capitalize on current corporate culture and strengths.
- Finding suitable merger and acquisition opportunities.
- Developing strategic thinking in the organization.

Human Resources

The human resources division supports senior management in developing the skills, professionalism, identity, and commitment of employees. In particular, human resources assists senior management in developing the corporate culture and systems of value and rewards. It does this through

- Providing a continuing flow of suitable candidates for corporate jobs and positions.
- Providing succession planning for every job in the company.

- Providing training and development for employees to assure continual personal growth.
- Building employee identity specific to the company.
- Designing compensation systems that pay for performance, share corporate business risks, and share corporate success.
- Assisting senior management in developing policies and beliefs based on the organizing principle and in creating stakeholder value.

Information Systems

The information systems division provides the means for integrating business functions throughout the corporation in its pursuit of creating stakeholder value. It does this through

- Providing access to information necessary to drive production systems, management control systems, decision support systems, and executive information systems.
- Assisting functional organizations in creating, standardizing, managing, and sharing the corporate information asset.
- Building the corporate information infrastructure in partnership with senior management and the functional organizations.
- Promoting the appropriate use of information technology to leverage business performance through education and example.
- Providing corporate information utilities.

Integrating and Uniting Business Functions

The common thread running through each of these mission statements is the need for overall integration and uniting of the corporate business functions. Chief information executives have the largest potential role because of their direct involvement in the infrastructure. They must consider every business process and every stakeholder relationship each time they modify the infrastructure.

Information systems executives who grew up in the central-ized data-processing and applications-development environment are facing a completely new role. This means a repositioning of both the information systems organization and the executive in charge.

To begin a process of repositioning, information systems executives must first determine their current position and the current movement toward better positioning. They can then begin to plan for the proper positioning of their I/S organization so that it will be able to carry out its mission.

Figure 5–3 shows a questionnaire that we have used with both information systems executives and members of the exec-utive committee to discover current positioning and possible future positioning of the I/S function in the business. The objective is to build better overall corporate understanding of the transition necessary for building a new role for I/S execu-tives and their staff.

The "Individual and Organizational Profile" gives insight into the way senior executives, users, and the organization as a whole perceive the information systems function. It also gives the executive committee and chief information executive an idea of the preparedness of the I/S staff.

Each section has a range of responses ranging from low to high I/S effectiveness. To achieve high effectiveness ratings, the chief information executive must educate upwards, downwards, and across the organization.

The answers for most companies have tended toward the middle answer in each category. Such results indicate that chief information executives need to promote major educational ef-forts in their companies. These educational efforts must be directed at the business use of information technology, not at the technology itself. This is a completely new role for those who have grown up in the data-processing environment.

A Word of Caution

We have found that it is possible for I/S organizations to be too far out in front of the rest of a company. For example, in most department store retailing companies, the executive committee

FIGURE 5–3
Individual and Organizational Profile

Name: Title:
Company:
Address: Mail Stop:
City: State: Zip:
Telephone:(   )   Extension

There are four sections in this profile, each consisting of five paragraphs that make key distinctions in the roles that information systems (I/S) and information technology (IT) play in organizations. In each section, select the one paragraph that best describes the situation today in your company and check the appropriate box in the "Today" column. Then select the one paragraph that best describes the situation as you see it in the future in your company and check the appropriate box in the "Future" column.
RETURN TO: Jack A. Hamilton, Vice President, The Information Group, Inc. P.O. Box Q, Santa Clara, CA 95055–3756.

Senior Executives' View of I/S

Today   Future

☐   ☐   Have minimal needs for computerized information in managing the business. I/S is a technical support function included in corporate overhead expense. IT investment is based on a percentage of the annual overhead budget.

☐   ☐   Focus on automating information critical to controlling the day-to-day operation of the business. I/S is a backroom data processing function with a mission to reduce costs. IT investment is based on payback.

☐   ☐   Realize that information systems are essential not only to controlling the day-to-day operation of the business, but also to the marketing and sales functions. IT investment is ROI-based. Include I/S executive as a member of the senior management team.

☐   ☐   Support information and IT as strategic resources. Willing to live with a lower ROI from IT investments than from comparable investments elsewhere in the company because of their belief that probably there is value-added from IT investments that can't be calculated. I/S executive reports directly to the CEO.

☐   ☐   Realize that information and IT are necessary to support new organizational structures. I/S is viewed as the key component of the corporate infrastructure that delivers the corporation's strategy and culture. A new, cooperative relationship is formed between I/S, human resources, finance, and corporate development.

FIGURE 5–3
Continued

Client Business Units' View of I/S

Today   *Future*

☐   ☐   I/S, in its present mode of functioning, is an obstacle to the business. I/S isolates itself from the business. I/S is not only unresponsive to client requests, it also prevents clients from using IT themselves.

☐   ☐   I/S is a backroom function that exists strictly as a programming and computing utility. I/S responds adequately to requests, but otherwise is invisible to the business units.

☐   ☐   I/S is a source of major computer applications development and processing systems that reduce the costs of business and support revenue generating processes. Financial institutions use I/S to produce new financial products that result in reduced costs and increased revenue. Manufacturing companies use I/S to reduce inventories, automate production processes, and automate their sales and distribution functions.

☐   ☐   I/S is the primary source of expertise and information used to improve the performance of the corporation. Shared databases enable business units to work together to solve common business problems. I/S staff responds quickly to satisfy information needs of the business units. Decision support and executive information systems are key to improving business performance.

☐   ☐   I/S is a value-adding partner in the management of the business and is the primary source of strategies for applying IT to business goals. I/S is open to joint exploration of centrally- and client-managed IT solutions to business needs. I/S staff works with business units to enhance the value of stakeholder relationships.

The I/S Executive's Role

Today   *Future*

☐   ☐   As operating officer, focuses on managing the corporate data processing and telecommunications utilities as well as central applications development. Has developed a high level of applied technical and project management competence. Accountable for minimizing the total cost of IT to the corporation.

FIGURE 5–3
Continued

☐ ☐ As technology officer, promotes the use of advanced information technology in the business. Has developed a high level of competence in advanced information technology research and joint ventures with technology vendors. Provides centralized control for the technical management of the IT investment.

☐ ☐ As information officer, provides centralized control of the information investment by focusing on data administration and information resource management. Establishes standardized policies, procedures, reporting structures, and communication channels to provide for information availability and accessibility throughout the organization. Has developed a high level of competence in data and enterprise modeling, database management, and decision support systems.

☐ ☐ As senior corporate I/S consultant, focuses on using information technology to improve organizational productivity and competitive advantage. Promotes the proper use of IT in business units to achieve corporate goals and objectives. Has developed a high level of competence in business consulting as well as in information technology.

☐ ☐ As corporate integrator, brings together the company's strategy, culture, and infrastructure in order to forge an alliance not only within the company, but externally with customers, vendors, etc. Focuses on building partnerships between business leaders in the company. Has developed a high level of competence in corporate culture, strategic planning, information management, and human resources.

I/S Staff Members' Identity

Today   Future

☐ ☐ Programmers of single-purpose systems. Respond to business unit requests to enhance existing systems or to build new ones. Highly competent in programming languages and computer efficiency.

☐ ☐ Database specialists capable of supporting multiple applications from common, centralized, shared data bases. Highly competent in database programming, transaction-based systems, and data administration.

FIGURE 5–3
Concluded

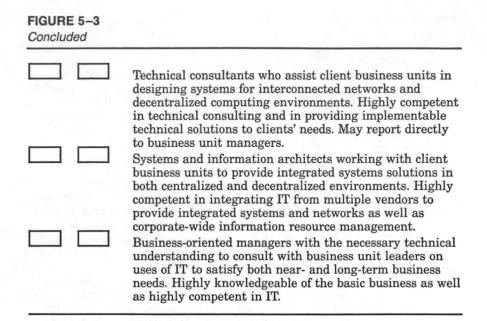

Technical consultants who assist client business units in designing systems for interconnected networks and decentralized computing environments. Highly competent in technical consulting and in providing implementable technical solutions to clients' needs. May report directly to business unit managers.

Systems and information architects working with client business units to provide integrated systems solutions in both centralized and decentralized environments. Highly competent in integrating IT from multiple vendors to provide integrated systems and networks as well as corporate-wide information resource management.

Business-oriented managers with the necessary technical understanding to consult with business unit leaders on uses of IT to satisfy both near- and long-term business needs. Highly knowledgeable of the basic business as well as highly competent in IT.

feels that it needs an operational executive in charge of I/S. Its emphasis is on the use of computers as production systems. The same is true for many banks and insurance companies.

In order for the I/S function to be positioned higher in the organization and to be a fully functioning member of the executive committee, the I/S executive will need to play a more active role in stakeholder management. This can be done through engaging in joint ventures and partnerships with the other executives that make up the executive committee.

Federated Department Stores, for example, tried for years to consolidate its data processing operations into a centralized corporate group. The executive committee hired a strong operational DP executive to set up the central organization. The new DP executive had hired over 200 people when he gave up the cause as lost. He had encountered resistance at every Federated subsidiary. In the end, he left, and the corporate group was disbanded.

Some time later, information systems executives from the subsidiaries began an initiative to set up an I/S company to serve the needs of the various subsidiaries. The presidents of the divisions that decided to join the initiative became members of the board of directors. The initiative achieved success, with almost all of the various Federated subsidiaries subscribing to the services of the new I/S company. Thus, the positioning of the new initiative succeeded where the attempted positioning of the corporate group failed.

As in marketing, positioning of the I/S function in the business can be the difference between success and failure. The mission statement for your I/S function helps to determine its proper positioning. If the mission statement is utility oriented, the positioning could be as a production/operations function. If it is control oriented, then positioning could be in the finance function. If it is oriented to integrating business functions and processes, its positioning could be as a distinctly separate corporate function.

CHAPTER 6

ENVIRONMENT, MARKET, PRODUCTS, AND SERVICES:
Creating and Delivering Value

THE ENVIRONMENT

Environmental issues are clarified by assessing the scope and nature of a corporation's stakeholders. By understanding global patterns and needs, one can better understand where a corporation's relationships with its stakeholders are going. This is a key step in establishing the information and information-technology elements of the infrastructure.

The market is a special subset of the global environment and deals with customer and competitive relationships. Information technology needs are clearer at the market level because the relationships are better defined.

Information technology needs must become a part of the products and services you offer. As you will see in the cases of Caterpillar and Federal Express, if you use information technology to add value to your products and services, not only will you be more competitive, you can actually increase your revenue stream. Competition based on product differentiation rather than on commodity pricing is the road to follow. And, the best part is that all stakeholders benefit.

Global Concerns

The environment most American executives consider for business planning is the U.S. economic, political, and regulatory climate. They assume that the rest of the world will experience more or less the same environment. As a result, American executives assume away important corporate relationships with global stakeholders. In the past, this has often led to management surprises. In the future, such assumptions could be fatal.

For example, Control Data Corporation made a $500 million trade agreement with the Soviet Union based on the economic cooperation section of the famous Helsinki Agreement in 1975. However, the economic cooperation hoped for in the agreement didn't materialize. The Soviet Union ran short of hard currency, and human rights issues slowed the implementation of the agreement. The $500 million agreement eventually died on the vine.

In today's global economy, corporations must pay as much attention to the overseas environment as to the environment at home. Global stakeholders include national, state, and local governments as well as global competitors, suppliers, and customers.

Building New Global Relationships

The cash-rich Japanese market is of particular interest to American firms. Entry into it for American firms is difficult because of long-standing stakeholder relationships. To gain entry to the Japanese market, your company will have to make a major long-term investment in developing and fostering relationships. One way to develop these relationships is for American firms to jointly develop products with Japanese firms. Another way is through combined marketing efforts. Without information sharing and innovative uses of information technology, these relationships are impossible.

Global Competition

Although there is a fine dividing line between global and national issues, there is value in making such a distinction because it focuses our conversation on which global stakeholders are involved. Because of its labor-cost advantage, China is likely to produce electronic components at a much lower cost than a corresponding American firm can. As a result, a Chinese firm might be able to sell its parts in the United States at a much lower price than does the American producer but still make a profit. The response from the American firm might be to employ one of the following strategies:

1. Seek regulatory relief.
2. Sell components at a loss to discourage the competitor.
3. Invest in product innovation to make the competitor's product obsolete.

The American firm might also find difficulties in selling U.S.-made components in China because of new, local competition.

In either of the above cases, the American firm has experienced a change in the global environment.

Therefore, when we speak of customers, we must define their environment. Customers in California have different characteristics than do customers in Singapore. Suppliers in Peru have different characteristics than do suppliers in the United Kingdom. For each of these customers or suppliers, there are different possibilities for establishing stakeholder relationships.

There are further distinctions within stakeholder categories beyond just the economic, political, and regulatory environments. These include the relationships that exist between stakeholders, changing stakeholders needs, and changing industry structures.

For example, the automobile industry hit one of its first peaks in the late 1940s. Until that time, all automobile transmissions were the manual-shift variety; the automatic transmission hadn't been widely introduced yet. There were a large number of potential drivers who hadn't yet considered driving because of the complexity and dexterity required by manual transmissions.

With the advent of widely available automatic transmission, a whole new category of potential drivers were enabled. The market size practically doubled overnight. It's such shifts in environment that cause changes in perceived stakeholder needs. And, for those of us who recognize them, they are windows of opportunity.

The Customer Environment

As illustrated by the advent of the automatic transmission, the customer environment includes external factors that will affect the customer's ability to buy and use your service or product. The assessment of the market is a special analysis of the customer environment, which is covered later in this chapter under "The Market."

The Investor Environment

The category *investor* includes

1. The board of directors, who nominally protect the interest of investors.
2. Shareholders.
3. Bond holders.
4. Note holders.

The category *shareholder* includes

1. Management shareholders.
2. Employee shareholders.
3. External shareholders who want long-term yield or growth.
4. External shareholders who are speculating on the short-term price of the shares.
5. External shareholders who wish to take over the corporation.

All of these are investors. All of these stakeholders contribute to the corporation's capital environment. Therefore, we must look for significant events in this environment, events that can impact the business. Examples of such significant events include

1. *Increases in interest rates.* The higher the rate, the more difficult it will be to cultivate equity investors.
2. *Decrease in interest rates.* The lower the rate, the more attractive it is to the company to use banks and bondholders as sources of capital.

3. *Uncertain business conditions.* The more uncertain the business conditions, the more difficult it is to raise capital of any kind.

The Employee Environment

The employee environment includes the following considerations:

1. Labor laws (the result of another set of stakeholders—regulators).
2. Availability of candidates.
3. Working conditions (such as telecommuting, flexible time, etc.).
4. The degree of automation in the workplace.
5. Senior management's attitude toward employees.
6. Unionization.

The employee relationship is an important leverage point for the corporation. Information can increase the ability for people to work from their homes, for example. This could result in significantly lower occupancy costs.

The Supplier Environment

The supplier environment includes the following considerations:

1. Competition in the supplier's market.
2. The ease of using substitutes.
3. The ease of entry into the supplier's market.
4. Regulation.
5. The use of just-in-time methods.
6. Electronic data interchange.
7. Interlocking boards of directors (e.g., a partially or fully owned subsidiary or sister company).
8. Availability of raw materials.
9. The value added by the supplier.

The supplier relationship is another important leverage point for the corporation. Many suppliers have built information systems that provide automated order entry from their customers. This speeds deliveries of products and services and reduces the need for inventory investment.

Consideration of the supplier relationship is the reverse side of considering the customer. This will be covered further in the discussion of the market.

The Competitive Environment

The intensity of competition determines, to a large extent, the ability of the enterprise to exercise control over the market. With intense competition, there can be little or no market control. With a lack of competitive pressure, the company has more leeway to dictate prices and conditions of sale.

Michael Porter in *Competitive Advantage* used the model shown in Figure 6–1 to describe the competitive environment. The intensity of competition increases as the buyer gains power from ease of entry into the suppliers market and from the availability of acceptable substitutes.

FIGURE 6–1
The Traditional Industrial Competitive Model

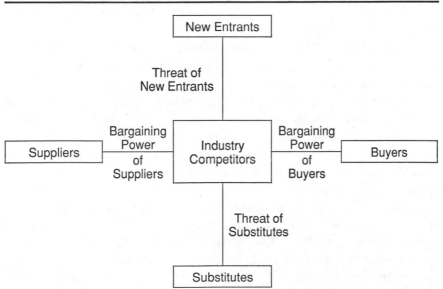

Reprinted with permission from *Competitive Advantage,* Michael E. Porter, The Free Press, New York, 1985.

Porter's basic assumption in his model is an adversarial environment. A strictly adversarial approach to competition assumes a win-lose proposition. In most cases, this attitude ultimately results in a lose-lose situation. The company loses because of tenuous supplier relationships. The competing companies lose because of lower prices and higher costs of selling. Consumers lose quality and value when competitors focus their attention on each other rather than on their customers.

A good example of this is the American automobile industry, which paved the way for the entries of Toyota, Honda, Nissan, and others. Ford, Chrysler, and General Motors ignored consumer wishes as they built bigger and bigger cars having less and less quality. By the 1970s, the market was truly ready for a quality, moderately priced car. The Japanese, who earlier had a reputation of low quality, came up with products that matched market needs.

The American automobile industry example suggests that the best way to better competitors is to do a better job of meeting market needs. In a new business era, this is best done by creating stakeholder partnerships for delivering outstanding value in the marketplace. In 1987, the Ford Motor Company did just that with its successful introduction of the Taurus and Sable models.

Notwithstanding the adversarial implications of Porter's competitive model, the model is useful in seeking business advantages. For example, when a company has used information technology extensively to strengthen its relationships with both suppliers and customers, it has created a formidable barrier to market entry. For example, McKesson Corporation, using its advanced distribution system, has captured 35 percent of the distribution market for ethical and over-the-counter pharmaceuticals.

Similarly, American Airline's Sabre system locked in 35 percent of the nation's travel agencies. In order to gain a similar competitive advantage, Delta Airlines chose to buy into American's system rather than to continue their own.

Manufacturers are getting more involved with their suppliers' manufacturing processes, even to the point where common information systems send information back and forth between suppliers' internal manufacturing systems and manufacturers' internal operations. In this book, this is called *supply-side competition,* and it is an effective barrier to entry for would-be competitors.

Chemical Abstracts is a case where the chemical industry has broadly cooperated on the supply side. The American Society of Chemical Engineers sponsors a large information-processing organization, Chemical Abstracts. The organizing principle of Chemical Abstracts is to provide chemical formulations and information to the members of the American Society of Chemical Engineers. One important factor in establishing Chemical Abstracts is the sharing of information. By sharing, all members can better understand alternative formulation possibilities including product substitution, one of Porter's competitive factors.

Chemical Abstracts has become so successful that it contributes substantial funds to the American Society of Chemical Engineers, which in turn has greatly reduced the cost of being a member. This is all made possible by one of the largest commercial information organizations in the world. Because of its advantage of size and information technology and its unique information investment, Chemical Abstracts is a virtual single-source international supplier of chemical information.

The Community Environment

The community environment is becoming more and more important as environmental issues grow in importance. Consideration of the community environment includes

1. Environmental and ecological issues.
2. Community support for attracting professionals and workers.
3. The community communications infrastructure.
4. The community's reliance on the company for the local economy.
5. Taxes.

Transborder Dataflows

A key regulatory environment issue in the information age is transborder dataflows. As regional economies recognize information as having value, they will also recognize its value as a source for tax revenue. Governmental restrictions and the additional costs associated with sending information across national borders pose a threat to the value added by information technology. American companies conducting business abroad should take an active role in international organizations that address this issue from a viewpoint of keeping free-trade channels open.

Government Privacy Laws

Another regulatory issue can be found in government privacy laws, which may restrict the information a corporation can legally store. For example, the West German government forbids keeping records on employee performance. In response, some companies keep their personnel records in other countries that don't forbid the keeping of such records.

France prohibits the keeping of certain direct mailing lists. Corporate response has been to follow the example of companies doing business in Germany and their personnel records: keep them outside the country. These obstacles ultimately raise costs to the consumer. There's a need for international agreement on the morality and legitimacy of creating data bases.

Summary

In assessing the environment, you must examine every corporate stakeholder relationship and anticipate its needs. By considering the full range of environmental possibilities, you will do a much better job of identifying key issues that you can turn into competitive advantages.

THE MARKET

The market is a special subset of the environment. The nature of the market, in large part, dictates what kinds of relationships are possible with customers. The extensive case studies in the literature attesting to companies that have gained a competitive advantage are, in fact, simply documentations of changes in relationships with the customer.

The market description also includes an analysis of the relationships that are grouped under the customer category. Figure 6–2 illustrates the group of relationships contained in the customer category for a pharmaceutical company. These represent the possible relationships for a pharmaceutical company selling ethical drugs in the current market:

1. Wholesaler and distributors buy the product for resale to pharmacies.
2. Large retail customers buy the product for sale in their stores.
3. Medical doctors prescribe the medication.
4. Pharmacists fill the prescriptions made by the MD's.

FIGURE 6–2
The Organizing Principle: Who Is the Customer?

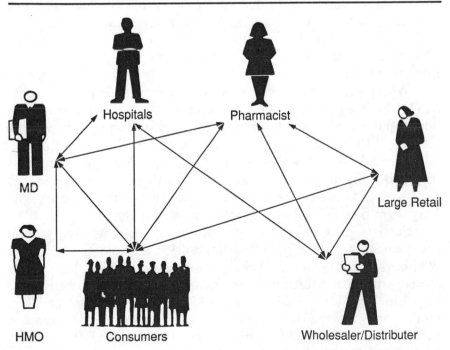

5. Health maintenance organizations have doctors and pharmacists working together.
6. Finally, consumers take the medication.

The relationship between the pharmaceutical company and the consumer is indirect. The company's employees never deal directly with the consumer. There are at least two other relationships involved with getting the medication into the hands of the consumer that are illustrated in the following case study.

Pharmaceutical Customer Case Study: G. D. Searle

G. D. Searle recently announced a policy that brings them closer to the consumer. Under the Searle plan, an M.D. prescribes a drug to a patient. If the drug doesn't work as intended (e.g., a medication to reduce blood pressure has no effect on the patient), the patient can go back to the M.D. The M.D. fills out a certificate saying that the drug didn't work in this case as hoped. The patient takes the drug back to the pharmacist. The pharmacist gives the patient credit toward another medication. The pharmacist returns the first prescription to Searle for reimbursement.

While this appears to be a real win-win situation, many M.D.'s don't agree that it is. They object to interference in the doctor-patient relationship and resent the extra paperwork. The success of this program is yet to be established.

Nevertheless, the Searle prescription refund program does offer a benefit to the consumer. The consumer is aware, perhaps for the first time, of the company making the medication. The long-term Searle goal is customer brand loyalty.

Such a program isn't possible without extensive use of information technology. The information needed to drive the reimbursement system also serves another crucial purpose. Searle will gain additional insight into the doctor-patient relationship. That is precisely why the M.D.'s are complaining. They don't want pharmaceutical sales organizations to leverage the sale of medications through special knowledge of the doctor-patient relationship. M.D.'s want a free hand.

Perhaps this program will work better if Searle invests more in the M.D. relationship. Perhaps Searle can provide information to the M.D.'s that will provide vital statistics about the effectiveness of a particular medication. Both parties need a critical element: the trust that comes from a perceived mutual benefit.

Electronic Markets

Electric data interchange (EDI) is becoming a major market consideration. In order to do business with the Ford Motor Company today, you must be able to receive orders, send confirmations, send invoices, and receive payment electronically. The linking of supplier and the purchasing firm is only beginning. In the future, suppliers and their purchasing firms will link quality, inventory, product planning, and other key information systems. The chief information executives of the two firms will act as partners in enabling the two companies, acting as one, to improve the ultimate relationship with customers.

Regional and Local Markets

The Wells Fargo Bank and its regional marketing strategy were discussed in Chapter 4. Wells Fargo is a regional bank serving California. But within California, Wells Fargo identified 185 markets, each with special market characteristics. This identification came about as a result of studying demographic information.

There are several marketing research organizations that sell demographic data with granularity down to the neighborhood level. By simply knowing a person's address, you can find out his or her buying habits, income, house payments, and so on. Let's suppose this person has a passbook savings account with your bank. A match of her address to demographic data might tell you that people who live in her neighborhood typically have certificates of deposit, safe deposit boxes, money-market accounts, mortgages, car loans, and investments in mutual funds.

You know that she has a passbook savings account with you and is doing the rest of her business with other financial institutions. Why isn't she doing all her business with you?

Relationship Marketing

Relationship marketing is used extensively by banks, where it is called *relationship banking*. The concept of relationship banking identifies a person using one of your products who could be sold on using more of your products and services. Many financial services companies have special market strategies that give incentives to the customer using multiple services.

Furthermore, you can tailor these services to demographic characteristics. Check-cashing services are important in low-income neighborhoods, Christmas club saving accounts are important in middle-class family neighborhoods, and personal service at the branch and by telephone is important in high-income neighborhoods.

Information and information technology make demographic marketing programs possible. Sophisticated banks like Wells Fargo have created a customer information file (CIF) that contains complete records on every bank customer. By matching the CIF to demographic data, Wells Fargo makes a new information base of customer potential with products and services that Wells can market to them. The revenue generated from such a program can be enormous.

Other consumer industries can benefit from relationship marketing: automobile manufacturers and distributors, department stores, insurance companies, brokers, real estate firms, and so on. The key is information on current and potential relationships.

Summary

Traditional market relationships represent only a part of the economic potential for your company. Using information and information technology, your company has new capability to explore the market, capability that was until now not even imagined. Customer information files and demographic data can provide a basis for your company to change old relationships in your current market and to create new market distinctions that will result in new market relationships. The result will be increased revenue, profitability, and win-win situations for corporate stakeholders.

PRODUCTS AND SERVICES

Products and services represent the value that the company delivers to its customers. In the financial statements, the value delivered appears as sales or revenue.

When a company enhances its products or services with information technology, it increases their value to the customer. Such was the case with the Morton Parts Facility of Caterpillar, Inc.

Adding Service Value with Information Technology: Caterpillar, Inc.

Caterpillar, Inc., makes earth movement equipment for construction, roadbuilding, and agricultural customers. Their Morton Parts facility delivers maintenance parts for Caterpillar equipment throughout the world. The Morton Parts Facility installed a large online network in the 1970s to track inventory at remote Caterpillar and dealer locations. The result was a profitable new service.

Because the Morton Parts Facility knew where any given part was at any time, it was now possible to deliver the part where it was needed within 24 hours. If the part wasn't in stock in the multibillion-dollar inventory at Morton, the part could be trans-shipped between field locations.

The result was a new service—24-hour delivery at a premium price. When road gear broke down and stopped work, the cost of lost time on the job far outweighed the extra delivery fee. Caterpillar was so sure of the 24-hour delivery that they reflected it in their policy: there's a healthy 24-hour delivery surcharge, but if the part doesn't get there on time, there's no charge at all!

A further benefit of the online system was inventory reduction. Morton was able to reduce the quantities of large, expensive parts. Parts could be shipped from the central Morton facility or trans-shipped between remote locations without any reduction in service.

Adding Product Value with Information Technology: Federal Express

One company that has used I/T to enhance the value of its product is Federal Express. Their overnight delivery is an outstanding service. Many of us use Federal Express because of their high reliability. But the clincher is the ability to trace packages quickly and easily.

Many organizations receiving Federal Express packages are so large that, even though a package is delivered to the correct address and building, there is no way to be sure that the intended person in the building will receive the package. Or, many executive's desks are piled so high with incoming mail and packages that, even if the Federal Express package is on their desk, they might not know it.

Federal Express has used I/T to create a special system to support package senders. You can call them at any time, and they can tell you exactly where a package is. If it has been delivered, they can tell you who signed for it. We have often assisted clients in finding Federal Express packages delivered to their site by giving them the information we easily received from Federal Express.

Conclusion

As we approach a possible no-growth decade, environmental, market, and product and service issues will take on new importance. We will all be contending for share of market while at the same time fending off environmental difficulties. Leveraging products and services with greater information content is one way that many companies will master both their market and their broader environments.

PART 2

DETERMINING ORGANIZATIONAL AND TECHNOLOGY INVESTMENT ACTIONS

CHAPTER 7

ESTABLISHING GOALS AND OBJECTIVES: Redefining the Economic Basis

When your executive team sets out to establish your corporation's goals and objectives, it considers all corporate stakeholders. The process of establishing your company's goals and objectives starts with setting stakeholder expectations. You then need measures that will determine corporate performance as compared to stakeholder expectations. New information sources and new information technology applications play key roles.

Corporate goals and objectives usually deal with financial results, including profitability, return on investment, and earnings per share. These traditional measures are important because they reflect the relationship with one very important stakeholder: the shareholder. For this reason, IT investments to measure corporate performance have focused on financial measurement systems accompanied by large, control-oriented staffs to administer these systems. With these systems, goals and objectives for profit, return, and earnings drive the day-to-day management of the corporation.

Today's corporation needs information technology to deal with a much broader spectrum of information that includes corporate performance as perceived by its stakeholders.

THE CHANGING ROLES AND EXPECTATIONS OF INVESTORS

Table 7–1 gives a generic list of corporate stakeholders and their general expectations for corporate performance.

TABLE 7–1
Expectations of Shareholders for Corporate Performance

Stakeholder	Expectations
Investors	
Long-term Shareholders	High yield, long-term stock growth
Traders, Speculators	Short-term growth, opportunistic dividends
Takeover Opportunists	Inexpensive company acquisition, quick turnaround, sell company on open market for large profit
Debtholders	Long-term interest payments
Customers	High quality, cost-effective products and services, long-term supply stability, after-sales support
Employees	Good working environment, rewards for effort, sense of accomplishment, security
Suppliers, Vendors	Long-term agreements, fair prices, forecasts of needs
Management	Rewards for risk, good working environment, security
Regulators	Compliance with laws and regulations
Community	Taxes, jobs, clean environment, stability
Competitors	Market share, fair prices, stability

The nature of one stakeholder, the investor, has changed dramatically over the past two decades as a result of advancing technology.

A brief examination of the stakeholders and their expectations in Table 7–1 points out a serious senior management dilemma:

> *The corporation must find a way to monitor and balance the short-term performance demands of traders, speculators, and turnaround opportunists instead of the long-term requirements of virtually all other stakeholders.*

What happened to create a set of investors focused on short-term results as opposed to the traditional long-term investors who want a stream of dividends or interest payments over time?

Long-term investors tend to judge corporate performance against the rates of return from safer investments in a bank or treasury bills. Short-term investors judge corporate performance by dividends and increases in share value *this year.*

Other stakeholders look to the long term. Customers want a reliable, quality-oriented supply of goods and services that they can count on over time. Employees want long-term, satisfying jobs that pay as well as or better than a series of jobs at other companies. Suppliers and vendors want long-term agreements that they can count on year after year. Managers want long-term jobs with a company that gives them financial rewards and status. Regulators simply want compliance. The community wants a strong financial base with stable jobs and without industrial pollution. Competitors usually want predictable market share and a chance to make a good return on their investment.

INFORMATION TECHNOLOGY AND CHANGING INVESTOR RELATIONS

In the 1970s, the Securities and Exchange Commission enacted a fundamental change that set the stage for our current stock exchange phenomenon. At that time, the amount of paperwork required to issue and reissue share certificates had become a bottleneck on the capacity of the exchanges. Around 10 million shares could be traded in a day at that time.

Then, taking a lesson from banking, the exchange commission allowed brokers to establish electronic accounts with share balances. As for banking, the electronic systems of keeping share balances don't require that actual shares be issued. Instead, the computer keeps electronic account balances for future trading.

Since the early 1970s, the numbers of shares traded each day have doubled, quadrupled, and multiplied until today's daily numbers sometimes exceed 150 million.[1] With electronic share account balances, another group of stakeholders—traders and speculators, including large investment firms, mutual funds, pension funds, and the like—took on new importance and has grown to represent some two-thirds of the capital market.

Speculators typically are individuals and small funds that hold stock for short periods of what they hope is rapid growth. Venture capitalists are a special kind of speculator who invest in start-up companies with hopes of cashing in on their investment in two to three years, selling their interest to yet other traders and speculators.

TRADERS AND SPECULATORS AS STAKEHOLDERS

Although traders and speculators have always existed, their influence on the market was limited by the volume of transactions that could be processed in a day. It was also limited by the amount and frequency of information publicly available from corporations.

As information technology removed limits on stock-transaction quantities as well as availability of corporate information, traders became a dominant force in the marketplace. Traders may own shares of a dividend-paying company for several years or for several minutes. Traders sometimes buy shares just long enough to be shareholders of record for a dividend payment.

A STAKEHOLDER DILEMMA

This presents a dilemma to the board of directors and senior management. There are now three major categories of shareholders:

1. Long-term shareholders such as management, employees, and individual investors who are interested in the long term.
2. Traders and speculators who are buying and selling shares for short-term gain.
3. Takeover opportunists.

These three categories of shareholders have conflicting interests. The long-term shareholders are interested in goals and objectives that take in the long-term prosperity of the enterprise. The traders have an interest that can best be served by maximizing short-term return. They don't have any stake in the long-term prosperity of the enterprise. The takeover specialists typically break up a firm, selling off unprofitable operations to pay off debt. Their objective is to acquire a firm at very low cost, turn it around, and sell it at a large profit.

There are two other classes of investors to be considered: bondholders and debtholders. Both of these stakeholders have an interest in the corporation's long-term prosperity and ability to service interest payments over time.

A DEBTHOLDER CASE STUDY: MEMOREX AND BANK OF AMERICA

In the 1970s, Bank of America became a major investor in Memorex Corporation. It started out with a commercial loan. Memorex manufactured and marketed computer peripheral equipment and supplies. Most of the equipment that Memorex made went out to customers on leases. Since lease revenue is spread over a long period of time, Memorex needed cash to finance the buildup of its leased equipment. Memorex borrowed money from Bank of America to finance its leased asset base. In the first few years, the Bank of America loan grew to about $80 million.

Over the next several years, Memorex encountered serious cashflow problems. Memorex made IBM-compatible peripherals. In their initial financial forecasts, they assumed that IBM's current pricing would prevail for the next several years. This proved to be naive. With competition from Memorex, IBM reduced its prices and marketed aggressively. Toward the end of the 1970s, the Bank of America loan had grown to around $300 million.

The Memorex board of directors, under pressure from Bank of America, brought in Bob Wilson, who had a reputation for turning companies around. Wilson started negotiating stakeholder expectations with shareholders, debtholders, customers, employees, and suppliers. In the end, he managed a set of goals and objectives that allowed Memorex to have a positive cash flow.

By the early 1980s, Wilson had substantially improved Memorex's position. The Bank of America loan had been dramatically reduced. Memorex is still in business today. Without Bank of America as a long-term stakeholder, this might not have been the case.

BALANCING CONFLICTING INTERESTS

Your company needs to recognize the interests of these dissimilar investors in the corporation's goals and objectives. Management and the board need to balance short-term and long-term needs.

Unfortunately, you can't always satisfy all these needs and wants at the same time. This means that senior management and the board of directors need to establish mechanisms for achieving stakeholder consensus on a periodic basis—each year or quarter, for instance. One such mechanism for investors is the annual shareholder's meeting. Some companies, such as NCR Corporation, have undertaken a bold new approach: stakeholders' meetings.

COMBINING STAKEHOLDER RELATIONSHIPS

Before any corporation can reasonably attempt an annual stakeholders' meeting, they must create an environment where it can be successful. This means going beyond simply discussing stakeholders' needs and hoping that all stakeholders can agree on the priority of needs. The stakeholders need to be involved in the business to an extent that they will truly understand the needs of the business and its aggregation of stakeholders. Stakeholders and corporate management need education to understand the concept of the organizing principle of the corporation. By understanding the interrelatedness of stakeholders' needs, the process of setting expectations becomes more meaningful.

The quickest way to gain stakeholder commitment is to build systems that interconnect combined business processes. To combine stakeholder relationships and to support them with information technology is to build a global vision of the business.

ELECTRONIC DATA INTERCHANGE (EDI)

Electronic data interchange (EDI) is a rudimentary form of linking stakeholder relationships. An EDI system electronically processes and communicates purchase orders, sales orders, confirmations, shipment notices, receiving notices, invoices, and payments. Supplier and seller use a common system. Figure 7–1 illustrates how EDI can link several supplier/seller relationships in a chain that ends with the consumer.

The EDI network connects suppliers to a manufacturer. It then connects the manufacturer to its distributors. When taken in its entirety, the network connects an entire chain of stakeholders serving the needs of a final consumer. The EDI network

FIGURE 7–1
The Emerging Industrial Model: The Electronic Data Interchange Network

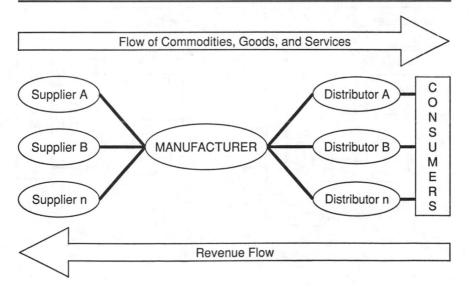

has the potential to become a powerful bond that unites the manufacturer, its suppliers, and its distributors into a chain of partnerships with a common vision for satisfying consumer needs. This is especially true for communicating quality and cost information and for after-sales support requirements.

The concept of EDI is today in its infancy. The factors driving EDI are cost and inventory reduction. As companies gain experience in dealing with one another electronically, they will begin to understand the potential that information technology makes possible—economic alliances for both supply and demand of goods and services.

Figure 7–2 shows an illustration of the economic alliances that will ultimately grow out of an EDI network. This extended EDI model depicts a flow of goods, services, and information in a chain from the earliest stages of material supplies to the

FIGURE 7–2
Economic Alliances: Supply-Side and Demand-Side Competition

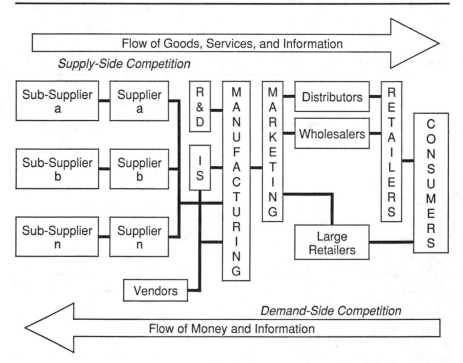

manufacturing, marketing, distribution, retail, and consumer stages. This forward-moving chain is what we normally think about when we consider Porter's value chain.[2]

The manufacturer, marketer, or distributor ends up being the leading partner, or integrator, of several processes including financial planning for the entire flow of goods, services, money, and information. The leading partner takes the responsibility for defining the technology environment in which other partners will participate.

In these economic alliances, there is new clarity of how market, distribution, and manufacturing can be applied. The nature of the market, competition, and the buying environment determines the prices that distributors can charge for a product and the volume that they can sell.

At this point, the revenue potential for the entire economic network is a given.

Take the market share, the unit volume potential, and the selling prices, and you have the total revenue potential for the entire chain of partnerships. This reality is known from the beginning to the end of the value chain through the shared information system.

There is also a chain that moves in the other direction that represents the flow of money and information. The economic alliance begins with a universal understanding that the ultimate consumers of the goods and/or services represent the entire potential source of revenue for all the businesses in the chain.

From the total potential revenue stream, the distributors, the manufacturer and its suppliers, and the marketers must make a fair profit. The employees and management throughout all the concerns must make a fair wage. The investors in all three areas must make a fair return on investment. To reach agreement on sharing the revenue potential from consumers, all participants in the network must make open disclosure and negotiate the revenue split.

Information technology makes a constant flow of revenue, cost, and performance information available to assess the distribution of profits. Each enterprise in the chain of partnerships has goals and objectives. Each enterprise in the chain has information about all others. Each has rewards for superior performance. Each sacrifices when its performance is substandard. This is a practice foreign to most American managers who are most concerned with maximizing their corporation's short-term financial results.

The constant communicating and updating of information up and down the value chain provide capability for rapid response to both demand and supply conditions.

SUPPLY-SIDE AND DEMAND-SIDE COMPETITION

American business schools emphasize the concepts of competitive strategies and advantage. The value chain goes from the manufacturer to the consumer. Product positioning, competitive positioning, and market control are all concepts that are involved in demand-side competition.

Equally important is the supply side of the equation. When manufacturers look at the value chain toward the consumer, their backs are to the suppliers. One of the most difficult transitions for American companies adopting just-in-time (JIT) manufacturing methods is understanding that their old adversarial role with suppliers is obsolete. JIT methods result in more intense relationships with fewer suppliers. The potential for supply-side competition is enormous. Intense relationships with the best suppliers in your industry can put your demand-side competitors at a disadvantage.

For example, a steel manufacturer that produces specialty alloyed metals can place its demand-side competitors at a serious disadvantage when the sources for alloys are restricted. By having a superior relationship with its suppliers, the specialty alloyed metals company enjoys a most-favored–customer relationship.

RELATIONSHIP DEPENDENCIES

Figure 7–3 illustrates the kinds of relationships that an enterprise can create. Assume that a manufacturing company is *A*

FIGURE 7–3
Relationship Dependencies: Interdependence versus Indifference or Conflict

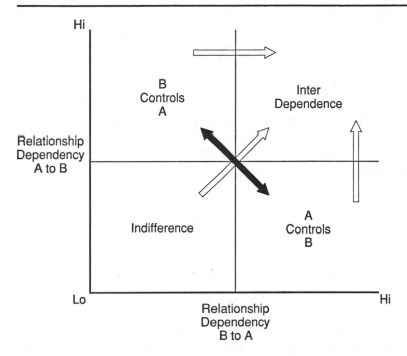

and its supplier is B. The vertical axis represents the degree to which manufacturer A is dependent on supplier B. The horizontal axis represents the degree to which supplier B is dependent on manufacturer A. When neither is dependent on the other, they are indifferent.

When manufacturer A is highly dependent on supplier B, then B controls A. American management usually considers this a desirable position for supplier B.

When supplier B is highly dependent on manufacturer A, then A controls B. Again, American management usually considers this a desirable position for manufacturer A.

Because management considers both positions desirable, they strive to achieve a controlling position for their company, thereby setting the adversarial state represented by the dark arrow. Manufacturers will play one supplier against another to get the lowest price. Suppliers each attempt to be the sole source for their product or commodity.

While we are taught that the achievement of these goals will bring business success, quite the opposite is often the case. Manufacturers drive suppliers out of business and later find they don't have enough sources. Suppliers force manufacturers to integrate vertically to protect themselves, leaving the suppliers with fewer customers.

When both parties realize that they are partners in an economic alliance, then achieving control is not as important as is the recognition of interdependence. Therefore, controlling relationships is likely to be more effective with the realization of interdependence. Indifferent relationships need new rationalization to find the grounds for interdependence.

NETWORKING AND TRUST: A CASE STUDY

In the late seventies, a large American financial corporation had many subsidiaries that were engaged in manufacturing, transportation, and even making movies. One subsidiary was involved in selling and servicing computer peripherals—we'll call it *American Peripherals* (AP) for this discussion. The AP management wanted to begin a point-of-sale terminal business. The point-of-sale business offered potential to build on the subsidiary's capabilities.

Therefore, AP management sought an American point-of-sale business partner. They found that the American point-of-sale terminal manufacturers were fully committed to established distribution channels. For American manufacturers, AP had nothing unique to offer. AP began to seek offshore manufacturers. A Japanese trading company, Kanematsu-Gosho, and a Japanese point-of-sale manufacturer, The General Corporation, showed a great deal of interest. AP management constructed a business plan to share with their potential Japanese partners.

AP management fully disclosed its planned revenues and expenses for five years. So did the Japanese companies. Together, they found that the first few years of the project would result in a net loss for both of them. The Japanese companies agreed to absorb their share of the loss. As the program commenced, AP and their partners fully disclosed the results. The initial losses turned out to be greater than expected. The Japanese firms again agreed to absorb their share of the loss.

The joint venture resulted in a point-of-sale terminal for grocery stores and one for bars. AP also worked together with a Japanese scale manufacturer to develop an electronic scale to sell in the United States. Today, the scale company imports these scales to the United States. The General grocery store terminal never gained market share. The bar cash registers were a hit and still represent a major export for General.

As it finally turned out, the financial parent company underwent restructuring. It sold off or closed down all nonfinancial enterprises. As a part of the restructuring, it closed American Peripherals. The Japanese venture ended.

Nevertheless, AP management and the people involved from the Japanese companies still conduct periodic business based on their current positions. They established a sense of trust that left them free to concentrate on the business rather than on which negotiating ploys they might use on one another. They had full disclosure and knew where they stood every step along the way. They're hopeful that once again, in the future, they'll find another major opportunity to work together.

SAMPLE GOALS AND OBJECTIVES

Figure 7–4 shows an example of stakeholder-based goals taken from a real situation at a chain of restaurants. The stakeholders include guests, employees, management, investors, inspectors, vendors, and competitors. The goals are shown across the top of Figure 7–4. Where a stakeholder is affected by a goal, there is a check mark. For example, by operating at 90 percent of capacity, the employees, management, investors, and vendors benefit. By providing service within three minutes, guests, employees, and management benefit. By building the restaurants' reputation as new wave establishments, the competitors are affected.

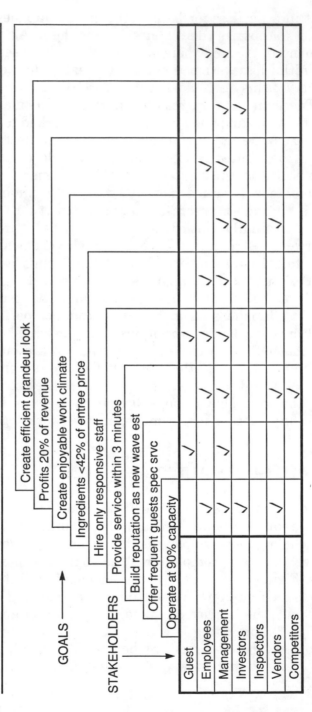

FIGURE 7–4
Stakeholder Relationships: Goals by Stakeholders

The following are sample goals and objectives you might use in your environment to construct your own version of Figure 7–4. These goals may then be used as guides for investing in the business, including the information technology investment.

Customers

Customer-related goals and objectives should reward customers for their relationship with your corporation. Customers should perceive that by purchasing your products and/or services, they have received

- High quality and value for the price.
- An ongoing, supportive, and valuable relationship.
- Recourse when expectations aren't met.

Investors

Investor-oriented goals and objectives should reward long-term shareholders, assure debtholders, and discourage speculation. The goals and objectives should reflect

- Increasing long-term return on investment.
- Consistently improving earnings per share.
- Maintaining a high market price multiple on earnings.
- Paying dividends that represent a good yield on market price.

Employees

Goals and objectives aimed at employees should reward the employees for performance, loyalty, and initiative. The goals and objectives should reflect

- Investing in employees to increase their value and potential for reward.
- Paying for individual and team performance.
- Involving employees in the success of the company through profit sharing and employee stock-ownership programs.
- Retaining exceptional employees.

Suppliers and Vendors

Supplier/vendor goals and objectives should emphasize the mutual goal of consistently meeting the expectations of the corporation's customers. Suppliers and vendors are business partners in supplying goods and services. The goals and objectives should reflect the mutual commitment to

- Consistently provide quality and value.
- Allow each other to meet reasonable goals and objectives.
- Work together to innovate highly competitive goods and services.

Management

Management-oriented goals and objectives should emphasize management's supportive role in creating value for stakeholders. These rewards must come from the value management adds to the corporation, not from the power they wield. The goals and objectives should reflect their responsibility to

- Unite disparate corporate functions in fulfilling their missions.
- Work together to build an effective strategy, culture, and infrastructure.
- Build an innovative and quality working environment.
- Lead and create followership.
- Balance long- and short-term business requirements.

Regulators

The goals and objectives concerning regulators should emphasize the importance of working together for appropriate regulations and then complying with those regulations. The goals and objectives should reflect the corporation's responsibility to

- Work together with regulators for effective regulations that benefit all stakeholders.
- Consistently comply with regulations in the most effective manner.

Community

Goals and objectives should also emphasize the corporation's role as a part of the communities in which it does business. The goals and objectives should reflect the corporation's responsibility to

- Preserve and enhance the environments of the communities.
- Work together with schools and universities to develop the communities' educational capabilities.
- Provide a source for jobs and tax revenues.
- Work together with the communities to nurture social prosperity for all their citizens.

Competitors

Many corporations have goals and objectives aimed at maximizing market share and minimizing competition. When these goals become all-important, the corporation suffers. For example, there is no one company that has a majority share of the shoe market. Kinney shoes has a market share of 15 to 20 percent, which makes it one of the largest. In order for Kinney to attempt to get another 10 percent market share, it would have to price its shoes at a near loss. This would not satisfy the expectations of corporate stakeholders.

An automobile parts manufacturer and supplier had a 90 percent share of its market. It attempted to improve this share by taking away the remaining market from its small competitors. The net result was 10 percent lower prices on the 90 percent share and a 2 percent share gain—a very poor trade-off.

The goals and objectives dealing with competition should take into account market position, regulation, and the welfare of other stakeholders. These goals and objectives should reflect the long-term benefits of

- Maintaining a market share that brings market stability.
- Discouraging regulatory intervention as occurred in the case of AT&T.

- Emphasizing positive competition by creating better quality and value rather than creating artificial market disadvantage.
- Cooperating in ventures that will provide benefit to the industry or nation (e.g., joint research).

INFORMATION TECHNOLOGY SUPPORT FOR A NEW MANAGEMENT DIRECTION

By establishing goals and objectives for each group of stakeholders, management communicates its commitment to creating stakeholder value. Most of the goals and objectives for stakeholders, other than those for the investors, are new in the corporate environment. For this reason, the corporation has never measured its performance for achievement in these areas. There is virtually no quantitative history for non-financial stakeholders.

The challenge is to create measurements for these new variables and begin their history. This is a new investment in information. Obviously, information technology plays a key role in providing capability to collect and disseminate the extended performance considerations. This will be discussed further in Chapter 14.

ENDNOTES

1. In the October 1987 stock market panic, the daily volume went over 350 million.
2. Michael E. Porter, *Competitive Advantage* (New York: The Free Press, 1985).

CHAPTER 8

CORPORATE IMPERATIVES:
Reaching Consensus on
Key Assumptions and
Corporate-Wide Actions

Corporate imperatives and assumptions deal with both the spoken and unspoken aspects of the business. Your executive management communicates for possibilities and action based on perceived and implied understandings of what is critical to the survival of the corporation.

For example, marketing and sales departments, with their focus on the relationship with customers, consider any factor dealing with this relationship to be the most critical in the entire corporation. Because of this focus, marketing and sales executives assume that the rest of senior management knows and understands the importance of these customer-related details as well.

Likewise, personnel executives focus on the legal aspects of the employee relationship to the exclusion of other pressing issues (such as designing new reward systems appropriate for a new business era). Thus, judging by their behavior, these personnel executives have made a key assumption: everyone else in the corporation also understands that senior executives must first, last, and always consider the legal aspects of employee relationships.

Similarly, executives from the other functional areas of the business focus on their critical areas, each assuming that the balance of senior management understands. As a result, when these executives meet and converse, they are making assumptions about the knowledge and understanding of the various critical elements of each functional area. In fact, the assumed knowledge and understanding seldom exists, and the functional executives are basing their conversation on false premises.

What we need is a way to uncover underlying assumptions and to expose them in truly meaningful conversations with our fellow executives. By focusing on corporate imperatives, we can accomplish this.

A clear agreement among functional executives on the corporation's imperatives and their underlying assumptions results in business conversations that support unity of action.

CORPORATE IMPERATIVES

Corporate imperatives arise from those few key areas of business activity in which positive results are essential to the success of the enterprise. They come, consciously or unconsciously, from the corporation's organizing principle, driving force, environment, and market. They are based on the corporation's products, services, goals, and objectives, and on management's assumptions (see Figure 8–1).

Accomplishing each corporate imperative results in the enterprise's perceived ability to satisfy each stakeholder's needs as outlined in the enterprise's goals and objectives. To further determine your corporation's imperatives, you will also need to examine your industry's dependencies and perceptions.

Corporate Imperatives and Stakeholders

Let's examine a set of stakeholders in a bank—its regulators. An imperative for a bank is to meet regulators' needs by being in compliance with regulations. To be out of compliance means risking fines or even closure of the bank. Furthermore, being out of compliance with regulators directly affects all other relationships. It may mean that bank stakeholders will decide to terminate their relationship with the bank: its depositors may withdraw funds, employees may leave, high-quality individuals

FIGURE 8–1
Corporate Imperatives: Looking Behind Them
Where Do They Come From?

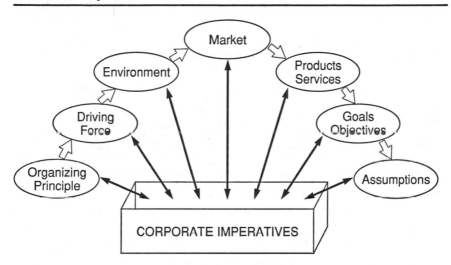

and organizations may not apply for loans, the Federal Deposit Insurance Corporation and the Federal Reserve Board may cause the bank to change its management, and so on.

The imperative for compliance with regulation has some very predictable consequences. It also has some less predictable consequences as a result of stakeholder perceptions. A troubled bank is a possible target for takeover. Traditional shareholders may sell out for a seemingly attractive price under the circumstances but ultimately lose because the bank's worth was really much higher than the price paid. Inadequate management of a corporate imperative leads to a perception of poor performance. Inadequate attention to an imperative often results in an overall unfavorable stakeholder reaction with a potential of a lose-lose situation.

Imperatives Exist at Each Level of the Organization

The overall corporation has a set of imperatives. So do each of the business units and functions within the corporation. Divisional imperatives are based on the special relationship with specific division stakeholders. Taken together, corporate and divisional imperatives must all add up to success for each and every corporate stakeholder.

Corporate Imperatives: Cause and Effect

Figure 8–2 lists examples of corporate imperatives for various industries. The first, *introduce relationship banking,* comes from the banking industry. The second, *improve product positioning,* applies to the retail business, whether it be in banking, cosmetics, or toys. And so on.

Each imperative has an expected effect or result. The result of successful relationship banking is increased business from current customers. The result of improved product positioning is increased market share.

In establishing corporate and functional imperatives, your executive team must be clear about the expected results. All too often, executive debates on alternative courses of action overlook the need for a common, agreed-upon expected result.

FIGURE 8–2

Corporate Imperatives: Cause and Effect (Getting results—various industry examples)

Cause (Imperative)	Effect (Results)
Introduce relationship banking	Increased revenue from current customers
Improve product positioning	Increased market share
Improve product differentiation	Increased revenue from current volume
Reduce product costs	Increased competitive strength
Reduce expenses	Increased earnings
Enter R&D alliances	Reduced risk, increased market share
Enter distribution	Increased revenue from current volume, increased earnings
Improve salesforce productivity	Increased revenue from current salesforce

Corporate Imperative Case Study:
Wells Fargo & Company

Until 1982, Wells Fargo was an international bank. It had offices in several foreign locations including Japan, Hong Kong, the United Kingdom, Germany, and France. The rationale for being in international banking arose from the relationships that Wells Fargo had with its commercial customers who were multinational corporations. A Wells Fargo corporate imperative was to service its multinational customers in foreign locations. The expected result was more business with western U.S. companies. The assumption was that Wells Fargo needed branches in foreign locations to satisfy this corporate imperative.

In 1982, a new Wells Fargo management team challenged this assumption. An examination of foreign branch business activity showed that less than 35 percent of the bank's combined business was with multinational firms having their U.S. account with Wells Fargo. The other 65 percent was marginal business with various firms local to the foreign branches. Further examination revealed that, because it was regarded as a necessary service to retain large, multinational accounts, the international division was not considered a profit center. In fact, some of the foreign activity was very unprofitable. Some of the Third World loan portfolio later resulted in large write-offs that significantly impacted 1987 results.

Wells Fargo's shareholders were largely institutional investors. Their ownership was about 64 percent of the bank's outstanding shares. They had no vested interest in Wells Fargo's international activity. They did have a vested interest in Wells Fargo's profitability. Multinational commercial customers did have a need for service in foreign areas, but Wells Fargo had an alternative: establishing interbanking relationships with foreign banks, a new class of stakeholders. The only other stakeholders who had a vested interest in international operations were Wells Fargo's employees in its international division. Most of these were easily transferred to domestic operations.

The decision became obvious once the basic assumption that Wells Fargo had to directly provide international service was put aside. The new management team closed the international division, sold or disbanded the foreign branches, and established interbanking relationships with foreign banks. One of these interbanking relationships developed into a major benefit later on. Wells Fargo made a business arrangement with a United Kingdom bank, Midland Bank, in order to acquire the Crocker Bank in California.

Thus, Wells Fargo set aside a corporate imperative that was based on a false assumption: international banking would result in expanding the bank's portfolio of industrial customers. The expected result was better served by establishing new international relationships while redeploying capital to domestic operations.

Corporate Imperatives: Sources

Figure 8–3 lists some of the formal and informal sources you can use for deriving your corporate imperatives.

The best source for discovering corporate imperatives is in the beginning of annual reports where the CEO discusses the state of the business and the outlook. Almost always, corporate imperatives figure in this discussion. Further information is available in the 10-K supplements and minutes from the annual shareholders meeting.

Many companies publish their corporate imperatives along with their organizing principle and business purpose. They have

FIGURE 8–3
Corporate Imperatives: Sources (How to determine what they are)

Formally	Informally
Annual reports	Minutes from executive
10-K supplements	committee meetings
Annual shareholder's meeting	Internal memos
Press releases	Executive interviews
Company meetings	Competitive analysis
Company newsletters	Consultants
Published corporate purpose/	Industry publications
mission statements	Industry meetings
Official management memos	Research organizations

found that this creates unity of action by management, employees, and other stakeholders. It makes good corporate image marketing material, too.

Informal sources, such as management meetings and memoranda, provide clues for determining the corporation's imperatives. Industry meetings and publications provide insight on industry issues and courses of action. Consultants and competitive analysis also yield fresh insight into corporate imperatives.

Before you can use your list of imperatives as a guide for action, you need consensus from executive management. This calls for a focus on imperatives in executive meetings and conversations. Achieving consensus at this level also means dealing with a common set of assumptions about the business and its stakeholders.

ASSUMPTIONS

People create assumptions whenever there is imperfect knowledge about the environment, which is most of the time. We can only guess what will happen in the future based on our knowledge of previous happenings. When Coca-Cola executives announced New Coke, they assumed that their regular customers would accept the change while Coca-Cola tapped into a new, younger market. The assumption turned out to be wrong. The old customers rebelled, so we now have New Coke and Classic Coke.

Assumptions guide actions. When planning ahead as to which actions to take, people use assumptions to steer their course. When executives of different functions, specializing in different stakeholder relationships, use differing assumptions to guide action, it's no wonder that information executives experience frustration and stress when attempting to implement cross-functional systems.

This is why the first step in the process leading to action is to expose all the assumptions being made by the participants. The second step is to negotiate a common set of key assumptions as a basis for planned action. Agreement on key assumptions is necessary to achieve unity of action.

As soon as any key assumption changes, typically as a result of new knowledge, executives must reassess the plan. Examining and communicating potential changes in assumptions consumes a great deal of executive energy. Nevertheless, when this is done in combination with cross-functional coordination, it is a vital activity.

With consensus on key assumptions, long-term business investment projects are more likely to contribute to management's expected results for corporate imperatives. Without consensus, investment projects will seldom deliver the expected results.

Information systems development projects are an example of business investment projects that often disappoint executive management. As a result, development projects are suspect whenever I/S management proposes them. At stake are the needs of the business and the credibility of senior I/S management.

The Never-Ending Systems Development Project

Many corporations have experienced the never-ending systems development project. The symptoms of such a project are clear:

- The systems development project timeframe is 18 months to 2 years.
- The developers complain of a never-ending stream of changes from the business unit requesting the systems.
- The business unit complains about the time frame being too long to meet the needs of the business.
- In the end, the systems never get delivered.

Every company has had several of these, so you can find examples of these in your own systems development organizations. Just look for the symptoms described above.

Further analysis of this syndrome typically leads to the following discoveries:

- There wasn't a clear set of agreed-to assumptions.
- The project wasn't tied to a clear corporate imperative to spell out what corporate action the project supported as well as what results were expected.

- New knowledge was continually received by the business unit, but the systems developers, because of isolation, were unaware of the impact of changing assumptions.
- Systems limitations perceived in the design stage were often overcome with additional understanding about the technology being used and with new technology available from vendors.

The never-ending systems project is, therefore, the result of a lack of clear, communicated assumptions by all executives involved. Business unit executives change their assumptions as they receive new knowledge. This translates into requests for changes in the system. The systems developers receive new technical information. This translates into new systems capabilities. By continually requesting changes in the systems, the business unit executives delay delivery. By continually making changes to accommodate the latest technical knowledge, the developers delay delivery. The combined activities of both groups ensure that the system will never be completed.

When examining your own applications development portfolio, look for differing assumptions about the business and its needs. This will give you clues to start resolving these predicaments.

Overcoming the Never-Ending Systems Development Syndrome

To avoid the never-ending systems development syndrome, or to overcome it once it has been discovered, the information systems and business unit teams must take the following actions:

1. Create a development team that is comprised of both I/S developers and key business unit staff.
2. Establish as a part of the systems specifications a clear and agreed-to set of business and technical assumptions that are continually updated, communicated to all team members, and agreed upon by all team members and their management.
3. Identify the corporate imperative satisfied by the project and the project's impact on expected results.

4. Divide the large system into several smaller ones that can be delivered in shorter periods of time (e.g., four to six months). This also opens up the possibility for the purchase of systems available on the open market that could be substituted for internally developed systems.
5. With every change in key assumptions, reassess priorities for the portfolio of potential systems, emphasizing the priority for those with higher value-added impact.

The above actions are the driving force behind dispersion, which places development staff within the business unit. By creating systems capability at the business-unit level and providing closer relationships between I/S and line staff, many companies have improved the assumption-making process. By better identifying the corporation's imperatives and achieving consensus on assumptions, the company can overcome the never-ending systems development syndrome.

Mission-Critical Systems Versus Business Support Systems

Dispersing systems development responsibility to the business units doesn't preclude senior management's responsibility to maximize the return for systems investments. There are many systems that should still be developed on a centralized basis or purchased from vendors.

For example, does it make sense for your company to design its own general ledger system when there are more economical, ready-developed packages available on the market from vendors such as MSA or McCormick & Dodge? By developing its own general ledger, does your company satisfy the need of a corporate imperative or create an enhanced stakeholder relationship?

In a recent meeting of the Committee on Information Management of the Financial Executives Institute (FEI), John Stewart, head of internal auditing at IBM, and Silvio Lanaro, also of IBM and a member of the FEI committee, described a program under which IBM is realizing savings of millions of dollars annually.

At IBM, the general ledger is considered *mission critical* in that it standardizes the unique IBM culture at thousands of locations around the world. The problem in the past was that IBM was running about 50 different general ledger packages around the world!

Under Stewart's and Lazano's leadership, the number of general ledgers was reduced to a total of six. The reason for not getting down to one general ledger was that IBM recognized the need for regional differences around the world as a result of different societal and accounting practices. However, by eliminating the duplication of tasks in building and maintaining the myriad general ledgers, IBM will realize significant cash savings this year and in each future year as well.

SUMMARY

By establishing and communicating your corporation's imperatives, the various business functional units can bring greater focus on cooperative efforts. The merit of investment in information and technology can be assessed in terms of its ability to satisfy corporate imperatives. When your corporation has clearly communicated its imperatives, executive time is spent in achieving them, not in trying to find what they are or, even worse, in making wrong assumptions about what they are.

CHAPTER 9

ESTABLISHING ACTIONS AND PRIORITIES: Translating Corporate Imperatives into Action

Corporate imperatives are statements of key areas of activity that your corporation must accomplish in order to achieve its goals and objectives. A typical set of corporate imperatives for a consumer manufacturing and marketing business might be:

1. Achieve product differentiation to provide sales leverage.
2. Attain product positioning to achieve first or second place in the market.
3. Repurchase equity to consolidate ownership and protect the corporation from takeover.
4. Reduce costs to protect earnings during a period of strong price competition.
5. Create research and development alliances with other companies to spread the risk and costs of product discovery and development.
6. Enter the distribution business to decrease dependency on independent distributors.

As you can see, these corporate imperatives are statements of action at the highest level—at the board level and in the executive committee. There is no equivocation. These action-oriented statements are to be used as the ultimate guide for creating priorities throughout the corporation.

Each business-unit executive produces a list of divisional imperatives from the set of overall corporate imperatives. Divisional executives then convert their imperatives into programs and projects, many of which need supporting information technology and systems to implement them.

Figure 9–1 shows a spreadsheet that matches new systems development project spending to corporate imperatives. Since some projects affect more than one imperative, their cost is distributed between the affected imperatives. The totals across the bottom of the spreadsheet reflect total spending for the imperative heading each column.

Figure 9–2 shows a pie chart illustrating the total new information-technology (IT) spending by imperative. Note that 12 percent of new IT spending isn't related to any of the corporate imperatives. This spending is suspect and should be examined for possible cancellation or deferral.

Figure 9–3 shows spending by corporate imperative graphed in priority order. *Differentiating products* is the highest priority, *positioning* the second, *takeover protection* the third, and so on to *no imperatives,* which is, of course, last.

Management review of this last graph will generate key questions:

1. Why are there discrepancies between the priority of certain imperatives and the amount spent on them?
2. Why does the spending on projects unrelated to imperatives exceed the spending on four projects that are related to corporate imperatives?

Few information systems organizations can relate their activities to corporate imperatives. The huge gap between the corporation's imperatives and the project statements of the I/S division leave the I/S organization disconnected from the business. What accounts for this?

I/S development groups preoccupy themselves with responding to requests from business-unit clients whether or not these requests are related to corporate imperatives. Their focus is on the technology that creates systems, not on the business process that drives the systems. The data center, telecommunications, and end-user computing groups focus on delivering a utility

FIGURE 9–1
Corporate Imperatives: New Development Spending

Acme Companies, Inc.
New Systems Development Budget
Fiscal Year 1989

Budget Allocation ($000) by Acme Companies' Corporate Imperative

New Development Project	Differentiate Products	Position Products	Takeover Protection	Reduce Product Cost	Reduce Expenses	R&D Alliance	Enter Distribution	No Imperative	Total
Automate accounts receivable			$ 600		$ 150				$ 750
Field inventory control			$ 130	$260	$ 130		$ 130		$ 650
Electronic data interchange	$300			$100	$ 200		$ 300		$1,000
Customer information base	$168	$168			$ 336	$100	$1,008		$1,680
Electronic mail system					$ 125			$125	$ 250
Sales reporting system	$ 90	$ 90	$ 60		$ 60				$ 300
Common operating systems					$ 160			$640	$ 800
Shareholder database			$ 300						$ 300
Customer support system	$190	$190							$ 380
Automated budget system			$ 50	$ 25	$ 150			$ 25	$ 250
TOTAL	$748	$448	$1,140	$385	$1,311	$100	$1,438	$790	$6,360

142

FIGURE 9–2
New IT Spending $(000) By Corporate Imperative

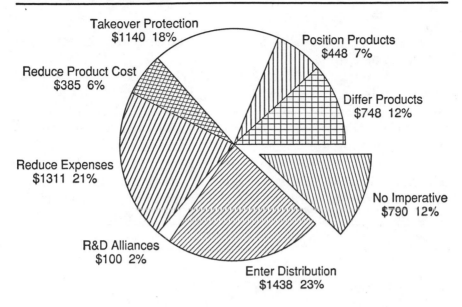

FIGURE 9–3
New it Spending $(000) by Corporate Imperative

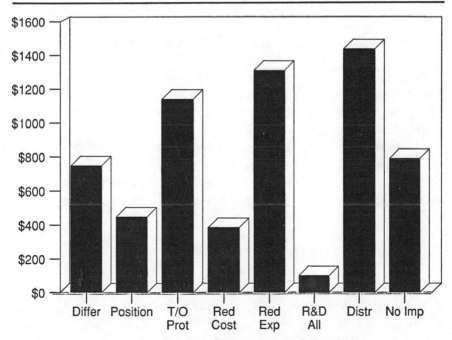

service. How these utility services serve corporate imperatives is seldom asked.

This chapter describes how the I/S organization can enter into a viable partnership with business units in helping to fulfill corporate imperatives. To do this, the I/S executives must first understand the corporate imperatives and then work together with the business-unit executives to trace through the supporting divisional imperatives to the various development projects. The I/S executive, in partnership with the business-unit executive, must assess each systems project in terms of its effectiveness in ultimately fulfilling divisional and corporate imperatives.

I/S AS TECHNOLOGY PARTNER FOR FULFILLING CORPORATE IMPERATIVES

In Chapter 12, the I/S function as a portfolio of investments will be described. The I/S businesses are the data processing, telecommunications, and information utilities, as well as project management and consulting. All of these businesses contain information technology as a key ingredient. An overall positioning of the I/S function is as a technology partner with other business functions.[1] The financial function plays a role in the business as a financial partner, the marketing function as the marketing partner, and so on.

As opposed to simply responding to requests for service, I/S executives must take on a proactive role in the business. Their focus must be on helping business units apply information technology to better fulfill corporate and divisional imperatives.

WORKING WITH DISPERSION

Dispersion is a measure of the degree to which business units within a corporation make innovative uses of information technology to implement divisional imperatives.[2] Dispersion is not decentralization or the placement of I/S functions within the business units. Neither is it distributed processing or the placement of hardware and software in the business units.

The advent of the personal computer, with corresponding computer literacy at the departmental level, is a key factor in dispersion. As a result of the increased power and proliferation of small computers, business units are beginning to take the lead in finding new and innovative uses for information technology. High-dispersion organizations are experiencing a shift in the locus for the application of information technology from a centralized I/S function to business groups below the departmental level. Low-dispersion organizations, however, remain dependent on the central I/S function to develop innovative uses of information technology.

I/S organizations in high-dispersion environments are rapidly changing their role in the business. The checklist for typical actions to take in the high-dispersion environment includes

Preparation
- Decide what and what not to disperse.
- Build standards for data architecture, networking, and maintainability.
- Design new career systems for I/S professionals.
- Choose the receiving organization(s).
- Design the organization for dispersed systems.
- Choose the I/S professionals to disperse.
- Plan the migration of systems and people.

Readiness Work
- Selection and training for receiving managers.
- Briefings for senior management, I/S management, and user management.
- Business and communications training for dispersed I/S staff.
- Location planning for dispersed staff.
- Business-unit briefing for dispersed I/S staff.

High-dispersion business units are characterized by intense activity with stakeholders. An example is the sales and marketing function and its chief stakeholder, customers. Innovative uses of information technology to achieve a competitive advantage yield increased revenue and fulfillment of the corporate imperatives that deal with customers. The sales and marketing organization is driven by the immediate need for performance. Immediacy of performance is further evidenced by the reward system used for the sales force. Salespeople receive direct and immediate rewards for producing revenue—sales commissions.

Because they are performance driven, salespeople are open to innovation. At the same time, they can't tolerate interruption of their day-to-day tasks. If new technology can be made simple, if it can be handed over with the very minimum of difficulty, and if there is immediate performance benefit, salespersons will readily take to using new technology. If the new technology is cumbersome and requires a great deal of effort for little or no gain, they will not be bothered with it.

Marketing people march to a different drummer than do salespeople. Marketers typically focus on the analysis and improvement of product positioning. Quite often, marketing people come up with sales systems that help the analysis of the sales process rather than the sales process itself. If such systems place any burden on salespeople, chances for the systems' success are slim because salespeople will undermine them.

When sales and marketing people work together to conceive new systems, the results are much different. Acting as a technology partner, I/S staff can add significant value to the process as well. Key to this partnership is understanding on the part of I/S staff of what the marketing and salespeople really want out of the process. This means digging into the jobs themselves to find out how personal performance can be enhanced, both on the front line of sales work and in the marketing-strategy and tactical-support areas.

ORGANIZING TO MAKE EFFECTIVE USE OF NEW TECHNOLOGY

To become an effective technology partner, an I/S executive must organize both the central I/S unit and the dispersed I/S units for action. Add to this the building of the corporation's network infrastructure for communications and moving information and you have an outline of the emerging role of the chief information officer (CIO). To earn a seat on the executive management committee and to merit the title of CIO, the information systems executive must lead the I/S function in taking the following actions:

1. *Position I/S as a proactive technology partner.* In contrast to simply responding to requests, IS should participate in the planning of future activities in corporate and divisional business units. By attending regular executive and planning meetings, I/S executives can gather information to guide new technology development.

2. *Plan and execute projects based on corporate imperatives.* The basis for interaction between corporate and divisional I/S groups is the company's corporate imperatives. By focusing on imperatives and the new technology required to achieve results, consensus on actions and priorities is readily achieved. Furthermore, I/S groups avoid serious gaps in planning.

3. *Focus on high-value–added projects.* All new technology projects undertaken internally should yield a higher value added than that of the corporate average. Lower value-added projects are candidates for external development or even deferral.

4. *Focus on the timing of new technology.* I/S executives should optimize the use of new information technology by first establishing the possible timing for introduction. By the time a corporate or division business group requests a development project from I/S, the ideal time-frame for implementation has already passed. The need to apply new information technology to prevent further losses has become immediate. I/S organizations have disappointed their clients mainly by not adequately anticipating the need for new information technology.

5. *Build a network of technology experts.* An important I/S effort is to identify and qualify both internal and external experts for anticipated areas of new technology. This effort will dramatically speed up results in the future

and will also cut out expensive and lengthy duplication of work already done outside the corporation.

6. *Build I/S staff's knowledge in corporate and divisional business activities.* I/S organizations are inbred groups. Most I/S staff members haven't worked in a company's various business units and don't readily identify with those units' missions or imperatives. They are insulated from the pressures of day-to-day business-unit activities and thus fail to understand the issues facing business-unit managers.

   To undo the inbreeding, central I/S executives and staff should be rotated in and out of the various business units on a periodic basis (perhaps every two years). This would build a solid and extended team that is knowledgeable about the business and strategically located throughout the organization to make the maximum contribution. This process also provides a career path for developing I/S management staff.

7. *Integrate corporate-wide I/S activities.* When there are two or more information-technology groups that have regular meetings, the central I/S group can play a significant role in integrating their activities. Central I/S, working together with the business units, should determine whether each new technology project meets the following conditions: (*a*). it impacts corporate imperatives, (*b*). it enhances high-value–added work, and (*c*). it eliminates low-value–added work.

   If a project has an impact on all of these, it should receive high priority. If it doesn't relate to a corporate or divisional imperative, if it has no impact on high-value–added work and doesn't reduce or cut out low-value–added work, it should be given low priority.

8. *Build a corporate-wide communications infrastructure.* The communications infrastructure is for all voice, data, and image movement. The objective is to connect all your company's information workers so that geographic location doesn't make any difference. Whether they are situated at central headquarters, at remote plants and offices, at home, on the road, or at work, information

workers must have access to appropriate information
and communication facilities. This is essential to productivity.

ESTABLISHING PRIORITIES FOR NEW
INFORMATION TECHNOLOGY

Figure 9–4 presents a spreadsheet that illustrates how
information-technology projects can be matched to corporate
imperatives. The corporate imperatives are listed along the top
of the spreadsheet and the projects are listed in the left-hand
margin. The budgeted amounts for each project are listed under
the corporate imperatives that are satisfied by the project.

The spreadsheet summarizes the IT project investment for
each project and the total investment for each imperative. The
amounts planned for each imperative can then be compared
with the relative importance of that imperative. Projects that
aren't aligned with corporate imperatives are suspect and
amounts spent on them are likely to be cut or reassigned to the
investment in established imperatives.

In overseeing the IT investment, the central I/S executive
monitors each divisional I/S organization to ensure that it
matches its projects to corporate and division imperatives as per
Figure 9–1. Central I/S executives maintain an overall priority
summary supported by divisional summaries. Corporate and
division I/S executives filling in the chart in Figure 9–1 show
their projects as they relate to divisional imperatives, which in
turn help to achieve corporate imperatives. Central I/S executives then establish regular meetings of a new-technology–
development steering committee to review corporate and divisional imperatives vis-à-vis project priorities.

REPOSITIONING THE CHIEF I/S EXECUTIVE

In their classic book on positioning, Al Ries and Jack Trout
discuss the difficulty in changing people's minds.[3] Once they
have placed a particular product, person, or organization in

FIGURE 9–4
Corporate Imperative: Project Analysis

Acme Companies, Inc.
New Systems Development Budget
Fiscal Year 1989

Budget Allocation ($000) by Acme Companies Corporate Imperative

New Development Project	Enter Distribution	Reduce Expenses	Takeover Protection	Differentiate Products	Position Products	Reduce Product Cost	R&D Alliances	No Imperative	Total
Automate accounts receivable		$ 150	$ 600						$ 750
Field inventory control	$ 130	$ 130	$ 130			$260			$ 650
Electronic data interchange	$ 300	$ 200		$300		$100	$100		$1,000
Customer information base	$1,008	$ 336		$168	$168				$1,680
Electronic mail system		$ 125						$125	$ 250
Sales reporting system		$ 60	$ 60	$ 90	$ 90				$ 300
Common operating systems		$ 160						$640	$ 800
Shareholder database			$ 300						$ 300
Customer support system				$190	$190				$ 380
Automated budget system		$ 150	$ 50			$ 25		$ 25	$ 250
TOTAL	$1,438	$1,311	$1,140	$748	$448	$385	$100	$790	$6,360

their minds, it is very difficult to change. I/S executives are generally viewed by other executives as "techies." To convince people otherwise is no easy task.

The actions I/S executives need to take in repositioning their function are to talk, act, and look like business people. The old adage, "If it walks like a duck and quacks like a duck and looks like a duck, it probably is a duck," is especially applicable here. By focusing on corporate and divisional imperatives, I/S executives can talk, behave, and be perceived as business people.

IS YOUR COMPANY READY FOR A CIO?

In working with our clients, we find that many are not yet ready to have a CIO to integrate the various business units into what we call the *new corporation*. Our clients are in various stages of company development and in a variety of businesses that have varying competitive pressures.

For example, companies in a commodity business typically have less need for a CIO than do product-marketing companies. The marketing-driven company readily recognizes the need for creating and sharing information as an investment for its marketing and distribution efforts. Stakeholder relationships have a high priority in a market-driven company, especially those relationships on the demand side.

On the other hand, the capability-driven commodity company focuses on its investment in its mills. The commodity company recognizes internal information needs if they have to do with production. The only other information needs critical to the business are financial because management tends to be fixed on the investor relationship for return on investment.

Nevertheless, a commodity company whose executive committee decides to become more market driven will soon encounter expanded information needs. This is the kind of environment in which a CIO can make a real contribution.

If your company is ready to recognize the business possibilities that go with enhancing stakeholder relationships, then it is probably ready for a CIO.

IS YOUR I/S EXECUTIVE CAPABLE OF BECOMING A CIO?

Whether or not a particular I/S executive is capable of becoming a CIO is a ticklish issue that all executive committees will have to deal with sooner or later. In many companies, the I/S executive has grown up in the data-processing function and has performed well over the years in managing the DP utility. The tendency of executive committees is to simply promote the DP utility executive, providing little or no development and preparation for the new job. In fact, the executive committee usually doesn't realize that as the company develops and grows, the top I/S job changes. The result often is that the traditional DP executive, who hasn't perceived the need to change his or her thinking to resemble that of a business executive, fails and is replaced with a non-DP executive.

POSITIONING THE CIO

The chief information officer has a position analogous to that of the chief financial officer. The CFO is responsible for the company's capital investment, financial reporting, and financial controls. The focus is on money.

The CIO is responsible for the company's investment in information and information technology. Just as the CFO is charged with optimizing the return on invested capital, the CIO is responsible for optimizing the investment in information and information technology. In Chapter 11, we will see just how big this investment is—in most companies, it exceeds the net worth! Like the CFO, the CIO should report to the chief executive officer of the company. In the case of a holding company, the CFO and CIO report to the head of the holding company, with separate CFO's and CIO's in each of the subsidiaries or business divisions. This allows the CIO, like the CFO, to participate in determining policy and to participate in conversations about business alternatives at the highest level.

A key responsibility for both the CFO and CIO is integrating the company's business units. The CFO uses the general ledger as the vehicle for integrating the financial elements of the business. The CIO uses the communications backbone and information-based business systems to integrate disparate business functions.

A CRUCIAL PARTNERSHIP: THE CFO AND THE CIO

The CFO and the CIO in partnership can provide the necessary ingredients for a company to succeed. This partnership is *crucial* to the health of the enterprise. When this isn't the case, and when information systems are out of synchronization with financial records, the integrating potential of both functions diminishes.

SUMMARY

I/S executives, acting in partnership with business-unit executives, must use corporate and divisional imperatives as a frame of reference for taking action. By insisting that all information-technology investments be based on achieving success of corporate imperatives, I/S executives will begin a new conversation with business-unit executives. As opposed to performing strictly in a provincial technical role, I/S executives can reposition themselves and their staffs as crucial business partners.

ENDNOTES

1. Al Ries and Jack Trout, *Positioning: The Battle for Your Mind,* (New York: First Warner Books, 1986).
2. Kay Lewis Reditt and Thomas M. Lodahl, "Leaving the IS Mothership," *CIO Magazine,* October 1988, pp. 54–60.
   Kay Reditt and Tom Lodahl are performing some excellent research that is sponsored by the Society for Information Management and endorsed by the Financial Executives Institute's Committee for Information.
3. Al Ries and Jack Trout, *Positioning: The Battle for Your Mind* (New York: First Warner Books, 1986).

PART 3

CHARTING THE TRANSITION

CHAPTER 10

RESOURCE MANAGEMENT:
People, Information,
and Capital

In Chapter 9, we examined how corporate and divisional imperatives channel a company's energy into actions that are essential to business performance. But it will take a careful marshalling of your company's resources to accomplish those actions.

Your company is made up of three basic resources: people, information, and capital. It's the weaving together of these resources to execute your corporate plan that makes your company unique and competitive. This chapter addresses the role of information technology in helping you to combine, ready, and manage these three basic resources.

RESOURCE MANAGEMENT IN THE INDUSTRIAL AGE

Think back to the time before the industrial revolution, when company sizes were very small and labor was the largest ingredient. Much less capital was required than was later needed to fuel the industrial revolution. Information, needed mostly for commercial transactions, distribution, and trade, was otherwise incidental to business processes. It was limited by the scarce human labor available for such work.

In the industrial age, labor became standardized and simplified. Large numbers of people could earn their livelihood through the performance of repetitive tasks aided by machinery.

Capital became a much larger component because of the large investments in plant and machines.

Information work took on a more important role in the industrial era and expanded with the advent of industrial engineering, cost accounting, and the new, massive distribution systems. Information work was still limited by the capability of human labor and the small number of educated people required.

Today, capital continues to be a major component of businesses as we move into the information age. Information technology has arisen as one of the largest capital items in any corporate budget.

RESOURCE MANAGEMENT IN THE INFORMATION AGE

In today's information age, information technology is propelling business processes and the way people work in three basic stages. Each stage involves the ability of people to do information work and the resultant job and organizational restructuring.

There are three stages in which organizations synthesize information technology into the workplace:

In the first stage, organizations use information technology to replace people.

In the second stage, organizations use information technology to expand people's capability.

In the third stage, organizations use information technology to create new forms of organization, work, and economic systems.[1]

In the first stage, begun in many organizations in the 1960s, computers were typically used to replace clerical labor. Their cost was justified by labor savings. In commercial organizations, the first application of computers was for payroll and other accounting activities, thereby minimizing the need for scores of accounting clerks. In research organizations, computers were first used to make complex mathematical calculations, thereby minimizing the need for armies of research assistants.

In the second stage, during the 1970s and 1980s, organizations began to justify computers and telecommunications investments on the basis of new information-based products that were enhanced by new analytical and engineering capabilities. For example, companies used information technology to make distribution systems more efficient. In capital markets, brokerages and stock exchanges used information technology to handle more volume and diversify capital instruments.

American companies are just getting started with implementing the second stage. Artificial intelligence, expert systems, decision support systems, and executive information systems are all designed to enhance human capability. This makes them a part of the second stage. They also are helping to usher in the third stage.

Today, we are just beginning to understand stage three, in which new forms of organization, work, and economic systems are possible. As was discussed in Chapter 6, electronic data interchange (EDI) is evidence of a new economic structure that suppliers, manufacturers, distributors, wholesalers, and retailers are building together to realize new economies of production and distribution (see Figure 10-1).

To be competitive in stage three, we must learn more about information work and how it contributes to the economic alliances as shown in Figure 10-2. These economic alliances will pose numerous challenges to us:

- *Legal.* Antitrust laws will be reexamined in light of new information-technology capabilities and their use.

- *Economic.* Barriers to market entry will be strengthened by the added complexity of economic alliances.

- *Regional economic systems.* The impending European Economic Community implementation, Canadian–U.S. trade agreements, Pacific-basin trading communities, communist-bloc agreements, and the like will favor economic alliances by region.

The key to becoming a player in these new arenas will be in establishing corporate alliances through the use of information technology. Within the corporation, information and knowledge work will take on new importance.

FIGURE 10–1
The Emerging Industrial Model
The Electronic Data Interchange Network

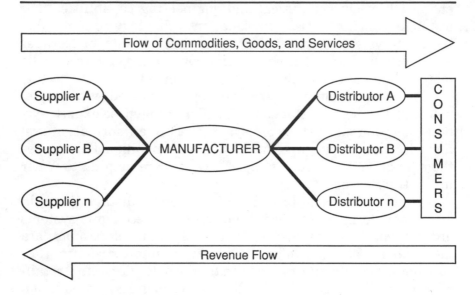

Yet, today's corporate economics treat information work as overhead, found in huge departmental chunks. This outdated view underlies management decrees for 10 percent budget reductions in hard times. Management doesn't understand where and how information work is accomplished.

Reward systems are even more at odds with reality. Bureaucratic, point-based job-rating systems lead to yet more inefficiency and lack of effectiveness.[2]

PEOPLE

Using Information Technology for People Management

Professor C. Northcote Parkinson spent much of his life lecturing and writing about his famous Parkinson's Law:

Work expands to fill the time allowed for it.

FIGURE 10–2
Economic Alliances
Supply-Side and Demand-Side Competition

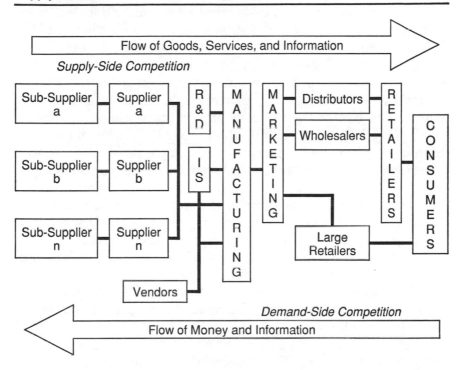

Professor Parkinson observed that people in the Royal Admiralty were rewarded for building large staffs and controlling large budgets. If the large staffs and budgets didn't exist, then prospective supervisors created them to the fullest extent they were allowed by their superiors. Since their superiors also benefited from expanding their staffs and budgets, approval was always forthcoming.

Parkinson further observed that bureaucracies grow so that the people in them can increase their personal rewards. Conventional wisdom dictates that heads of large departments are worth more than heads of small departments or people who aren't heads of anything.

American industry and government clearly developed this behavior during the industrial era; unfortunately, it shows no signs of lessening as we enter the information age. In our government, we can see ever-increasing spending deficits. In our industry, the bureaucratic reward system is embodied in point-based job-rating systems, such as the Hay Point System.

Point-based job-rating systems give more points for jobs that have supervisory responsibility for subordinates and for budgets and spending. The more people supervised, the more points. The bigger the budget and the more money spent, the more points. The more points, the higher the job rating and the higher the pay and other rewards such as private offices, secretaries, and the other spoils of winning the point-based pay game.

In a recent *Fortune* article, the author demonstrated that corporate executives have rationalized their reward systems to the point that they get outstanding rewards in both good times and bad.[3] It's the janitors and clerks who are at risk in economic downturns—they can actually lose their jobs.

Companies that want to be competitive today will have to do away with archaic bureaucratic reward systems exemplified by point-based job-rating systems. In their place, we need new measures of performance that we can tie directly to personal and team reward systems. We have the information technology to do it. We seem to lack the will to make it happen.

But, there's hope. The Gramm-Rudman Act in Congress put spending limits on our government. A global economy and free currency exchange rates put limits on what American producers or, for that matter, any producer can charge for products and services. This is forcing American manufacturers to reexamine their underlying business assumptions.

Just-in-Time People-Management Concepts

Increasingly popular just-in-time (JIT) manufacturing systems represent a complete change in basic assumptions about the manufacturing process and the way people work at all levels of the organization. Industrial age manufacturing companies divided labor tasks and skills so that the least-capable worker could still specialize in one task—and do well at it. As more and more of the simpler and routine tasks in manufacturing were automated, workers with low skill levels were displaced by automated lines.

The scope of today's worker is potentially broader but is kept artificially narrow by a management philosophy that doesn't permit initiative and capability at low levels in the organization. This legacy of the industrial age management philosophy stresses control.

JIT concepts foster a new attitude toward workers on the production line—they will participate and take initiative if they are given the objectives and tools. JIT begins with enabling, rather than controlling, the frontline worker. Rather than continuing expensive control and oversight departments, the JIT-based company makes production employees responsible for self-measurement of output quantities and quality, for preventative maintenance, and for involvement in the total process with the rest of the manufacturing team.

JIT also promotes a new conversation among production line workers. They learn to share a concern for quality—something that can't be mandated or inspected into the product. The workers also are encouraged to hold new conversations with management and technical support groups. Maintenance mechanics become instructors instead of mechanics, with the production worker assuming the responsibility for maintenance of production equipment.

Manufacturing engineers also become instructors and work with production workers to overcome technical and quality problems. The key difference is that the role of the production worker is enhanced, with those who previously performed control roles now playing teaching roles.

In addition to the investment in training and teambuilding necessary to implement JIT manufacturing concepts, there is a need for the creation and distribution of information. Production workers need measurement information for their operations. Support technical groups to change their focus from overseeing production workers to their planning information needs.

JIT Applied to Information Work

At present, JIT systems focus on direct manufacturing support and what has traditionally been direct labor. To get the full benefit of applying JIT thinking to our corporations, we need to focus on the huge indirect, or overhead, category. Focus in this area will lead to new work measurement and personal reward systems. Applying JIT thinking to information work begins with new assumptions about information workers and the way they contribute to implementing corporate imperatives.

Jobs and Imperatives

Each information job should relate directly to corporate and divisional imperatives. The output quantity and quality of each job should be measured by each information worker for the degree to which they satisfy the achievement of imperatives, just as JIT imperatives are measured in manufacturing.

Individual rewards should be based on individual and team success in satisfying corporate and divisional imperatives, as they are in the JIT environment. This is very much like management by objectives, but it is taken all the way out to the frontline.

With comprehensive performance measurement of information work based on corporate and divisional imperatives, we can neutralize a major Japanese competitive advantage—one that came from America and has been forgotten. That is, at least 40 percent of pay should come from demonstrating individual and team contributions toward company and divisional success.

The way we work and communicate must be directed to actions necessary to satisfy corporate and divisional imperatives. Information technology can help this process by improving communications, coordinating the efforts of teams and groups, providing action-oriented information for decision making, and enabling measurement of information-work processes.[4]

INFORMATION

Information and human resources are inextricably linked. Quality people working toward corporate and division imperatives produce quality information. For this reason, the design of information work and the corresponding individual and team performance must be related throughout the corporation. This means that information and people management is a line, not staff, function.

Using Information Technology to Manage Information: Information Resource Management (IRM)

Managing the organization's investment in information significantly increases its value for improving the competitiveness and performance of the company. There are two key IRM principles: The management of the corporation's information integrity, availability, and quality is primarily the responsibility of the user community. And policy direction, data definitions, and technical support are provided by the central information-resource management organization.

There are two other, related IRM principles:

- The corporation must view the various types of databases as an integrated activity rather than as separate functions.
- Effective communications between the user community and the central IRM staff must take place on a continuing basis.

Figure 10–3 shows the basic IRM functions: planning, administration, and the information center.

Information Planning

Information, as is shown in Figure 10–4, is more than just defining the internal uses of data. It means planning the

FIGURE 10–3
One Approach to IRM

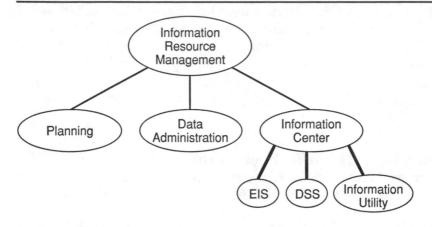

FIGURE 10–4
Information Planning Is More Than Defining Internal Uses of Data

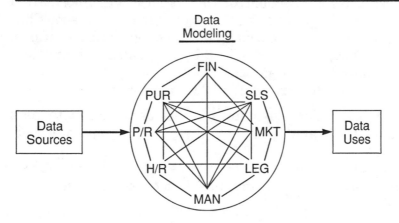

information that the corporation needs to ensure satisfactory achievement of corporate and divisional imperatives. This success is driven basically by corporate stakeholder relationships (Figure 10–5). To satisfy stakeholder needs, your company performs a number of business functions. Business function models are helpful to understanding the organizational units responsible for determining policy and those responsible for

FIGURE 10–5
The Organizing Principle: Defining Simple Relationships

execution. The objective of performing business function analysis is to determine what information is needed by which organization to conduct the company's business.

Restaurant Case Study

In the example set forth in Figure 10–6, a restaurant chain performs the various tasks as shown in this business process model. The actual processes may be conducted in one or more of the various company organizations, such as planning, personnel, or accounting.

In Figure 10–7, the process *Perform Strategic Planning* is conducted in all the restaurant's various functions including finance, operations, personnel, and I/S. *Manage Guest Services* is primarily the responsibility of the operations group, but I/S, finance, and personnel also have roles to play in this process.

FIGURE 10–6
Business Process Model

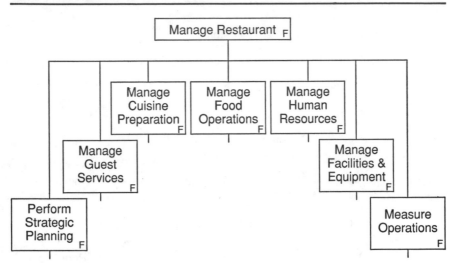

In constructing the various business processes, you need to identify the function having the prime responsibility for carrying out each process. Let's continue with the restaurant example.

For the process of *Analyze Trends* in Figure 10–7, the planning function has the responsibility both for the policy for this process as well as for performing the task. Moving down the list of business processes, the responsibility for the policies governing the process *Present Bill* belongs to operations while the performance responsibility belongs to the waiters. Thus, we can begin to understand how the business establishes policies and executes its various processes. The IRM concept spans all the company's information and data activities, including their use in

- Office automation and executive information systems.
- Decision support systems.
- Production data processing.

The IRM concept also deals with classifying the information as it relates to the various functions performed by the company. Figure 10–8, based on information from the restaurant chain,

FIGURE 10–7
Business Process Analysis

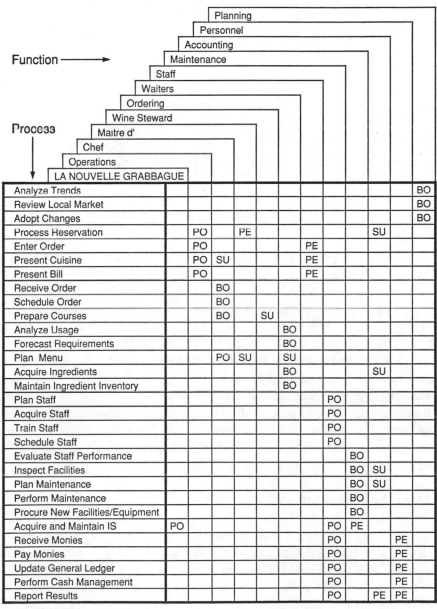

Function →

Process ↓

Diagonal function headers (top to bottom): Planning, Personnel, Accounting, Maintenance, Staff, Waiters, Ordering, Wine Steward, Maitre d', Chef, Operations — LA NOUVELLE GRABBAGUE

Process	Operations	Chef	Maitre d'	Wine Steward	Ordering	Waiters	Staff	Maintenance	Accounting	Personnel	Planning
Analyze Trends											BO
Review Local Market											BO
Adopt Changes											BO
Process Reservation			PO	PE					SU		
Enter Order			PO			PE					
Present Cuisine			PO	SU		PE					
Present Bill			PO			PE					
Receive Order		BO									
Schedule Order		BO									
Prepare Courses		BO		SU							
Analyze Usage					BO						
Forecast Requirements					BO						
Plan Menu		PO	SU		SU						
Acquire Ingredients					BO				SU		
Maintain Ingredient Inventory					BO						
Plan Staff							PO				
Acquire Staff							PO				
Train Staff							PO				
Schedule Staff							PO				
Evaluate Staff Performance								BO			
Inspect Facilities								BO	SU		
Plan Maintenance								BO	SU		
Perform Maintenance								BO			
Procure New Facilities/Equipment								BO			
Acquire and Maintain IS	PO								PO	PE	
Receive Monies									PO		PE
Pay Monies									PO		PE
Update General Ledger									PO		PE
Perform Cash Management									PO		PE
Report Results									PO	PE	PE

PO = Policy
PE = Performance
BO = Both Policy and Performance
SU = Support

FIGURE 10–8
Business Information Model

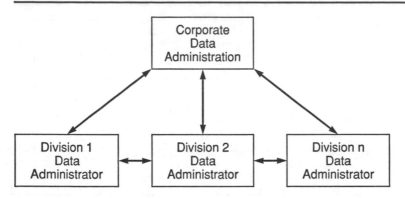

illustrates the various information classes as they relate to business functions.

Figure 10–9 shows the flow of information as the various business functions are performed by the company's organizational units. These information models can quickly become very complex. For this reason, we have found it best to select one segment of the business at a time for performing business-function analysis and information modeling.

Unfortunately, it is very easy to lose sight of the stakeholders in this process. When information elements rather than stakeholder needs dominate conversation, the planning exercise has become too esoteric and will not meet management expectations. For this reason, we have found that the success of the information-planning effort is highly dependent on the business orientation of the planning leadership.

Data Administration

In the next chapter, I will make the case for information as an asset. The data administration function parallels the corporate controller's function. Data administration has the same responsibilities for information as the controller's functions have for budgets and spending. The data administration organization, therefore, parallels that of the controllers, with a corporate data

FIGURE 10–9
Information Model

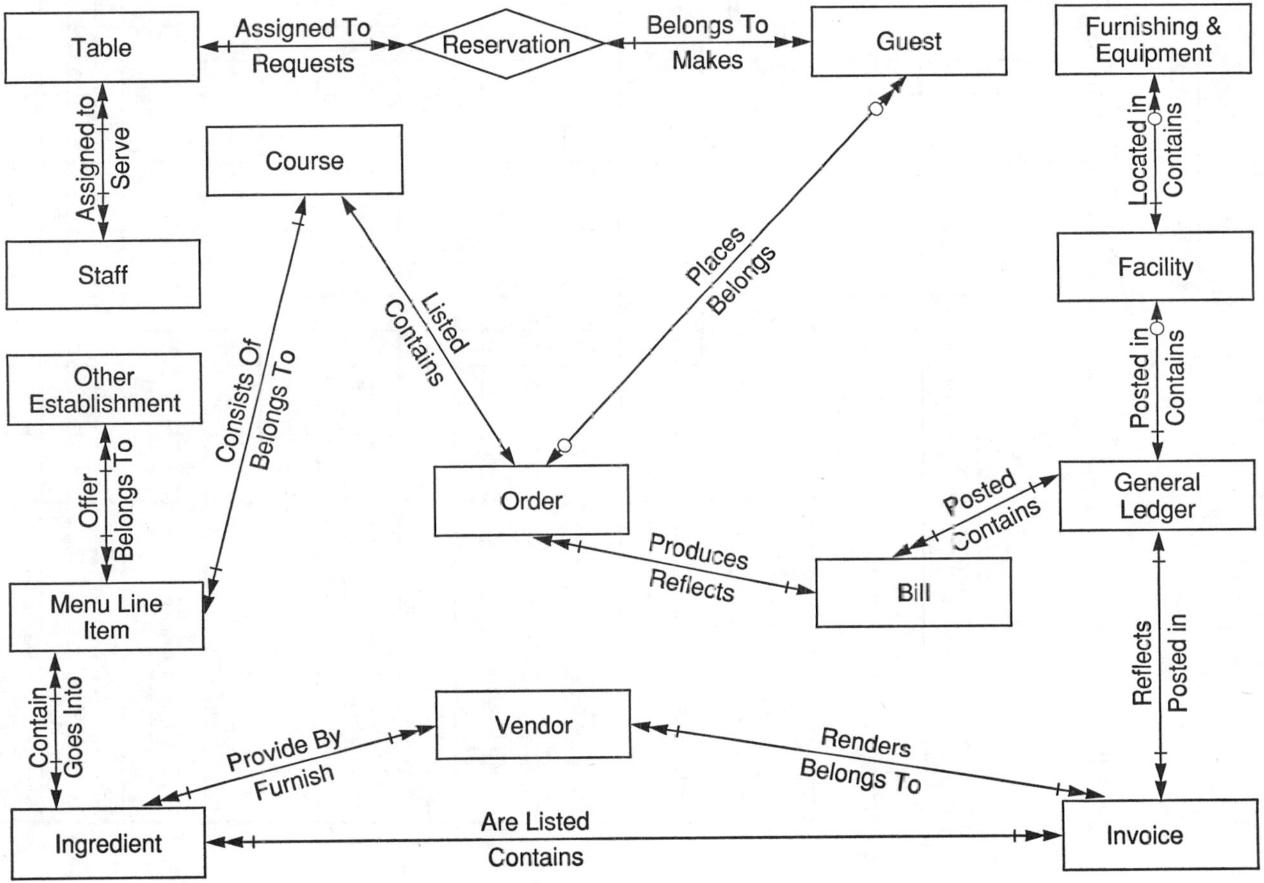

FIGURE 10–10
Data Administration: A Key Corporate Investment

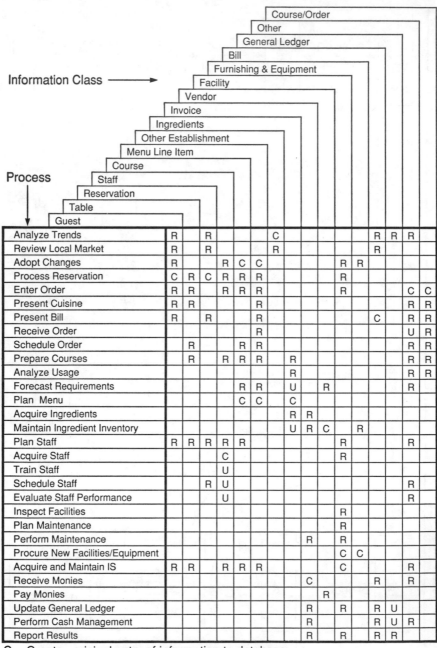

C = Create - original entry of information to database
R = Retrieve - read only use of information in database
U = Update - modify information to keep database up to date

administrator and divisional data administrators to manage and control the company's investment in information as shown in Figure 10–10.

The elements of the corporation's information-technology investment strategy will then evolve from its information strategy and the appropriate technology strategy (see Figure 10–11). Key to the technology strategy are the economic alliances with providers of information-technology services and vendors of computing and telecommunications hardware and software.

Establishing IRM

To establish a formal IRM function in the Information Systems organization, you must first select a senior-level manager from your organization to lead the effort. This senior-level manager must be fully conversant with information technology, organizational concepts, and the business functions throughout your company. In addition, this person must be a good listener and a skillful negotiator.

Furthermore, users must appoint data administrators in their areas to oversee the integrity and quality of data and to assure compliance with corporation-wide IRM policies. These data administrators must be senior-level managers who are especially conversant with both the business and systems functioning in the respective user organizations.

FIGURE 10–11
Elements of IT Strategy

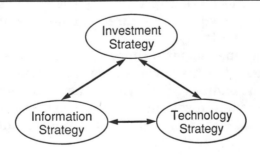

In implementing the IRM program, there are four important initial phases:

- Identify a corporation-wide IRM strategy that would identify the corporation's short- and long-term information needs.
- Propose an IRM program to senior management.
- Establish the central IRM staff, its leadership, and its charter for defining data definitions and policy.
- Establish the user data administrators and their charter for assuring the integrity and quality of data in the user organizations.

IRM at the World Bank

In the mid-1980s, Mel Ray served as director of IRM at the World Bank. During his tenure at the World Bank, Mel established a bankwide IRM capability.

The World Bank is largely bureaucratic in nature, with a driving force of research capability. Because of the bank's large size, the sharing of information was minimal. In addition, the bank's functional areas had developed strong feelings about information ownership and territorial imperative. Thus, when Mel was brought into the bank in 1981, he encountered mushrooming and loosely controlled databases located throughout the bank's operating and administrative units.

In 1982, the bank's management committee agreed that IRM concepts should be integrated into the bank's operations. They agreed to the underlying IRM concept that would be communicated throughout the bank. This was that management of the bank's information resources is the responsibility of the user community, with policy direction and technical support being provided centrally.

The bank's management committee also agreed to two other key principles—that the various types of technology being used throughout the bank would be viewed as an integrated activity, and effective communications between the user community and the central IRM staff must take place on a continuing basis.

A first step was the appointment of data administrators for each of the major business functions (e.g., finance, personnel, research, and operations). A second step was the study of what information was needed by the business units to support their day-to-day activities. A third step was to achieve consensus that the quality of information was a bank imperative.

Dispersed IRM at the bank allowed the business units to give up part of their territorial imperative associated with information in return for more complete and better-quality information. The business units also agreed to central coordination of technology and standards in turn for increased information-technology capability within the business units.

IRM education at all levels increased the awareness of the bank's interdependencies and need to share information. It also made bank staff more comfortable with information technology and enabled them to use IT more effectively.

Appendix 2 describes in detail how the World Bank established the IRM function. Due to the World Bank's political nature and size (and because it also conducted a full business systems plan), the IRM program took several years to establish there. Nevertheless, the World Bank experience is useful because it outlines a general approach that will succeed in many environments.

At your corporation, the needs are probably much nearer term than they were at the Word Bank. Assigning responsibility for the information resource and getting buy-in from the user organizations will quickly improve the integrity and quality of information and data at your company. This, in turn, will make your information-technology investment far more effective. It will result in reduced expenses, and, ultimately, in improved financial performance.

In the final analysis, information planning and its direct relationship with information work are key to achieving improved corporate value-added products and services. Information planning and the use of information technology to support economic relationships will result in leveraged corporate relationships (see Figure 10–12).

FIGURE 10–12
Information Planning and Information Work Inextricably Linked . . . .

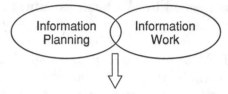

LEVERAGING CORPORATE RELATIONSHIPS

CAPITAL

Using Information Technology for Capital Management

Information technology's role in capital markets in the past two decades has been nothing less than miraculous. Stocks are bought and sold in subsecond time. Exchanges are wired for global action. Today's volumes on the New York and American exchanges were unthinkable just ten years ago. The London, Tokyo, and Hong Kong exchanges are a part of every stock broker's daily scope.

American investors, two thirds of whom are tied in with pension, mutual, and insurance funds, are wired for access to every exchange and every conceivable capital instrument. These include bonds, common stocks, preferred stocks, warrants, puts, calls, index options, commodities, and commodity options, to name just a few.

What more can information technology do for capital markets? Most likely, the global capital market will change in the next ten years just as much as it has in the past ten years, with new entrants coming from Soviet bloc countries and the People's Republic of China. The European Economic Community will also have a major impact as it consolidates currencies and removes provincial trade barriers.

Notwithstanding all these macro economic changes, internal capital management in corporations is also undergoing a fundamental change. Two events in the past two decades are especially significant: the rise of the holding company to provide internal capital markets and the electronic treasurer's terminal that allows corporations to manage their cash online.

A new phenomenon in the evolution of holding companies is the leveraged buyout (LBO). LBO's actually reverse the process of multiple mergers that resulted in the holding company. To the surprise of business professionals, many subsidiaries become inefficient as a result of being held. The result is that the portfolio management game has added some new rules. The subsidiary management, usually backed by an outside source of capital, proposes an LBO to the holding company management. The holding company management, looking at each subsidiary as a portfolio investment, decides whether the offer represents an appropriate return on their investment. Sometimes, the holding company invites competition to bid the price up.

In the final analysis, the subsidiary management buys out the company from the holding company, incurring significant debt along the way. If subsidiary management can do better on their own, they win. If they can't, they lose.

Both holding companies and their subsidiaries can benefit from economic alliances. This allows more flexibility in tapping capital sources and more autonomy for subsidiaries acting in various economic alliances. But the real benefit for economic alliances is for small and medium-size companies that wish to maintain their independence in a tougher economy. Economic alliances will allow smaller companies to participate in a chain of alliances by specializing in products and services that become part of other products and services.

Today, electronic data interchange (EDI) is the first step in building economic alliances between corporations in a value chain servicing a common market. In the future, capital could be shifted between corporations and up and down the value chain to support investment that will bring the best return to all the corporations participating in an economic alliance. EDI is already connecting showroom floors and retail outlets to manufacturing facilities. The leverage information technology brings to the economic alliance is crucial.

One effect of JIT manufacturing techniques has been to reduce inventory levels. The result is another internal source of capital. Freeing capital from inventory makes it available for other, better-return alternatives.

In today's market, General Motors' vertical integration is a handicap. Ford Motors' policy of creating economic alliances rather than owning the sources of their components has allowed them to stay lean when it really counts. The real test will come when the government tests antitrust and price-fixing laws with such economic alliances. The field of corporate law will be an active one in the next decade.

SUMMARY

As we move into a highly competitive and global economy, it's essential that you begin to manage the corporation's three basic resources—people, information, and capital—as investments to be applied for return as opposed to being controlled. Today, people are managed as legal liabilities and information is managed as throw-away expense while the focus is on capital management.

Innovative *people management* involves viewing information work as plannable, measurable, and rewardable. Innovative *information management* involves creating a corporate climate for participating in formation of the information base and for sharing the resultant information resource. Innovative *capital management* looks for new internal sources, as in the case of companies implementing JIT concepts, and for new external sources through new stakeholder relationships.

ENDNOTES

1. Masuda, Yoneji, *The Information Society as Post-Industrial Society,* Bethesda, MD: World Future Society, 1980), pp. 59.
2. "Job Evaluation: A Critique," Edward E. Lawler III, Center for Effective Organizations, Graduate School of Business Administration, University of Southern California G 85-7 (73).
3. Graef S. Crystal, "Where's the risk in CEOs' rewards," *Fortune,* December 1988.

4. A growing technology, *groupware,* is an emerging information technology area that will provide methodologies and tools for this. Groupware is communications software designed for coordinating the activities of teams. Notable among these is *The Coordinator,* produced by Action Technologies, Inc., in Emeryville, California. This coordinating program is designed to incorporate the communications research done by Fernando Flores at the University of California at Berkeley and at Logonet, Inc., also in Emeryville.

CHAPTER 11

INFORMATION AS A CORPORATE ASSET: A New View of Corporate Worth

So far, we have been concentrating on the information-technology investment. But, in an internationally competitive environment, the new corporate challenge is to realize value from the investment not only through the information-technology infrastructure but also through information itself. So, before giving further consideration to the technology investment, we need to explore the value and benefits of information as an asset.

RECOGNIZING THE ASSET VALUE OF INFORMATION

To help senior executives recognize the asset value of the information investment, a fundamental change in perspective is necessary. We must begin by working with the economic, financial, and accounting communities to develop ways to determine the asset value of information. These communities need substantial proof that information is an inventoriable and capitalizable commodity in commercial and governmental enterprises.

A change in attitude on the part of these communities would undoubtedly affect tax laws. Assets are subject to sales and property taxes. If new taxes were to be levied, information asset taxation would also affect the return on investment to investors.

Historically, investors have resisted any efforts to reduce their return on investment, and they will likely do so in the future. This will then become another case of stakeholders' conflict before a new business equilibrium is achieved. The business community, along with regulators and lawmakers, will have to deal with this issue.

The real need is to develop financial and economic theory that will govern the use of this emerging asset. The purpose of this chapter is to enhance your understanding of the value and use of information.

Although information is often invisible to the eye, it is essential to operating a business. Let's examine the four physical properties of this vital asset:[1]

1. *Information is not consumable.* Products and services are consumed as they are used; information is not.
2. *Information is copiable.* When goods move from point A to point B, they are physically transferred to point B. When information is electronically transferred from point A to point B, it then exists in both places.
3. *Information is indivisible.* Utilities such as gas, electricity, and water are divided and distributed for use. Information needs context and must be used as a set.
4. *Information is accumulative.* The accumulation of goods only happens when they aren't consumed at the rate at which they're produced. Because information isn't consumable and because it's copiable, new information always adds to the already-accumulated base.

This last property of information is probably its most important aspect. Information's accumulative nature is what causes it to be such a unique corporate asset.

The following are the essential characteristics of the information investment that qualify it as an asset. They are a logical extension of economic and accounting theory used to define other corporate assets.

INFORMATION AND ACCOUNTING THEORY

According to the Financial Accounting Standards Board, an asset has three essential characteristics:[2]

1. It embodies a probable future benefit that involves a capacity, singly or in combination with other assets, to contribute directly or indirectly to future net cash flows.
2. A particular enterprise can obtain the benefit and control access to it by other enterprises.
3. The transaction or other event giving rise to the enterprise's right to control of the benefit has already occurred; that is, the enterprise has already made the investment, it is for exclusive use by the enterprise, and it is in usable form.

How then can we relate information to this classic definition of an asset?[3]

PROOF OF CREATING FUTURE CASH FLOW

We can cite many examples in which information determines whether future business transactions will take place. If a specific information investment creates future cash flow, it meets the first criterion above for classifying an entity as an asset. An example of such information may be as simple as a customer prospect list made by a salesperson. Or, it may be as complex as customer intelligence files containing information for strategic market planning. In either case, the intended result of investing in such information is to create future sales.

Let's look at the sales example in more detail. Many selling efforts are numbers games. The more extensive the list and the more complete the information, the higher the hit ratio for the target market. In respect to a particular market segment, many companies maintain extensive client lists in addition to lists purchased from other firms. These companies can use statistical data to calculate an expected return from each 1,000 customers who were mailed sales letters.

For example, companies in the seminar business expect that 0.5 percent of the persons receiving a seminar flier will attend. If the fee for attendance at the seminar is $500, the return on mailing 1,000 fliers would be $2,500. Assuming that the cost per seminar attendee is $400, the future net cash flow per 1,000 prospects would be $500. Without this information, the anticipated future cash flow would be impossible to calculate.

THE EXCLUSIVITY OF THE INFORMATION

Next, we must test the prospect list to see if it meets the second criterion of an asset, its exclusivity. If the information for a market segment were readily available from public sources, then the cost would be minimal. We would value the asset at cost or market, whichever is lower. For public information, the cost would be negligible and therefore of no asset value. On the other hand, if the information we collected were exclusively for the use of the enterprise and were not public, then we would have a case for valuing the information asset at cost. Since the information asset must be secure and safe from theft or misuse, it will require protection as would any other asset.

THE INVESTMENT HAS ALREADY OCCURRED

The information investment also meets the final criterion: the enterprise has already made the investment. Thus we already have the right to control it. The only remaining test is to audit the information. The audit will test its usability and determine whether it will lead to future cash flow.

THE ECONOMIC BASIS FOR THE INFORMATION ASSET

Economic theory contains ample support for the classification of information as an asset. Economic theory defines a good or commodity as something useful or valuable. An owner's ability to sell and deliver it to a buyer and to provide post-sales support enhance its value.

Businesses regularly sell information commodities such as mailing lists, research reports, market studies, patents, trade secrets, and software programs. They deliver the information product after the sale, with the delivery often taking place over a telephone line. The seller's financial success depends on selling multiple copies to many information users. For this reason, the seller places restrictions on the buyer or licensee to maintain the privacy of the information. The seller holds the buyer liable for any disclosure to a third party.

Information businesses have developed and automated medical and legal libraries for sale or lease. Such information commodities and delivery systems easily meet the foregoing criteria for classification as an asset.

An example of such an automated medical system is INTERNIST/CADUCEUS, developed at the University of Pittsburgh. This system covers more than 80 percent of all internal medicine, including information on 500 diseases and 3,500 manifestations of those diseases.

An example of a legal system is an automated legal library, LEXIS, developed and marketed by the Mead Corporation in Dayton, Ohio.[4] Another legal library is WESLAW, marketed by the West Publishing Company in St. Paul, Minnesota. Attorneys lease services such as LEXIS and WESLAW, which include the databases and the delivery mechanisms for lawyers preparing legal briefs. They need only to enter the subject area from remote terminals, and they have access to all the necessary case information.

INFORMATION-DRIVEN COMPANIES

There are some industry sectors especially driven by information. Their only product is an information-based service. These are the firms that we called *information-driven companies* in the results of a survey we conducted of 100 companies in 1985, and they include

- Banking and financial services.
- Insurance and security services.

- Most government agencies.
- Marketing and sales organizations.
- Accounting and auditing firms.
- Software development firms.
- Investment houses.

The most common characteristic of all the above businesses is that their end product is information. They are also labor intensive and they rely heavily on information systems. The results of their efforts are either read, heard, or recorded for future access.

As with other assets, information has a useful life that may be extended by updating and maintaining its usability. If the useful life of information is a year or less, then it doesn't make sense to capitalize it.

Information that we can classify as an asset would likely have a useful life of three to five years depending on the frequency of required updating. We would expense the maintenance of such information, as is done with the maintenance of any other asset.

The expansion of an information asset, however, could qualify as an addition to its asset value. We would then amortize the expansion over the same period as the base information asset.

The above analysis shows that the information investment can pass the test as an asset. Information, however, is relatively intangible when compared to plant, equipment, raw materials, and consumer hard goods. Nevertheless, executives working in an information-based economy can overcome the tangibility issue. To do this, they need a methodology for assessing the value of the information asset. They need to know how to plan for it, manage it, control it, and report it.

VALUATION OF THE INFORMATION ASSET

So far, we've examined how information can be considered an economic commodity and an asset. It's not unusual to find corporations that have invested at least 75 percent of their annual payroll in the information asset. Our research has shown that the information investment in those companies is even greater than imagined. We've also found that the corresponding investment in information technology doesn't adequately reflect the potential value of the information investment. Here are some observations that come from our experience in working with our client companies:

1. In order for the information investment to be considered an asset, it must clearly have value. This means that the result of investing in information will clearly yield future revenues. This is difficult to prove. Nevertheless, the evidence suggests that IT plays a key role in making information valuable.

2. The actual information investment, depending on the industry, is in fact much larger than originally estimated. The findings are presented in Table 11–1 for those industries driven by information (banks, insurance companies, service organizations) and manufacturing-based organizations.

3. The ratio of the information investment to that of the annual IT expense varies according to industry type—that is, the IT investment as compared to the information investment is higher in information-driven organizations than in manufacturing organizations. This ratio has value-added implications.

THE INFORMATION INVESTMENT
AND LABOR DEPLOYMENT

In 1984, we mailed a questionnaire requesting the information shown in Figure 11–1 to Fortune 500 companies and received over 100 responses. The results were printed in *Computerworld* in the same year.

The results of the study were dramatic. Some companies reported that as much as 80 percent of their payroll and related overhead costs were for creating and maintaining information. One of the world's most successful information-driven manufac-

FIGURE 11-1

Calculating Your Investment in the Information Asset

1. Total number of people in your corporation = _____
2. Percent of total people working with information = _____ %
3. Net equivalent information workers (1 × 2) = _____
4. Percent of time spent creating and maintaining information (this normally runs 60–80%) = _____ %
5. Net equivalent workers creating and maintaining information (3 × 4) = _____ %
6. Average salary per information worker (this normally runs $20–40,000) = $ _____
7. Average general expense per information worker (plant, equipment, fringes, taxes, utilities, etc.) = $_____
8. Total cost per information worker (6 + 7) = $ _____
9. Total annual information investment (5 × 8) = $ _____
10. Capitalized cost of information investment (it would take 3–7 years to build an information base equivalent to the one that now exists) $ _____

Analysis: Key Statistics

A. What is your annual budget for hardware, software, and telecommunications? $ _____
B. What is the amount spent on information technology per year per information worker? (The Grace commission recommended $4,000 annually for the U.S. Government) $ _____
C. What is the ratio of the capitalized information investment to your annual budget for hardware, software, and telecommunications?
D. How does the capitalized information investment compare to your corporation's net worth (is it more or less)?

turing companies estimated that their information investment might be as high as $45 billion.[5]

The results were combined into two basic categories:

1. Information-driven companies—banks, insurance and financial service firms, and marketing organizations.
2. Manufacturing companies.

The survey results are shown in Table 11–1. The results pointed to a trend in the amount invested in information and the annual expenditure on hardware and software. This trend has held in companies The Information Group has worked with since then.

TABLE 11–1
Information Investment versus IT Annual Budget

	Information-Driven Industries	Manufacturing Industries
Average Information Investment/IT Annual Expense	18:1	36:1
Average Information Technology Investment	$4,200 million	$1,200 million

The information-driven industries investment per worker expressed as an annual figure was about $4,000 per year. This is the same figure that the Grace Commission recommended to President Reagan to reduce government spending as a result of their study of the U.S. government.

The $4,000 annual IT expense per employee may be a low investment, at least when compared to the banking-industry figures reported in Chapter 2 of over $8,000 per information worker. Of course, the banking industry's higher investment per employee was a result of two factors—the decreasing number of employees as well as increases in information systems expenditures.

To give a sense of what this means on a macro-economic basis, our economy employed about 56 percent of the labor force as information workers in 1988. The 1988 U.S. gross national product (GNP) was $5 trillion. Our 1988 national income, excluding rents, corporate profits, and interest, was $3 trillion. This means that $1.7 trillion, or 34 percent of GNP, was spent on information work.

What value was produced by this $1.7 trillion? This is the central issue that needs to be addressed by economists, politicians, and businesspeople in the next decade. Otherwise, the 1990s may go down in history as the time when America became a Third World country.[6]

In order to achieve the productivity gains and to address the challenge of the 1990s, we need to improve the ways we handle and manage information. If workers are limited to using information in paper form, it's no wonder that we have difficulty placing a value on it. Such paper-based information might even be reducing productivity, and the value of information can be measured only when it contributes to organizational productivity. Automated information systems make this process easier.

In a 1984 study, Kodak found that there are 21 trillion pages of information stored in desks, files, and archives (see Figure 11–2). When the Kodak statistics are priced out at a nominal $1.00 per year per piece of paper stored , $.25 per page of computer printout, $.10 per photocopy, and $8.00 for each letter, the costs are astronomical (see Figure 11–3) and too high to be real. However, the example does give an idea of what waste we create in our businesses and government with too much unautomated data and insufficient technology to manage it.

Kodak further estimated that the annual growth rate for paper-based information is about 20 percent. This is frightening!

FIGURE 11–2
Some Information Facts

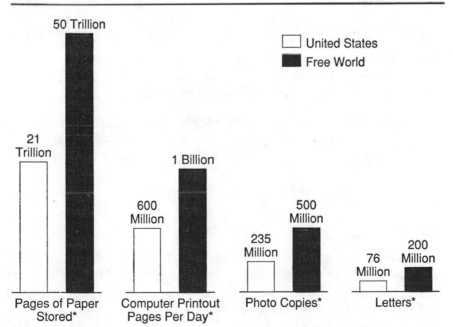

* Scales Are Not Proportional

FIGURE 11–3
Cost to Create

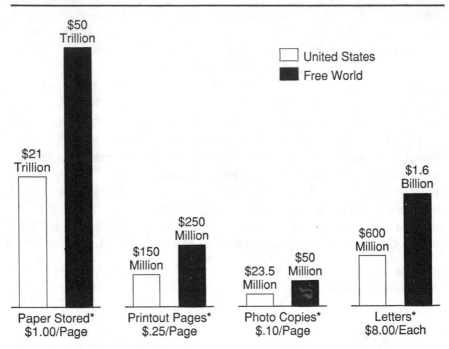

* Scales Are Not Proportional

COST TO STORE

	United States	Free World
Cost to Store Per Year	$.25 X 21 Trillion = $5.25 Trillion	$.25 X 50 Trillion = $12.5 Trillion

US G.N.P. ~ $4 Trillion

A few years ago, we interviewed the chief information officer of a large telecommunications company. He told us that his corporation had too many people, resulting in an overload of information. This reduced the value of information produced. Not all information has value. If information doesn't help the information worker in performing tasks critical to the organization, it is worthless. Too much information can be worse than not enough. The remedy in this case was a significant reduction in the number of information workers.

How then might a company go about deciding whether it is spending the right amount on IT? Or, for that matter, is it spending too much for information? Does it have too many information-generating workers? The purpose of this chapter is to start the process of answering these questions.

BANKAMERICA'S INFORMATION INVESTMENT: A CASE STUDY

In 1988, BankAmerica had a banner year. Its return to profitable operations and excellent financial performance—.76 percent return on assets and 20 percent return on stockholders' equity—has gone a long way toward overcoming some very difficult years.

Using Figure 11–1 and BankAmerica's 1988 annual report, let's calculate the bank's information investment, availability of information, and IT investment per information worker.

At the end of 1988, BankAmerica had 53,700 employees. Virtually all of BankAmerica's employees are information workers. We can conservatively estimate that 75 percent of their time is spent on creating and maintaining information (e.g., adding to the information investment). This nets out to an equivalent of 40,275 information workers who are adding to the bank's information investment.

According to its income statement, the bank spent $1.9 billion on personnel costs, $420 million on occupancy costs, and $1.2 billion on other noninterest expense. Excluded is the equipment, or information-technology, expense. The personnel, occupancy, and other costs amounted to $62,200 per employee when divided by the average headcount for the year (1988 began with 59,500 workers).

By multiplying the 40,275 equivalent information workers, who are continuing to add to the information investment, by the annual cost per worker, excluding IT, the resultant annual information investment rate is $2.5 billion!

If BankAmerica had to build its information base up from scratch, how long would it take with the current staff available for adding to the information investment? Let's say for this example that it would take four years. This means that Bank-America's information base viewed as a capital investment is about $10 billion. This is two and one-half times its net worth!

Since BankAmerica is a viable, profitable, and ongoing enterprise, we could reasonably assume that the value of the bank's investment in information at least equals its cost. Nevertheless, the balance sheet and book value of BankAmerica don't include the value of the information investment. If they did, BankAmerica's net worth would be about $14 billion.[7]

Expressed in the investor stakeholder's terms, the book value per common share would increase from $22 a share to $75 a share. The market value of a BankAmerica share at the end of 1988 was about $20. This further illustrates the market's lack of understanding, and, consequently, its lack of interest in a full valuation of BankAmerica Corporation that includes the information investment. In this case, the difference between understood value and potential is about $55 per share.

Now, let's look at the information investment as compared to BankAmerica's annual IT expense. To calculate this, we use the $10 billion information-base figure and divide it by the annual equipment (IT) expense of $329 million. The result is the ratio of 30:1.

What does this ratio mean? When compared to other information-driven businesses in our survey, BankAmerica's information is probably less accessible (e.g., it is not in automated form).

What is BankAmerica's annual IT expense per information worker? We can calculate this by taking the equipment expense of $329 million and dividing it by the 53,700 continuing bank employees, all of whom are information workers. The result is $6,126 per information worker, higher than the 1987 figure of $5,672 but still lower than the expense per information worker of Citicorp or Wells Fargo.

What does this mean? The possible conclusions that Bank-America management might reach are

1. There are investments being made in information that have limited value because they aren't generally available (e.g., the information investment isn't accompanied by a corresponding IT investment).
2. BankAmerica would benefit from further restructuring and reductions in the number of people required to run its business.
3. There might be some significant benefit gained by making the information investment more available through increased IT investments.

The optimum course of action might be a combination of all of the above. Of course, this is only speculation, but it points out the need for more analysis of the information investment as it relates to the bank's performance. This is why we believe that in the near future annual reports will contain this sort of analysis.

DETERMINING VALUE OF THE INFORMATION INVESTMENT

The first step toward determining the value of the information investment is to find out the business reason for the collection of information. The second step is to assess the ability of the information-handling system to provide the right information (as determined by the first step)

- At the right place.
- At the right time.
- In the right form.
- At the right cost.
- In the right quality.

The resulting assessment will help to document the impact of information on the success or failure of the enterprise. Ultimately, accountants will assess the value of the information investment and the added value provided by information systems by measuring the future cash flow.

In good times, little thought is given to useless information that may be created or to the fact that vital information may be missing. As long as profits and/or return on investment goals are met, the information investment remains in the background.

In times of economic stress, companies reduce payroll costs in order to protect the viability of the enterprise. In reducing payroll, the organization doesn't consider value of its information asset. Therefore, the weeding-out process of nonvital costs is haphazard at best.

The conscientious valuation of information is a necessary practice in both good times and bad. The corporation should consider the value, the useful life, and the future costs of maintenance when creating the information base. The investment includes all labor and information technology costs.

A CAPITAL INVESTMENT VERSUS A BURIED OPERATING EXPENSE

At present, the information and IT investments in our corporations are simply buried in operating expenses. This accounting treatment reduces current earnings. As a result, senior executives who attempt to maximize short-term profit or return on investment won't make necessary investments now for the long run. Rather, they will force I/S to patch older, less-efficient and incomplete information-handling processes. The result almost surely will be reduced future revenues, reduced profits, and low returns on equity—and, ultimately, new corporate management.

The valuing of the information investment and the IT investment must be conducted as any other construction project, such as a building. The accounting principles for construction are standard project accounting principles. The value of the building includes the total cost of the project, including material, labor, and overhead. The building's ultimate value will be determined by the rents produced.

RISK VERSUS GAIN

The valuation of the information base as an asset may be valid. But it also contains risk—a risk contained in valuing any asset.

The foundation of the building might be inadequate, and government authorities might rate the building uninhabitable. Or, an inventory of precious metals may lose value in a future period because the market price has fallen. Or, an electronic component carried at high value in the inventory of an electronic manufacturer might become obsolete in the next accounting period.

Similarly, an investment in information might or might not achieve the desired effect. It's the job of management (later audited by the electronic data processing [EDP] and financial auditors) to determine the risk associated with making any significant investment. Ultimately, the financial community will decide whether investments in information and information technology increase the value of the company.

One approach to the accounting of information is to report expenditures for information in the same way as research and development expenses are reported. This would result in a new expense category on the profit-and-loss statement—information.

At the least, a footnote to the financial statements is in order, giving recognition to the information expense including all the above components (labor, overhead, and technology). Auditors could then test the effectiveness of this new expense category. Management could begin to observe whether the value added by IT is being optimized. Confirming the effectiveness of this expense will lead to the question of how IT will benefit future cash flows.[8]

Auditors must also search for the answer to another vital question: Which business processes suffer from a lack of investment in information? Perhaps the lack of an appropriate information base is a real concern for top management. Can you imagine a situation where critical information is neither created, maintained, nor available because management considers IT an undesirable expense?

SUMMARY

The information executive will easily earn a seat on the executive committee when he or she can clearly demonstrate the value added to the business by the information investment. But the information executive needs help from the economic and accounting disciplines to accomplish this.

ENDNOTES

1. Yoneji Masuda, *The Information Society* (New Brunswick, N.J.: Transaction Books, 1981), pp. 77.
2. Financial Accounting Standards Board, *Statement of Financial Accounting Concepts No. 3: Elements of Financial Statements of Business Enterprises* (Stamford, Conn., December 1980).
3. The Financial Accounting Standards Board (FASB) is a very conservative group. For this reason, it will take a long time with many deliberations to reach a point where information is capitalizable. Hopefully, in the near term FASB will recommend a footnote on the information investment in financial statements.
4. Mead Corporation also markets an information base, NEXIS, for business people.
5. Our experiences with working with the information investment are consistent with a study done several years ago and reported in *MIS Quarterly* (September 1981). In this paper, Dr. Franz Edelman, then vice president of Business Systems and Analysis at RCA, put forth some statistics from RCA concerning the cost of information. The study, made in 1978, was confined to RCA. It took a slightly different view of the information worker than is now used by such notables as John Naisbitt in *Megatrends* or Alvin Toffler in *The Third Wave*. Nevertheless, Dr. Edelman's statistics were easily modified to closely resemble our approach.

   Paul A. Strassmann published an earlier study, "Managing the Costs of Information," in the September–October 1976 issue of the *Harvard Business Review*. In this study, the ratio of information investment to the annual expense of data processing ran about 88:1. The data presented by Mr. Strassmann was a percentage of sales. We made an estimate for the information work as a percentage of sales and capitalized as an investment (e.g., five years cost). We divided information systems percent of sales into the capitalized information investment to yield the 88:1 result. This is consistent with the fact that, at that time, most systems were production batch oriented.

   In Dr. Edelman's 1978 study, the statistics for RCA showed a ratio of 53:1. Dr. Edelman also used a percentage of sales approach. RCA at that time had moved into the interactive systems mode for some of their applications. However, they were at the beginning of this endeavor, and Dr. Edelman anticipated significant changes. It is a pity that he retired shortly after, and that more recent statistics are not available.

Edelman's and Strassmann's studies showed that in the 1970's, information investment had been 88 and 53 times the annual hardware, software, and communications expense.

This is consistent with more recent work by Strassmann. Mr. Strassmann used a different approach in his book, *Information Payoff.* His basis is the value-added chain which computes the value added for each major process in an organization. For example, purchased goods add no value. Labor, technology and management add value. Mr. Strassmann's observation is that the value added by United States senior management during the past 20 years has been declining. Michael E. Porter in his classic book, *Competitive Advantage,* uses a similar approach in determining ways to create and sustain superior competitive performance.

In his book, Strassmann clearly shows that the investment in information systems has outpaced the expected improvements for return on investment. The continued heavy investment in information systems has reduced the ratios that I calculated, especially in the information-driven companies. That these IT investments haven't, in many cases, yielded an improved ROI is a result of the wrong focus.

Strassmann shows that a company with poor potential for improved ROI will not benefit from investment in IT. We agree.

Nevertheless, those companies with limited potential for ROI will benefit from controlling the investment in information. How much useless information can be found choking the arteries of low-information–payoff enterprises!

6. Smithian economics has traditionally viewed three labor divisions (e.g., agriculture, manufacturing and service). We need to add a fourth: information. By lumping pizza chefs, bank presidents, and information workers, economists give a very warped and often dismal view of our economy. Many even predict that we will become a nation of lazy "Big Mac" flippers and consumers.

Some economists further predict that we won't invest in industries that will reduce our deficit in the balance of payments. Nothing could be further from the truth. Technology-driven "Silicon Valleys, Gulches and Prairies" are springing up to replace poorer rural economies. The technology produced by these new pockets of industry will improve the way other industries use information. The result: new potentials for industrial productivity in all sectors.

7. The information investment is being made to create future net cash flow. It is for the exclusive use of the bank. The bank will make additional investments to assure the security of the information. It will finance the investment out of its own internal funds. The bank has created what in future years might be considered a capitalizable asset—and it deserves to be treated as such. The bank's investors deserve to know the amount invested in these projects. Likewise, the IT planners need to be integrally involved in this process because it will be the IT systems that will make it all possible. Most leading edge banks have high technology groups to assess how new information technology can be used to serve a strategic need.

8. Appendix 1 suggests ways to report the information asset. The Committee on Information Management of the Financial Executives Institute and the Society for Information Management are both working on these issues.

CHAPTER 12

THE BUSINESS OF INFORMATION-TECHNOLOGY MANAGEMENT: Utilities, Project Management, and Consulting

---

INFORMATION SYSTEMS MANAGEMENT—MANY BUSINESSES IN ONE

Information systems have evolved through numerous phases: they have progressed from tabulating machines, to batch-processing computers, to online computing, to networks of dispersed computing. At each phase along the way, the function responsible for information technology has also shifted, changing from a backroom tabulating department, to specialized programmers, to operating systems' technical specialists, to business partners.

At each phase, the information-technology function's organizational placement has changed as a result of corporate recognition of its contribution to the business. Specifically,

1. The tabulating department was a backroom accounting function.
2. The computing or data-processing (DP) department was (and still is in many companies) an operating arm under the aegis of the finance department.
3. The management information services (MIS) department is an operating group—though with added man-

agement systems capability—that has still not become independent of the finance function.

4. The information management department, in addition to exercising responsibility for all the elements of previous phases, has the responsibility for managing the information and information-technology investment. This responsibility is central to recognizing that the information-technology organization has a new role as an equal with the finance function.

In the first phase, organizational positioning was not an issue. Tabulating departments were small and limited, performing routine accounting tasks such as posting to the general ledger or issuing payroll checks. The tabulating department staff were specialists with a narrow scope.

In the second phase, organizational positioning was little more than a minor issue. The finance function retained control of the computing or data-processing activities because most initial applications dealt with financial systems. As data-processing applications began to move beyond the financial organization, business units began to compete for scarce computing resources. Financial management encouraged hardware planning and charging business units for data-processing services so that the DP function could minimize the investment in computing equipment while delivering adequate service.

Corporations whose driving force is production, technology, or distribution capability can easily demonstrate that the most critical uses of data processing are in the operating departments that provide the capability. In some cases, the DP function was actually moved from the financial function to the operating function. This was especially true of distribution-capability companies. In many technology-capability companies, such as aerospace and research organizations, scientists and engineers often run the DP organizations.

During the second phase, specialized programming staffs were hired to develop large applications. IBM, in introducing its 360 architecture, gave major impetus to the development of large programming staffs that were to later number in the hundreds. Many large applications developed during the early 1960s are still in use today. Notable among these are the huge billing and trunk systems developed at Bell Laboratories for the Regional Bell operating companies (New York Telephone, Pacific Bell, Southern Bell, etc.).

In the third phase, MIS organizations began to assume a company-wide identity. Online systems brought with them higher organizational visibility for systems performance. While still typically reporting to the chief financial officer, MIS executives began to experience higher level involvement with the business.

During this phase, capacity and service-level management, a data center planning methodology, developed as a disciplines essential to managing centralized online systems. The telecommunications department grew out of previously separate voice and data communications. The applications-development function became more complex with the advent of database management systems. And throughout this time, continuing changes in a company's business processes required the development function to invest more and more in the maintenance and updating of old systems.

By the fourth phase, the MIS organization had evolved into an information-management organization with several relatively discrete information-technology–capability activities:

- *The data processing utility* (information-distribution capability).
- *The telecommunications utility* (information-access capability).
- *The information utility* (information-needs capability).
- *Project management* (technical/business information-systems capability).
- *Technical and business consulting* (applied information-technology and business-consulting capability).

Each of these information-technology activities has a circumscribed set of conditions that, when properly managed, significantly benefit the business. At the same time, these activities are interconnected with one another and with the activities in the business units. For this reason, it's essential that the corporation manage these IT activities on a corporate-wide basis.

In this fourth phase, the positioning of the information-technology function and its approach to information-technology dispersion are key to the corporation's ability to leverage its investment in information technology.

The central information-technology organization needs to be positioned high enough in the organization to integrate business divisions into corporate-wide systems when appropriate (general ledger, distribution, etc.).

At the same time, information technology needs to be dispersed sufficiently to enable the corporation's frontline to create and implement solutions to customer and other stakeholder needs.

As the fourth phase evolves, some corporations are using the title *chief information officer* (CIO) to describe the position of the top information executive. The emerging chief information officer position is a senior management position reporting directly to the chief executive officer.

The CIO is responsible for the use of information and information technology to improve corporate performance. To this end, the CIO works with other senior executives in establishing standards of performance for managing the five I/S business areas within the information management organization, whether they are centralized or dispersed.

UTILITIES

The Data-Processing Utility

The data-processing utility is an internal corporate utility that satisfies the corporation's need for computing services. The primary emphasis is on running computer applications required by the operating business units. These large business applications depend on a reliable, service-oriented, and cost-effective central utility.

The data-processing utility provides data processing and storage on demand for manipulation and analysis of the corporation's information base. Additionally, this utility provides the computer resources that support programmers who develop new applications and maintain existing ones.

The data-processing utility focuses on economies of scale to produce low overall costs for data processing and storage. The information-technology investment is consolidated in a large centralized facility and/or divisional facilities as shown in Figure 12–1.

The financial basis for justifying internal investment in the data-processing utility is return on investment and enhanced service to information workers. Companies face the make-buy issue because data-processing services are available on an open market from such companies as Electronic Data Services, Boeing Computer Services, Martin Marietta Data Systems, and McDonnell Douglas Information Processing. These external data-processing service companies offer computing based on a rate schedule for their various classes of services. In addition, they will also manage onsite facilities for their customers.

In resolving the make-buy decision, you will need to consider the up-front capital required, the resulting internal rates versus those available externally, and the quality of internal versus external service. The quality of service from large external providers of data-processing services is improving as telecommunications-technology capability improves.

By contracting out this utility, your company can use the capital that would otherwise be invested internally in large computers for business investments with higher cash-generating potential. It can also transfer management attention from internal data-processing operations management to con-

FIGURE 12–1
The Data Processing Utility

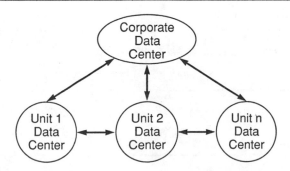

sidering information-technology applications for business opportunities.

If the decision is to keep this utility in-house, internal investments in the data-processing utility can be funded as any other utility. The services provided by the utility are an integral cost of doing business. To determine these business costs, a utility funding analysis helps to understand how the utility is used and how future investments in this utility can be funded. Figure 12–2 shows an example of a utility funding assessment made on a monthly basis for expense accounting.

The Telcommunications Utility

While the data-processing utility emphasizes the ability to process and store electronic information, the telecommunica-

FIGURE 12–2
Information Technology Investment Assessment

DATA PROCESSING UTILITY—SUMMARY
COMPANY: Acme, Inc.
DATE: January 31, 1989
Prepared by: Dave Vincent

Funding Distribution $(000)

Function	CPU	Storage	Other	Total
Marketing	$ 225	$ 325	$ 20	$ 570
Sales	215	350	40	605
Customer Services	275	375	75	725
Distribution	175	295	15	485
Finance	150	175	25	350
Operations	245	200	150	595
Research	195	50	85	330
Total Funding	$1,480	$1,770	$410	$3,660

Data Center Monthly Costs Versus Plan/Funding

	Plan	Actual	Funding
CPU	$1,500	$1,435	$1,480
Storage	1,600	1,800	1,770
Other	250	385	410
Total	$3,350	$3,620	$3,660

tions utility emphasizes access to electronic information. This utility started as the company's switchboard for answering incoming telephone calls and routing internal and outgoing calls. The switchboard service was typically administered by the personnel or plant facilities function. The advent of online systems created the need for electronic data transfer. And so the data-processing department leased from the telephone company lines that were dedicated to data transfer.

Today, most large corporations have combined the responsibilities for voice and data communications and placed them with the information-technology organization. The telecommunications function currently focuses on a three-phase voice and data network for corporate communications:

- *Voice* (desk sets, long distance, analog and digital voice transmission).
- *Data* (digital data transfer).
- *Image processing* (document storage and retrieval, facsimile).

Most companies have traditionally contracted with telephone companies to provide telecommunications services. Companies then paid the telephone company's monthly bill for telephone services. More recently, corporations have invested in their own telecommunications systems. In some cases, they have even bypassed the telephone company. These moves have resulted in a much larger internal capital investment in the information technology that supports telecommunications, much of which simply replaces an external monthly utility bill.

In a recent *Harvard Business Review* article, the chief information officer's role was described as that of a network manager,[1] a role that includes managing the investment in and contracting for information technology. The future of the telecommunications function will likely require more internal capital investment in information technology. By contrast, large DP utility investment funds will be converted to smaller annual operating expenses by contracting with data-processing companies that supply alternative DP services.

The telecommunications utility, like the data-processing utility, can be funded by a utility billing to users (Figure 12–3).

FIGURE 12–3
Information Technology Investment Assessment

TELECOMMUNICATIONS UTILITY—SUMMARY
COMPANY: Acme, Inc.
DATE: January 31, 1989
Prepared by: Dave Vincent

Funding Distribution $(000)

Function	Voice	Data	Other	Total
Marketing	$ 215	$ 150	$ 15	$ 380
Sales	375	250	10	635
Customer Services	300	150	25	475
Distribution	250	300	35	585
Finance	175	150	5	330
Operations	200	250	35	485
Research	100	50	5	155
Total Funding	$1,615	$1,300	$130	$3,045

Telecommunications Monthly Costs Versus Plan/Funding

	Plan	Actual	Funding
Voice	$1,600	$1,620	$1,615
Data	1,275	1,300	1,300
Other	125	130	130
Total	$3,000	$3,050	$3,045

The standards of performance for the data-processing and telecommunications utilities form the basis for managing these functions. The objectives are to provide service that satisfies the utility user's expectations while staying within budget limits mandated by the financial condition of the enterprise. This is the same economic dilemma encountered by public utilities for electricity, gas, water, and telephone. Service, and its cost, should bear a relationship to the needs of the business. Therefore, utility management should be focused on matching service levels to business needs.

Information-Technology Utility Management

Information systems are provided to meet an organization's business needs. They service the basic business of receiving all the business data and information inputs and providing for all data and information outputs. A methodology has evolved to match the business needs for data and information with the capability of information systems to service these needs. This methodology is similar to that used by utility companies to plan and provide service to their customers. Utilities such as water, electricity, natural gas, and information must balance their need for capital investments in equipment against the service needs and economic status of their customers.[2]

Establish Accountability for the I/S Investment

The I/S function is a corporate utility. Investments made in I//S are made to any of the following:

1. Reduce computer user budgets.
2. Reduce other forms of investment (such as inventory).
3. Provide revenue-generating opportunity.

The I/S function is not a business in and of itself. It is intended solely to support the business of its owner (an exception to this is the service bureau, which serves many diverse businesses). All I/S expenses are in fact business-unit expenses. The amounts spent for I/S are for the benefit of the business unit that uses the services. Therefore, these units should be held accountable for the I/S expenditures they have required.

In establishing a chargeback policy, I/S and their business unit clients must understand that I/S expenses are relatively fixed during a budget cycle, whether they are used or not. This means that if business units find cheaper alternatives to I/S, the real costs can be avoided only at investment windows. These windows occur at times when there is a major upgrade (or downgrade) in equipment. During investment windows, I/S and its users can revise their agreements to reflect changed business conditions.

I/S executives have found that companies can enjoy the most benefit from centralized computing facilities when they are limited to applications enjoying economy of scale. These are typically large-batch and online production jobs, including the large databases upon which the business depends. In some cases,

large databases may be distributed in business-unit environments with corporate standards. These distributed databases
tend to be located in large data centers and still require
service-level management.

By putting information systems resources in the hands of
business units, the business units assume part of the planning
responsibility for corporate investment in I/S resources. By
taking an active role in I/S planning, they will further realize
the implications of I/S costs versus business-unit operating
costs. The optimal use of information technology will add to
operational return on investment (ROI). Service requirements
for operational systems must be based on improved ROI.

Most large organizations recognize that the service-level
management issue is one of education for both I/S and the
business units. The objective is to make a joint transition to
enlightened service management. The process involves a two-
fold strategy:

1. Get computer users more involved by teaching them to
    become proponents of their own information systems.
2. Get chief information executives and their senior man-
    agers more involved in the business by helping them to
    thoroughly understand business-unit workloads.

By being more involved in the business, the I/S executives
can help the organization more effectively integrate information
technology. Business units will find more opportunities to benefit from information technology as they become more involved
in the information systems utility. A real win-win situation
emerges when I/S and its users understand how to balance I/S
resources, service requirements, and the needs of the business to
achieve the optimum I/S investment.

The DP Telecommunications Utility as a Profit Center: A Case Study

Let's examine the case of one I/S group at a utility company that
was faced with problem of measuring ROI from I/S. It was a real
dilemma in which I/S was constantly underfunded. Its strategic
importance was not clear. I/S had minimal perceived value.

To begin correcting the situation, the I/S executive decided to let business units participate directly in the funding of the data-processing utility by paying monthly usage bills prepared by I/S. The motivation for billing the business units was not to control or reduce the usage of the data center. Rather, it was to build a cooperative model in which the business units would assist the I/S group in understanding the business reasons for the DP investment. The I/S group was then able to explain to management the investment requirements and the distribution of amortized costs to the business.

The I/S group first researched the prevailing competitive market rates from outside service bureaus. They then consolidated the quotes and averaged them. From the average rates, they subtracted 25 percent to arrive at a rate that was far below market *value*. This allowed comparison of internal data-center costs to costs of companies competing in a defined market. The initial comparison showed clearly that the internal rates for data processing were much lower than were the average rates from outside service bureaus. The net effect was a definite cost reduction to the company by using internal data-processing services.

The new rates were proposed to management for use in evaluating I/S resource distribution and effectiveness. Management agreed that the proposed rates were more than fair and should be used in charging the business units that used the I/S utility. The I/S group had created a competitive revenue stream for funding the I/S operations.

The second step was to determine how much of the revenue should be invested in I/S and how much should be returned to the corporation. Accordingly, I/S created a profit-and-loss plan as well as a statement of assets employed. The analysis relied on the book value of assets employed including the capitalized value of leases.

Management agreed with the I/S objective to achieve the same return on assets employed as the rest of the company achieved. A target profit was established as a percent of assets employed. The target profit, when subtracted from the internal revenue generated by usage of the I/S resource, yielded the I/S budget.

As the investment in I/S grew, the I/S group had to make sure that the increased investment matched the increased quantity of work. Cost control was important to keep I/S services competitive with their discounted market value. The business units absorbed the charges from I/S as expenses in their operations. Each business unit, in turn, matched its portion of I/S expenses to its ability to generate revenue or to control costs. Essentially, the judgement of I/S investment was passed on to the business units' users in the form of expenses they had to absorb in the process of making their profit and ROI objectives.

The rates used for transferring I/S charges were not at issue—the rates were based on competitive market value. What was at issue was how the I/S resource was used. The only people influencing I/S resource usage were the business units. If they were unable to show a productivity gain while increasing I/S resource consumption, the burden of explanation rested with them.

This process is analogous to the transfer-price mechanisms used in large manufacturing organizations where many facilities are involved in producing a few kinds of end products. The transfer-pricing mechanisms are used at each plant to measure performance that contributes to the end product. Likewise, data-processing and information bases for business-unit use are just two of many corporate resources used by the larger organization to produce an end product.

The utility company top management changed its perception of I/S. From being a drag on overhead, I/S became a vital earning activity of the company. The I/S executive gained stature and became more involved in business decisions.

Nevertheless, there are pitfalls in establishing I/S as a profit center. The profit-center concept might lead to disastrous results if objectives are not well defined. Profit-oriented I/S and business unit managers might squeeze out vital services such as security and disaster recovery as a result of short-term profit maximizing. In addition to the funding received from business units, the larger corporation will have to fund any I/S activity that doesn't have short-term benefit to business units.

Profit centers favor high-volume, complex applications. These transactions take up much of the I/S resource and generate very profitable revenue but are used by only a limited number of business groups. On the other hand, time-sharing transactions are less complex, use less resources, and are far less profitable. Collectively, time-sharing may use large amounts of the I/S resource, but this is spread over many business units. When a profit-oriented I/S group favors the more profitable transactions, service may suffer on time-sharing. A problem arises when the degraded service on time-sharing is at odds with business objectives.

A key to matching service to business objectives lies in changing the way I/S professionals are paid and rewarded. If I/S professionals continue to be paid and rewarded under obsolete and bureaucratic systems, there is little hope of aligning their actions with I/S business objectives. I/S management needs to restructure I/S jobs and reward systems. The restructuring of jobs and reward systems is made easier when an identifiable contribution is used as the basis.

Finally, I/S executives in charge of a profit center need to be involved more than ever in the business of the organization in order to optimize the results of the new I/S business unit. If the I/S profit center views itself as an independent business, it might turn away from day-to-day involvement with the organization it serves. Running I/S as a profit center should enhance the stature of I/S in the larger organization, not diminish it.

The Information Utility

The electronic-information utility is new on the corporate scene. Its origins are in the corporate library. Most large corporations, particularly those with a technology-capability driving force, have a large investment in the corporate library. It serves as the central source for information on patents, formulas, research, and so on.

Chemical companies discovered early on that they needed a corporate library containing complete information on chemical formulations, so they cooperated as an industry through the American Society of Chemical Engineers and its Chemical Abstracts subsidiary. Today, Chemical Abstracts maintains the largest online library in the world.

During the past several years, most large corporations have invested in an internal-information utility for access to company databases. The beginnings of this utility were in helping business units to locate data and to get it in a form that could be used on personal computers (PC's) or with fourth-generation mainframe languages. The information-utility function staff concentrated on teaching business professionals how to use fourth-generation languages and PC's.

As this utility evolves into a key corporate role, it is having more and more influence on technical and business management of corporate-wide database management systems. The focus is on

- Helping business units to define information needs by determining data needs for action and building information requirements to support corporate stakeholder relationships.
- Providing access to internal and external data sources.
- Ensuring the control and security of the information asset.
- Maintaining the corporate-information encyclopedia.

The information utility, like the data-processing and telecomunications utilities, can be funded by a utility billing to business units (Figure 12–4).

PROJECT MANAGEMENT

The project-management function provides information-technology project managers and specialists that can provide systems and information-engineering services for the corporation. The focus is on the management of large systems projects for additions to, and changes in, the corporate infrastructure.

Project management services include

- Large/small systems development.
- Life-cycle management of the corporate investment in the infrastructure.
- Planning for the corporate applications-portfolio investment.

FIGURE 12–4
Information Technology Investment Assessment

INFORMATION UTILITY—SUMMARY
COMPANY: Acme, Inc.
DATE: January 31, 1989
Prepared by: Dave Vincent

Funding Distribution $(000)

Function	Download	Data Adm	Program	Other	Total
Marketing	$ 50	$ 30	$ 15	$ 5	$100
Sales	10	15	5	5	35
Customer Services	45	55	20	10	130
Distribution	15	25	15	5	60
Finance	25	10	5	5	45
Operations	15	20	15	0	50
Research	25	30	25	5	85
Total Funding	$185	$185	$100	$35	$505

Data Center Monthly Costs versus Plan/Funding

	Plan	Actual	Funding
Download	$190	$185	$185
Data Adm	175	180	185
Program	80	100	100
Other	30	35	35
Total	$475	$500	$505

Information-technology project management costs are typically treated as annual expenses. They are budgeted on an annual basis as an expense item of the information-technology budget. This expense-oriented view of applications development is shown in Figure 12–5.

Over time, the annual budget for maintenance of old applications increases while the amount spent on new applications decreases as a percent of the total budget. The expense view of applications ignores the investment base of the applications portfolio. The current budget is only the tip of the iceberg, as shown in Figure 12–6.

Viewing investments in the applications portfolio as expenses results in a lack of planning for the enhancement and

FIGURE 12–5
The Expense View of Applications Development

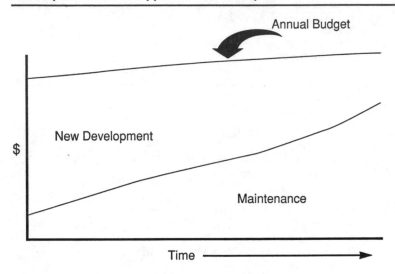

FIGURE 12–6
The Corporate Applications Portfolio Investment

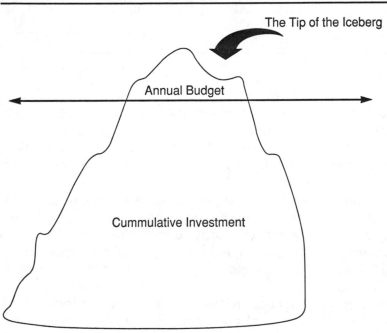

replacement of systems as they approach the end of their useful lives. Imagine building new factories on an emergency basis to handle unanticipated order sizes and rates. By the time the factories are built, it is too late to satisfy current demand. Nevertheless, this is just what companies do when they treat their applications-portfolio investment as an annual expense. As a result of this approach, information-technology organizations are trapped into being fire fighters as opposed to being solid business planners.

Application-Portfolio Analysis

To break out of this dangerous business cycle, information-technology organizations need to adopt a project-management basis for assessing the information-technology investment in applications. Figure 12–7 shows the investment in the order entry application for the customer-service function. The initial investment in the application was $2.6 million, including labor, computer time, outside contractors, software packages built into the application, and other expenses.

The order entry application was completed and put online in 1975. It costs $1.2 million each year in data-processing and telecommunications-utility expenses to run it and another $90,000 a year to keep it up-to-date. In 1989, the application will need a major enhancement costing $595,000. By 1991, the order entry application must be replaced at a cost of $3.5 million.

Figure 12–8 shows the total current application-portfolio investment of $112 million. The project costs $26.7 million a year in data-processing and telecommunications utilities to run and another $540,000 a year to maintain and update. The portfolio will require $12.9 million in major enhancements over the next few years and another $141.5 million to replace.

The applications-portfolio analysis illustrates the full economic impact of the investment in the infrastructure. Major enhancement and replacement costs can be enormous. For the first time, a corporation has a picture of its current investment in applications. The annual run costs are placed in perspective, presenting a meaningful picture for information-technology equipment investment. By giving management an idea of future

FIGURE 12–7
Information Technology Investment Assessment

APPLICATION PORTFOLIO ANALYSIS   Page 1 of 63

COMPANY:	Acme, Inc.
DATE:	January 5, 1989
Prepared by:	Dave Vincent
FUNCTION:	Customer Service
APPLICATION/MODULE:	Order Entry System
RELATIONSHIPS	
INTERNAL:	Sales, marketing, finance, manufacturing
EXTERNAL:	Consumers, retailers, wholesalers, distributors

$(000)

PROJECT START YEAR: 1973
YEAR IN PRODUCTION: 1975

Project Cost

Person Hours	35000	
Rate per Hour (@$35.00)		$1,225
Computer Expense		950
Outside Contractors		150
Outside Package		50
Other		235
Total Project Costs		$2,610

Annual Ongoing Costs

Data Center Run Costs		
Maintenance/Updating Person Hours	2000	
Rate per Hour (@$45.00)		$90
Total Annual Ongoing Costs		$1,290

Major Enhancement Year 1989: Major Enhancement Costs

Person Hours 6000	
Rate per Hour (@$45.00)	$270
Computer Expense	175
Outside Contractors	90
Outside Package	25
Other	35
Total Major Enhancement Costs	$595

Replacement Year 1991: Replacement Costs

Person Hours 30000	
Rate per Hour (@$50.00)	$1,500
Computer Expense	1,250
Outside Contractors	400
Outside Package	200
Other	150
Total Replacement Costs	$3,500

FIGURE 12–8
Information Technology Investment Assessment

Page 1 of 1

APPLICATION PORTFOLIO ANALYSIS

COMPANY:	Acme, Inc.
DATE:	January 5, 1989
Prepared by:	Dave Vincent

Installed Applications Portfolio = 63

Project Cost	*$(000)*
Internal Personnel Costs	$ 32,725
Computor Timo	28,050
Outside Contractors	15,150
Outside Package	25,050
Other	10,235
Total Installed Portfolio Project Costs	$112,110

Annual Ongoing Costs

Data Center Run Costs	$26,700
Maintenance/Updating	540
Total Annual Ongoing Costs	$27,240

Estimated Major Enhancement Costs

Internal Personnel Costs	$1,620
Computer Time	7,675
Outside Contractors	1,590
Outside Package	1,000
Other	1,010
Total Major Enhancement Costs	12,895

Estimated Replacement Costs

Internal Personnel Costs	$51,500
Computer Time	39,250
Outside Contractors	5,400
Outside Package	25,200
Other	20,150
Total Replacement Costs	$141,500

information-technology investment requirements, the IT organization assumes a role as a proactive business function as opposed to being purely reactive and technical.

CONSULTING

Technical and Business Consulting

In addition to utilities and project-management services, information-technology organizations find that they must also provide consulting services to the various business units. Business and technical issues arise as a result of finding more and better ways to apply information technology. The I/S organization in most companies is expected to provide specialized help in resolving these issues.

During the past few years, these consulting services have focused on finding ways for the corporation to increase its competitive edge. Additionally, the consulting efforts achieve significant payback in helping business units to

- Reduce costs.
- Identify new product opportunities.
- Develop new relationships.
- Discover new sources of capital.

The consultants may come from internal or external sources. Some corporations identify outside consultants whom it uses as needed to address certain kinds of issues. Others hire a basic staff capable of dealing with most internal issues. These corporations then hire external consultants for very special issues and for training internal consultants.

Both approaches can be effective. The ultimate determiner is how best to add value to the corporation.

I/S Value Added per Employee

The make/buy decision for internal versus external utilities and resources is, in part, a value-added issue. In Chapter 2, we calculated value added for the corporation and the value added per employee. If the value added per employee for a given task is equal to or higher than the corporation-wide value added per employee, the corporation will benefit from internalizing the task. (see Figure 12–9).

The value added for each information-technology organization business area is calculated by taking its output at market value less the passthrough costs of creating the value. The net result is then divided by the number of employees for that IT business function.

For example, if the data-processing unit produces $1,500,000 worth of activity at market value (as was done by the utility I/S executive mentioned earlier in this chapter), the results might be as shown in Table 12–1.

FIGURE 12–9
Information Systems
Value Added per Employee

Data Processing Utility:	$\dfrac{\text{Revenue @ market} - \text{purchases}}{\text{\# employees}}$
Telecommunications Utility:	$\dfrac{\text{Revenue @ market} - \text{purchases}}{\text{\# employees}}$
Information Center:	$\dfrac{\text{Revenue @ market}}{\text{\# employees}}$
Project Management:	$\dfrac{\text{Revenue @ market (exclude computer \$)}}{\text{\# employees}}$
Consulting:	$\dfrac{\text{Revenue @ market}}{\text{\# employees}}$

TABLE 12–1
Data Processing—High Value Added

CPU units = 10,000,000 @ $0.10 each	=	$1,000,000
Storage units = 25,000,000 @ $0.15 each	=	3,750,000
Output @ market value	=	$4,750,000
Less passthrough costs (equipment leases, etc.)	=	2,600,000
Data-processing value added	=	$2,150,000
Number of data-processing employees	=	20
Value added per DP employee	=	$ 107,500

Let's say that the corporation's value added per employee is $100,000, figured using the methods illustrated in Chapter 2. Using the formula from Figure 12–9, we have calculated a value added per data-processing employee of $107,500. Since the value added per data-processing employee is slightly higher than that of the value added per employee for the corporation, data processing should clearly be retained as an internal function.

On the other hand, either a change in market rates resulting in less revenue or an increase in passthrough costs could substantially lower the value added per data-processing employee. Let's take the above example and calculate revenue at $.08 per CPU unit and $.12 per storage unit. Let's also say that the passthrough costs are $2,800,000. The new calculation would then be as shown in Table 12–2.

In a company that has an overall $100,000 value added per employee, it doesn't make much sense to internalize a function that adds value at only half that rate. Management and professional time is diluted by taking time away from high value-adding activities. In this second case (all things being equal, e.g., data security and protection of proprietary rights), we should seriously consider contracting the responsibility for operating the data center out and have it performed by an external group.

In a new business era, a guiding business principle is that business activities that improve a company's value added should be internalized to the business, while those that don't should be farmed out.

This same analysis should be performed for the telecommunications and information utilities, project management, and

TABLE 12–2
Data Processing—Low Valued Added

CPU units = 10,000,000 @ $0.08 each	=	$ ·800,000
Storage units = 25,000,000 @ $0.12 each	=	3,000,000
Output @ market value	=	$3,800,000
Less passthrough costs (equipment leases, etc.)	=	2,800,000
Data-processing value added	=	$1,000,000
Number of data-processing employees	=	20
Value added per DP employee	=	$ 50,000

technical and business consulting. In each case the value added by internalizing the function versus contracting it out is a guide to how you should invest in employees. The corporation focused on increasing its value added rather than simply growing in size will realize enhanced stakeholder relationships through clearer alignment between stakeholder expectations, internal business-function performance, and the corporation's long-term financial results.

SUMMARY

The information systems organization is a complex mix of businesses, many of which have suitable alternatives in the marketplace. The days of the highly centralized, highly internalized information systems organization are over.

With the evolving role of chief information officer comes the responsibility for using outside services, dispersing information technology throughout the organization, and demonstrating the economics of each choice to business-unit executives.

ENDNOTES

1. John J. Donovan, "Beyond Chief Information Officer to Network Manager," *Harvard Business Review* 66, no. 5 (September-October 1988), pp. 134–140.
2. *Little's Law*—All utilities behave according to a simple observation: investment in power provides the capability to provide the utility service. In 1962, Dr. John D. C. Little of Massachusetts Institute of Technology put forth a rule for systems behavior that illustrates how service is achieved:

$$L = \lambda W$$

Where

   L = the number of jobs of transactions in a system.
   λ = the arrival rate of jobs or transactions.
   W = the time it takes a job or transaction to get through the system.

   Business units generate demand for I/S services based on the needs of the business. This demand, λ (Lambda), the arrival rate, is the amount of work coming into a system during a given interval of time, let's say a second. The arrival rate is determined solely by the service needs of the business and the work generated by people in the business units.

Business unit computer users experience a delay each time they give work to the computer. This is generally called response time. Response time is the time it takes a job or transaction to get through the system. The time for a job or transaction to get through the system is the sum of the time a job or transaction waits to get service from computer and telecommunications systems plus the time it must wait to be serviced. The service and wait time is directly related to the investment made in the power of information systems resources—in general, the larger the investment, the better the service.

The number of jobs or transactions in a system are then determined by their arrival rate and by their processing and waiting time. Queuing theorists have derived performance models from Little's Law. The most basic one is the M/M/1 model:

$$W = \frac{1/\mu}{1 - \lambda/\mu}$$

Where W $=$ response time,
λ $=$ arrival rate.
μ $=$ service rate.
$1/\mu$ $=$ service time.

This may be expressed more simply as

$$\text{Response time} = \frac{\text{service time}}{1 - \text{utilization}}$$

Response time is generally an objective set by management and is the service criterion most often at variance with business-unit computer-user expectations. The response time requirements come from the business units, which are responsible for the outputs of the business. Information executives must meet the mandated response-time requirements to fulfill their business.

Utilization is a function of the amount of work received. The greater the amount of work received (from the computer-user community for a given computer configuration), the busier the computer resource will be. The utilization of the computer resource is directly under the control of its users. Information executives are expected to receive and act on all demands for service by both computer users and management.

The only variable over which the information executive has direct responsibility is the amount of information system resource that will be provided to meet the response time objectives and the computer user workloads. The service rate, μ, is directly related to the investment in hardware and software. Through the use of capacity planning techniques, the information systems group can determine the requirement for processing power when the service objectives and the workloads have been established for the present and for the future.

The message, in short, is that effective information executives must know how to establish management response time objectives and computer user acceptance of their responsibility in the forecasting of future workload demands. Only then will I/S planning efforts result in business efficiencies.

CHAPTER 13

CORPORATE PRODUCTIVITY:
Imperatives for the 1990s

In the next decade, corporate survival hinges on corporate productivity improvements that will result in increased product and service quality and enhanced stakeholder value. Such productivity improvements can only come from restructuring the organization and being able to take advantage of the potential of information technology. To do this, senior executives need to be committed to organizational change.

COMMITMENT TO ORGANIZATIONAL CHANGE: CREATING THE FRONTLINE

The very first commitment is to recognize that your company has a frontline. The frontline consists of all the employees who deal with the corporation's stakeholders. They must be prepared to act whenever necessary and need the full support of the company.

As an executive responsible for your company's information-technology investment, you need to use IT to ensure support to the frontline that will give your company an edge over its competitors. On the supply side, frontline support includes helping those responsible for suppliers of materials, services, employees, and capital. On the demand side, it includes helping those responsible for distributors, wholesalers, retailers, and the ultimate consumers of your products and services.

Supporting the Frontline with
Information Technology

In Chapter 2, in an analysis of the banking industry, it was argued that banks making the right IT investment combined with management skill and strategy produce superior results. Enabling the frontline to take action predicated on access to information is a basic necessity for excellence in service industries.

Scandinavian Airlines advertises their flexibility at the frontline—a result of information access and action. Federal Express supports its frontline with complete routing information on express shipments. The result is larger market share and outstanding financial results.

Be aggressive in applying technology at the frontline—this is the area with the greatest potential for return.

COMMITMENT TO NEW REWARD SYSTEMS

The next important commitment is to replace industrial-era and bureaucratic pay systems with reward systems that more appropriately reflect employees' and management's responsibility for stakeholder relationships. The new reward systems should reinforce actions that improve stakeholder relationships and penalize actions, motivated by narrow and unenlightened self-interest, that degrade stakeholder relationships.

The new reward systems should ensure that all stakeholders will be considered whenever employees and management take an action. If reward systems are based on measurements of how well stakeholder needs are fulfilled, employee and management behavior will conform to the new measures of success. This means that all business units in the corporation need information that is continually updated regarding the status of stakeholder relationships. They also need systems that will allow them to predict the impact of decisions on stakeholders.

The new reward systems should be tied to systems that measure individual and team performance against corporate and divisional imperatives. The amount of pay tied to performance versus base salaries should be at least 20 percent and even as much as 40 percent.

USE INFORMATION TECHNOLOGY TO CHANGE THE NATURE OF WORK

The result of developing and using technology in the industrial age was a productivity increase by a factor of about a hundred. The information age has already seen productivity gains by a factor in information-based technology. And, the end isn't yet in sight.[1] This productivity potential can be a blessing or a curse to your company—you can aggressively take advantage of it or be buried by your competitors.

But, to take advantage of it, you must do more than just invest in technology. You must also invest in the people who will use the technology.

Concurrent with changing reward systems, you need to reward innovation in redesigning work. Encourage the use of information technology when it will improve quality, service, and the level of work performed. Use the frontline as key players on the work-design team. Their involvement will ensure success for new and innovative uses of information technology.

With this proactive approach, you can benefit from the forces of IT dispersion, thereby placing more technology in the hands of people on the frontline. They will help you to find innovative uses of IT in the workplace. And, you'll be using the full capability of your workforce to realize the productivity potential of your company.

EXPAND HIGH VALUE-ADDED INFORMATION WORK

A sure way to improve corporate productivity is to expand those areas of the business adding high value and farming out those that produce lower value.

To determine which areas add high and which add low value to the business, you need to begin measuring value added for each business function throughout the corporation. Then you can compare internal costs to the costs from outside suppliers of similar services.

As a guide for identifying functions and activities that add the most value, locate those that support your driving force. If your company is market driven, then marketing will likely add the highest value. If your company is technology driven, then research and engineering will likely to be high value-added functions. If your company is manufacturing-capability driven, look to manufacturing operations for the highest value added. If your company is results driven, look to the financial function for high value added.

FARM OUT LOW VALUE-ADDED WORK

Many of our client companies already have a policy of farming out low value-adding work. Security guards are almost always employees of outside vendors that supply this service. Office janitors and cleaning people are, in many cases, hired through small entrepreneurial companies providing these services.

In 1985, Wells Fargo Bank had only two economists, compared with the dozens their competitors had. Wells Fargo's management decided that having their own large staffs of economists wouldn't add a penny's worth of value. Instead they preferred to rely on the economic studies produced by competing banks, including the Federal Reserve Bank, which had large staffs of economists.

In a new business era, business alliances with small companies are often far easier to manage than are employees who would provide the same functions. The legal and adversarial focus of the employee relationship is replaced with the interdependence of two companies filling roles in which they have comparative advantage. The security company specializes in protecting access to company premises, while its customer concentrates on what it does best. This is a win-win scenario.

USE INFORMATION TECHNOLOGY TO SUPPORT NEW CAPITAL SOURCES

Seek out innovative uses of technology that will help provide new capital sources. Freeing up inventory, reducing accounts receivable, and reducing investment requirements to deliver products and services are all examples of freeing up capital so that it can be put to work in better ways.

For example, just-in-time inventory systems provide capital by decreasing capital requirements for inventory. Electronic data interchange speeds the transfer of funds between economic partners and leverages relationships.

IMPLEMENT INFORMATION-RESOURCE MANAGEMENT

By making available the information needed to take action on stakeholder relationships, the corporation is prepared to compete in the information age. It's important that you keep in mind that too much information is worse than not enough. Not only is too much information a waste of money and a drag on overhead, it also obscures the information really needed to drive the business. The way to ensure that the information investment is within economic limits is to insist that all information be related to an action with a stakeholder. Information that doesn't lead to an action or positive result is suspect.

USE INFORMATION TO IMPROVE DECISION MAKING

The use of information to support decision making falls into two broad categories:

Executive Information Systems (EIS) are comprised of summary and exception reporting systems that specifically address the needs of the executive management team.

Decision Support Systems (DSS) provide for information together with models and expert systems to give middle management and the frontline insight into decision alternatives.

Executive Information Systems

Rick Crandall, CEO of Comshare, Inc., began the internal implementation of the company's commercial EIS product, Commander, with a simple first step. He put his briefing book on his PC. The briefing book, started in the 1950s by Booz Allen, is a widely used concept for top-executive reporting.

Initially, briefing-book reports can be specially converted ("keypunched") for presentation on executive PC's. Such reports should focus on measurements of company performance, including those dealing with the 1988–1990 strategic imperatives. This will provide a basis for putting parameters around the scope of EIS inquiry and reporting. With this understanding, extended EIS capability can be developed and installed.

The goal of the EIS program is to have all members of the executive management team use EIS. Therefore, you should take the following action steps to begin the introduction and implementation of EIS:

- Assign responsibility for EIS to a senior-level information systems person who understands the reporting capabilities of fourth-generation languages and EIS reporting techniques. This person must be conversant with the kinds of reports now used by executive management as well as sensitive to future needs.
- Convert the information contained in briefing books to a PC–presentation format, including exception reports and graphics. The Comshare product, Commander, is an excellent example of what senior executives will expect over time.
- Create an EIS architecture that includes a top-down query capability, access to internal and external databases, and exception reporting.
- Provide executive education on the use of EIS.

Decision Support Systems (DSS)

The use of analytical and expert systems can significantly improve company performance. In the financial services industry, for example, relationship banking, a typical banking corporate imperative, is actually a sophisticated decision support system. The object of relationship banking is to leverage customer and product relationships. The success of the relationship-banking imperative is highly dependent on having comprehensive customer, prospect, and competitor information in a form that permits the analysis of the following relationships:

- Customers.
- Banking products.
- Demographic information on all potential customers.
- Financial-product availability and usage by both the bank's as well as other banks' customers.

Another potential DSS application is the financial-performance analysis of each banking product by geographic location. Each product or service offered at each geographic location is assessed for its financial viability. The results of this analysis will help in determining the kinds of relationships that need emphasis under the relationship-banking program.

Another area of opportunity in banking is the Lending Advisor (LA), an expert system that was especially designed to improve decision quality, loan-officer productivity, and performance of junior staff. LA also streamlines loan approvals and enhances the overall understanding of the credit-granting process.

The price tag for systems such as the Lending Advisor is high. Nevertheless, the potential savings are of even greater magnitude, as illustrated by the large reserves that the banking industry is required to maintain in the event of bad loans.

The obstacle to DSS application lies in potential resistance by senior management. This can be overcome by an effective internal-education effort aimed at the executive management team. In the case of the Lending Advisor, facts, figures, and results from banks using the Lending Advisor are necessary to build the case. First Wachovia and Wells Fargo, who were the first LA implementers, have benefited from the use of this expert system and are a source of such documentation.

To implement DSS, your company should take the following action steps:

- Assign responsibility for DSS to a senior-level person in information systems.
- Construct an architecture for a business-based DSS that includes databases and tools for analysis.
- Build an education program for company employees that will use DSS systems.
- Measure results of DSS use, and publish them in a DSS newsletter.

OFFICE AUTOMATION

Office automation means different things to different people. For our purposes we will deal with electronic communications that include

- Word processing.
- Electronic and voice mail.
- Analysis and report generation.

Word Processing

Using PC's simply to replace typewriters is commonplace. Word processing on PC's improves clerical efficiency and quality. Typewriters with built-in memory and advanced features also improve clerical productivity and quality.

However, simply replacing the typewriter is not enough. When properly managed through redesign of work tasks and work relationships, word processing can provide leverage on departmental performance. When secretary/typists are empowered to act as administrative assistants, a fundamental relationship has changed. For example, a manager might create the basic text for a letter and then hand the diskette to his assistant who can format, edit, and prepare it for transmission/mail.

Electronic and Voice Mail

Electronic and voice mail offer substantial opportunities for performance improvement. However, if they are used without being properly managed, significantly higher expenses can result with no corresponding gain in productivity.

Voice mail, far less expensive than electronic mail, offers most of the benefits of electronic mail. Electronic mail requires a desktop terminal, special wiring, and an ongoing hardware/software commitment to handle messages and storage for an amortized cost of around $100–150 per month per workstation. Voice mail can require as little as a new PBX but usually involves new telephone instruments as well for an amortized cost of around $35–50 per month per station.

Voice mail is appropriate for general employee use except in those cases where immediate response is necessary (e.g., customer support and service organizations). Charles Schwab & Company realized significant productivity gains from voice mail for both internal and external communications.

Electronic mail requires a more cautious approach. Because it doesn't discriminate between good and bad communication practices, initial use must be limited. Senior-level executives are the most productive users of electronic mail where the following conditions exist:

- Calendars are coordinated.
- There is rapid exchange of information when one or both parties are not easily contacted.
- There is exchange of information outside normal business hours.
- Records are kept of important conversations.

Executive management is an ideal organizational setting for implementing the initial phase of electronic mail.

As you expand the electronic mail network, education on communication concepts is very important. Executives and professionals need to be taught to replace unproductive communication with communication for action. Poor communication habits should not be automated.

Analysis and Report Generation

The analysis and report-generation capabilities brought about by office automation offer opportunities for substantial productivity improvement. On the other hand, they also offer the opportunity for the loss of data integrity and even greater paper-report generation.

Candidates for the use of PC's and necessary extended support, such as data administration, training, and technical service, must demonstrate a clear business need. When this technology is used to support such programs as relationship banking and credit analysis, the business need is clear. When a corporation's divisions use PC's to create parallel reporting systems, however, the business need isn't clear. Moreover, when primary reporting systems are circumvented, there is a potential calamity in the making. At issue is the integrity of the primary reporting system and the information/data supporting it.

Parallel reporting systems should be examined carefully. Their existence may be pointing out a need for modifications to the primary reporting systems. Or they may represent an attempt to circumvent the company's management-control system—making them strong candidates for elimination.

THE ROLE OF THE CHIEF INFORMATION OFFICER

Because information technology is used to build a system's infrastructure, and because the corporation itself is a living system, executives dealing with systems must also deal with integrating the functional entities of the corporation. This is the essence of understanding how to leverage the information-technology investment.

The designation of chief information officer (CIO) to describe the executive function of those responsible for the investment in information and information technology is gaining some ground. However, responsibilities accompanying this title are continually evolving as the organizational aspects of the position evolve. In one corporation the CIO may be a technical wizard, while in another the CIO is an integrating force. The role the CIO plays has no real precedent, and how this executive role is defined is largely up to the person who is placed into it.

Those CIO's who can demonstrate their role in integrating the corporation's business units to function as a whole, thereby fulfilling corporate and divisional imperatives, will have an identity linked with success and achievement.

ENDNOTE

1. These statistics are based on a quote by Dr. Carver Mead of the California Institute of Technology which was included in an article, "Technology and Sovereignty", by Walter B. Wriston. Wriston's article appeared in *Foreign Affairs*, Volume 67, Number 2, Winter 1988/1989.

CHAPTER 14

MAKING THE TRANSITION:
Building the
Information-Based
Corporation

Throughout the book, we have examined various concepts ranging from stakeholders to functional executives to the frontline to intercorporate alliances. We have also built linkages between the information investment, the use of information technology, and business performance. This final chapter will help you integrate all these into your plan of action for building an information-based corporation.

The action plan covered in this chapter has nine basic steps that will help you in building an information-based corporation. The time it will take to accomplish these will depend on where your company is today. These steps will take at least one year and could take as many as three. The initial three steps should be accomplished within six months to a year after reading this book, or the information and technology issue will die from lack of activity.

Step 1. Create and participate in the executive committee.

Step 2. Determine which functional executives should be key participants in making the transition.

Step 3. Establish and participate in an information-resource council.

Step 4. Establish the information and technology needs potential for demand-side stakeholders.

Step 5. Establish the information and technology needs potential for supply-side stakeholders.

Step 6. Establish the information and technology needs potential for investor stakeholders.

Step 7. Establish the information and technology needs potential for internal stakeholders.

Step 8. Establish the information and technology needs potential for the community and regulators.

Step 9. Establish the information and technology needs potential for economic alliances, integrating both the supply side and demand side of the value chain.

Step10. Develop an information and technology plan that accomplishes the business objectives of steps 1–9.

STEP 1: CREATE AND PARTICIPATE IN THE EXECUTIVE COMMITTEE

To build an information-based corporation, you, as the CIO or other senior executive, need to start with the corporate imperatives and how they are created in your company through some form of an executive committee. The executive committee process is critical both to your success and to that of the corporation. Your role as a participant in the executive committee is pivotal—it can make or break you as an effective corporate leader.

If your company doesn't have a functioning executive committee, you may participate in creating one. Executive committees have been known to have evolved out of other group activities:

- An executive group that meets periodically to discuss company-wide issues.
- A group of senior executives that meet for planning the activities of the various functions.
- A management committee that meets to discuss monthly financial results.
- A director's forum for senior functional managers to update their management skills.

Regardless of how an executive committee begins, it eventually must address important company issues and demonstrate its effectiveness by gleaning information and commitments from its participants.

Figure 14–1 displays effective positioning of the executive committee as it relates to determining the company's organizing principle, driving force, and functional mission. It also displays the executive committee's role in creating

- A common understanding of the environment.
- A description of the market and the company's position within it.
- The scope and function of the company's products and services.
- The company's goals and objectives.

Chaired by the chief executive officer, the executive committee helps to decide the possible future actions that should be emphasized as corporate imperatives. From an internal point of view, establishing corporate imperatives as well as monitoring their implementation are the most important roles of the executive committee. Through the imperative process, the executive committee assists the various business functions in making sure that their actions are aligned with the goals of the business.

FIGURE 14–1
Building the Information-Based Corporation
Creating and Positioning the Executive Committee

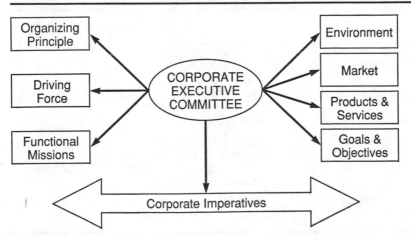

The executive committee's role in setting corporate imperatives especially benefits decision making for information and technology investments. As covered earlier in the book, all investments in information and technology must relate to the success of a corporate imperative.

STEP 2: DETERMINE THE FUNCTIONS THAT SHOULD BE THE KEY PARTICIPANTS IN MAKING THE TRANSITION

Figure 14–2 lists the key support functions that are necessary in building an information-based company. These centralized organizations are undergoing substantial change as we move forward in the information age.

The functional executive responsible for information systems and telecommunications will be a key player in helping an organization make the transition to an building information-based corporation. The information systems organization will be centralized for large databases and large production applications such as billing systems, payroll, and so forth. It will also be dispersed so that information can be used to make decisions and to support localized production applications in such areas as

FIGURE 14–2
Which Functions Are Involved in the Transition?

Organization	Potential Impact
Information Systems	Centralized/Dispersed
Operations	Business Unit Driven
Development	Business Unit Managed
Database	Information-Resource Management
Technical Services	Business Unit Driven
Telecommunications	Centralized
Human Resources	Line Driven
Recruiting	Business Unit Managed
Salary Administration	Business Unit Managed, Central Coordination
Relationships	Cultural Management
Strategic Planning	Decentralized
Finance	Centralized/Dispersed

personnel records, plant production systems, and marketing systems.

The centralized tasks will be driven by the business units that receive the benefits of the large applications and databases. Telecommunications, because of its crucial role in enabling information transfer, will tend to remain centralized.

The human-resources (HR) executive should also be a key player. In the next decade, HR will focus again on working with management in developing the potential of the human resource, thus returning to a line-driven function. Recruiting will be handled by line management. Salary administration will be a shared responsibility between line management and HR, with a focus on rewarding productivity. Relationship management with the company's internal stakeholders, employees, and management will be based on building cooperative and performance-based cultures.

The strategic-planning or organization-development executive will also be a key player. This executive role is also becoming more and more line oriented as it assumes responsibility for instilling strategic thinking throughout the organization.

The financial executive is also a key player who, like the information systems executive, will work in both a centralized and dispersed environment. The financial function has successfully worked this way for some time.

The balance of the key players come from the major line organizations such as sales and marketing, manufacturing, distribution, and operations. These line managers have the particularly difficult task of carrying out day-to-day line tasks while also managing the transition in their areas of responsibility.

These key players are your partners in building an information-based corporation.

STEP 3: ESTABLISH AND PARTICIPATE IN AN INFORMATION-RESOURCE COUNCIL

The information-resource council (IRC) consists of essentially the same participants as the executive committee. Its focus is more specific and functions as a steering committee for making investments in information and technology that support corporate imperatives and strategy.

This council will meet less frequently than the executive committee meets. An IRC generally meets once a quarter; the executive committee meets once or twice a month. The participants in the IRC are the same executives that compose the executive committee. The IRC should be chaired by the company's chief information officer.

Figure 14–3 illustrates the functioning and positioning of the IRC. The IRC deals with information and technology investments as they pertain to corporate imperatives, stakeholder relationships, and the business process that enables the company to achieve its goals and objectives.

The information and technology investments take the form of information bases, business systems, and integral components of the company's products and services. Underpinning the IRC process is the company's infrastructure and its reward systems. Information and technology investments become a part of the company's infrastructure.

To ensure effective implementation of corporate imperatives, stakeholder relationships, and business processes, the

FIGURE 14–3
Creating and Positioning the Information Resource Council

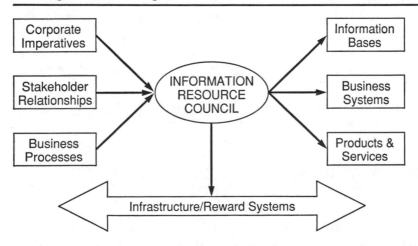

executive committee needs feedback. The IRC must provide for the measurement and reporting aspect of the corporate infrastructure. This measurement and reporting needs to have a strong connection to the company's reward systems. Otherwise, hoped-for productivity gains are not likely to be achieved.

STEP 4: ESTABLISH THE INFORMATION AND TECHNOLOGY NEEDS POTENTIAL FOR DEMAND-SIDE STAKEHOLDERS

Now, information executives can begin to do the homework necessary to play a leadership role in the IRC. By taking the initiative of examining stakeholder-based information and technology needs, information executives become partners with other corporate executives in improving corporate performance.

Figure 14–4 illustrates how information executives need to connect the information needs of demand-side stakeholders with the corresponding needs of internal corporate functions.[1] In assessing how well your company meets the demand-side information needs, you must look for

- Strengths and unique relationships that are supported by IT and specific information.
- Weaknesses resulting in poor stakeholder relationships.
- Opportunities based on cooperation rather than adversarial competition.

FIGURE 14–4
Building the Information-Based Corporation
Work from the Outside In—the Demand Side

Demand-side stakeholders

Internal functions

Distributors
Wholesalers
Small Retailers
Large Retailers
Consumers

INFORMATION NEEDS

Sales
Marketing
Finance
Manufacturing
R & D

Of special interest are complex stakeholder relationships of the sort we examined earlier for pharmaceutical companies. In situations where there are complex and diverse stakeholders on the demand side, there is great opportunity. If you find these in your company, chances are that this area will yield quick results.

To support the efforts on the demand side, your company might form a demand-side team, made up of key executives from the internal corporate functions and key executives from your external demand-side stakeholders. The purpose of this team would be to foster partnerships where there are mutual benefits to gain.

For example, a pharmaceutical company might form a team with executives from the sales and marketing, finance, manufacturing, R&D, and I/S functions to meet with key executives from distributors, wholesalers, large retailers, health maintenance organizations, M.D.'s, hospitals, and consumer groups. The focus of this team would be on how to improve all these relationships so that all might benefit from participating on the team.

These cooperative teams can provide a great deal of insight for executive committees in establishing corporate imperatives. They can also provide a valuable source of intelligence for the IRC.

STEP 5: ESTABLISH THE INFORMATION AND TECHNOLOGY NEEDS POTENTIAL FOR SUPPLY-SIDE STAKEHOLDERS

This step deals with territory less frequented. American companies have only recently faced fierce global competition—hence, the focus on the demand side. Nevertheless, attention to the supply side can yield benefits including lower costs, improved and more uniform quality, improved availability, and lower overhead costs.

Figure 14–5 illustrates the relationship between the information needs of supply-side stakeholders and the internal functions specializing in supply-side activity.

FIGURE 14–5
Building the Information—Based Corporation
Work from the Outside In—the Supply Side

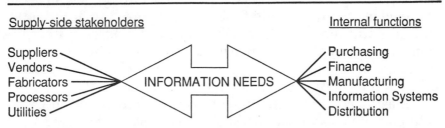

Supply-side stakeholders   Internal functions

Suppliers   Purchasing
Vendors   Finance
Fabricators   INFORMATION NEEDS   Manufacturing
Processors   Information Systems
Utilities   Distribution

Your relationships on the supply side are your partners in providing goods and services for the demand side.

Internal functions, such as purchasing, finance, manufacturing, and so forth, should manage those partnerships as opposed to establishing adversarial relationships. Like the demand side, the supply side could greatly benefit from a team made up of internal executives responsible for supply-side activity and key executives from supply-side companies. As in the case of the demand-side team, your company's executive committee and IRC can benefit greatly from this valuable source of intelligence on needs and possibilities.

STEP 6: ESTABLISH THE INFORMATION AND TECHNOLOGY NEEDS POTENTIAL FOR INVESTOR STAKEHOLDERS

The information and technology needs of investor stakeholders and the company's internal functions involved with them are subject to yet other important stakeholders, the regulators. The Securities Exchange Commission is key among these. Other quasi-regulatory bodies such as the Financial Accounting Standards Board (FASB) and the American Institute of Certified Public Accounts (AICPA) influence regulatory activity.

Thus, most of the information requirements in this step are focused on meeting regulatory and professional standards. Nevertheless, new sources of capital and opportunities for leveraged equity (e.g., greater dependence on borrowing) offer enormous potential to the investor. The problem is risk.

Figure 14–6 illustrates information needs for investor stakeholders and corporate functions. Improved information in this area will tend to reduce risk. Therefore, improved information will tend to attract more and different investors. This same information will also enable the IRC to examine the cause and effect of information and technology investments.

Most executive committees have investor-perceived corporate performance at the top of their priorities. Improved measurement for corporate performance, early problem-detection systems, and improved capability to take action will greatly improve the effectiveness of the executive committee. With better information, the executive committee will better understand the cause and effect of possible actions. As a result, the committee members can better explain to investors the options available between short-term and long-term actions.

STEP 7: ESTABLISH THE INFORMATION AND TECHNOLOGY NEEDS POTENTIAL FOR INTERNAL STAKEHOLDERS

Perhaps the most sensitive stakeholders are those internal to the company. For this reason, information about internal stakeholder relationships is sensitive. Therefore, the internal functions that have access to and manage such sensitive information

FIGURE 14–6
Building the Information—Based Corporation
Work from the Outside In—the Investors

Investors		Internal functions
Shareholders		Finance
Bondholders		Management
Banks	INFORMATION NEEDS	Legal
Creditors		Personnel
Pensioners		Board of Directors

have a special power. Management, personnel executives, finance executives, and the board of directors have status and privilege attached to their control over information about internal stakeholders. Figure 14–7 illustrates these special relationships.

For the information executive, this will be the most difficult area in which to participate as a partner. Key functional executives will need to be convinced that the information executive has something to bring to the party.

STEP 8: ESTABLISH THE INFORMATION AND TECHNOLOGY NEEDS POTENTIAL FOR THE COMMUNITY AND REGULATORS

The community and regulators have always been important for businesses, even though many seemed to have not realized it until a major incident occurred. Exxon is more aware of its community responsibilities after the oil spill in Alaska. Occidental Chemical, even though the former management of its acquisition adhered to all federal and local chemical waste regulations, found that in the case of Love Canal new discoveries of what is safe and unsafe can weigh heavily on a company. Figure 14–8 illustrates the interaction between internal functions and the external stakeholders, community and regulators.

By continually working together with both the community and regulators and with full disclosure of vital information by all, times of crisis are more manageable. When the company

FIGURE 14–7
Building the Information—Based Corporation (Work from the Outside In—Internal Stakeholders)

Internal stakeholders

Internal functions

Employees
Management
Contractors

INFORMATION NEEDS

Management
Personnel
Finance
Board of Directors

FIGURE 14–8
Building the Information—Based Corporation
(Work from the Outside In—Community & Regulators)

demonstrates its full commitment to the community and to regulators through open disclosure and quick and appropriate reaction to emergencies, your company's value is protected and may even increase.

STEP 9: ESTABLISH THE INFORMATION AND TECHNOLOGY NEEDS POTENTIAL FOR ECONOMIC ALLIANCES, INTEGRATING BOTH THE SUPPLY SIDE AND DEMAND SIDE OF THE VALUE CHAIN

This step involves synthesizing diverse demand-side, supply-side, investor, and internal stakeholders into an overall economic model of alliances, as shown in Figure 14–9.

By combining the strengths of allies in developing, producing, and delivering products and services, the economic partners produce a formidable competitive model.

At American Airlines, such an alliance was created for air passengers, travel agents, American Airlines operations, and even other airlines. The integrating mechanism was the airline reservation system. The CIO in this case is now the chairman of a new company created from the reservation system.

These opportunities exist in your environment as well. By discovering such opportunities, initiating alliances, and unifying the alliances with information and technology, your company can also create new, viable, technology-leveraged ventures.

FIGURE 14–9
Economic Alliances (Supply-Side and Demand-Side Competition)

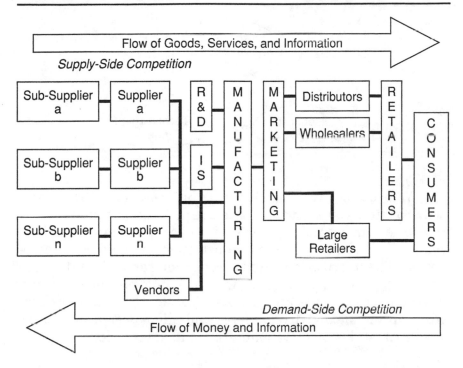

STEP 10: DEVELOP AN INFORMATION AND TECHNOLOGY PLAN THAT ACCOMPLISHES THE BUSINESS OBJECTIVES OF STEPS 1–9

In Chapter 10, we looked at resource management and at information-resource management in particular. The result was an investment strategy built upon an information strategy and a technology strategy, as shown in Figure 14–10.

This investment strategy will make sense only if it is based on the previous steps. Unfortunately, many companies initiate this step as an independent technology effort. The results are reams and reams of plans that have little to do with the business. Information and technology planning cannot be performed apart from the basic business planning and execution process.

FIGURE 14–10
Elements of IT Strategy

Your direct involvement in the business as outlined above will position you to succeed. We are in a new business era in which information and other senior executives must use information and technology to build a leaner, more effective corporation. The information-based corporation can be best described as a corporation that behaves with the efficiency of a thousand entrepreneurial units all working together with the same organizing principle and driving force and all dedicated to ensuring that each stakeholder benefits from the enterprise.

ENDNOTE

1. Demand-side stakeholders are enjoying a great deal of attention these days as a result of Harvard Business School and MIT's Sloan Management School emphasis on competitive advantage.

CHAPTER 15

CONCLUSION

In the next decade, more information will be available at speeds faster than we can imagine today. As we enter the 1990s, we are close to eliminating the time between an event and the transmission of information about it. At the same time, we're finding that it's becoming increasingly difficult to limit access to sensitive information by an increasingly informed and inquisitive society. That's why the Soviet Union's *glasnost* is more a product of the information age than just a benevolent change in ideology. As the result of a better informed community, the Soviet government is compelled to reexamine its relationship with its most numerous stakeholders—its citizens. This is a major shift from the past preoccupation with satisfying the exclusive needs of the Soviet upper-crust nomenklatura and party members.

Likewise, today's technology potential compels American executives to reexamine corporate relationships with customers, suppliers, community, employees, and other often neglected stakeholders. Some corporate leaders are beginning to realize that managing as some corporations do, with uncompromising self-interest as the basis, is the antithesis of sound competitive performance. NCR Corporation's CEO, Chuck Exley, is such an enlightened executive who is committed to stakeholder management. NCR demonstrates this commitment with a dedicated, top-level executive position responsible for overseeing stakeholder relations.

Today, the technology potential is helping to transform corporate and national ethics into a new global reality. Industrial-age ethics built on centralized, hierarchical power are reverting to pre-industrial age social and business ethics of smaller, more, localized economic communities. The resultant regional economies, in turn, are part of a developing global economy which links interactions between regional economic communities. The United States and Canada have formed an economic community. The Andean Pact ties together the economies of many South American countries. European nations are forging a truly unified economic community. Southeast Asian nations are beginning to form economic alliances.

The bonding of economic communities depends on mutual trust and respect. Technology helps to make this possible through constant information exchange.

Nowadays, when Manuel Noriega cheats an election process in Panama, or when Exxon has a major oil spill, or even when Japanese and American politicians skirt the law, the world's various economic communities and their citizens often know and react the same day these events happen.

While countries are creating economic communities, multi-national corporations cooperating with other multinational corporations are forging economic alliances. American, European, and Japanese pharmaceutical companies are entering joint-research ventures. Hitachi and General Motors have joined forces to market Hitachi's computers and EDS's services. Each of these economic alliances require assent and trust from each group of stakeholders of the corporations involved.

Stakeholder management concepts are based on mutual trust. Without trust, stakeholders will withhold support thus limiting economic possibilities. Eastern Airlines and its disparate unions failed to make a new possibility happen in the spring of 1989 with a new Eastern Airlines and with employee-owners, led by the successful and well-liked Peter Uberoff. The failure resulted from Eastern management's reluctance to share information during the takeover period by opening Eastern's books to the unions for their scrutiny and by the lack of union trust to operate without such disclosure. The transition to a new, unified Eastern was impossible with underlying trust missing on both sides.

With the help of today's technology, we can see the effect of information's availability or withholding through the actions of politicians, government, businesses, and voters. In the late

1970s Californians led a nation-wide revolt against galloping taxation. Since the present system makes it difficult to hold politicians accountable for spending, California voters placed limits on their ability to tax. On the national scene, the Gramm—Rudman Act put similar restrictions on spending by Congress. Even the US Congress canceled its 1989 salary increase when an outraged public learned of it. All of these political actions highlight the void of citizen confidence in elected representatives because of conflicting interests and lack of accountability.

Technology provides the capability for establishing accountability and monitoring performance in both business and government. The imperative is for corporate executives and politicians to sponsor this use of technology rather than resisting it for selfish reasons. Based on recent events, it seems that corporate executives and politicians often avoid such responsible action. To do so would violate their commitment to themselves as the most important stakeholders.

In 1989, Californians revolted against galloping insurance rates and demanded a rollback in rates. The insurance companies, in turn, sponsored legislation to limit the legal fees and awards involved in insurance litigation. California voters passed Proposition 103 in an attempt to force California insurers to open their books and demonstrate that they are making no more than a reasonable rate of profit.

This is only the beginning. In the next decade, we will likely question whether the present representative form of government is any longer viable. Our press is filled with examples of politicians elected and sent to Washington only to march to the beat of a different drum after they get there—a drum beaten by special interest groups, influence peddlers, and political parties. Technology makes possible a viable federal government without having to send representatives to live in Washington D.C. thus leaving politicians free to spend more time in their real constituency. Even now, a direct, participatory democracy is technically possible which would obviate the need for many of such elected officials.

History has presented us with a continuing panorama of change:

- The agricultural revolution with its growth of cities and states.
- The industrial revolution with its urbanization and new forms of transportation and communication.
- The information age with yet more possibilities for change in life styles and values.

When a new form of business or government is technically and economically possible and when it's viewed by stakeholders and constituents as good it's only a matter of time until the corresponding social and economic changes will occur.

As our corporations move into the new business era, we can reap the biggest benefits when we deal directly with all our stakeholders in a constructive and open manner. Key to this is a vital network of systems that will enable information-based corporations to keep their stakeholders informed and involved. Thus, stakeholders can support their corporations by

1. Understanding overall corporate performance as compared with diverse stakeholder expectations.
2. Offering positive suggestions of ways to improve overall stakeholder prosperity.
3. Participating in systems that provide the checks and balances a corporation must have for long-term success.

In the next decade, today's simple electronic-data interchange efforts will grow into major economic alliances supported by networks of information-based corporations. Stakeholders who are unified by these technology-supported economic alliances will help their corporations achieve new heights of performance for American industry in an exacting global economy.

APPENDIX 1

INFORMATION-INVESTMENT ACCOUNTING AND REPORTING IN FINANCIAL STATEMENTS

This appendix is intended to provoke discussion on accounting and reporting the information investment. If American business is to succeed in gaining control over runaway overhead costs, we must first understand the nature and value of information work, how to measure it, and how to plan and control it in ways that improve the financial results of our companies.

This appendix will offer some guidelines and examples for accounting and reporting of the information investment. The actual costs that make up the information investment are the following:

Information-work personnel and related costs.
Communications costs.
Information systems costs.
Office costs.
Storage costs.

PERSONNEL AND RELATED COSTS

Personnel and related costs is by far the largest cost category. It has been shown that in information-driven companies, information work accounts for 70 to 90 percent of the personnel. The related costs include payroll taxes, insurance, education, vacations, and holidays.

COMMUNICATIONS COSTS

Communications costs include voice, data, and image communications. Telephone company costs, communications equipment, electronic mail, postage, and travel to and from company meetings are examples of communications costs. Shipping people to meetings is an alternative to other communications costs such as telephone, postage, or electronic mail. Taken together, these costs are intended to effect a transfer of information.

INFORMATION SYSTEMS COSTS

Costs associated with information systems include the central data-center facility with its computer (s), storage devices, terminals, lines, air conditioning, building facilities, and maintenance. Included in these costs as well are all distributed minicomputers, microcomputers, and word processors.

OFFICE COSTS

All office costs are information related. Copying machines, typewriters, calculators, furniture, filing cabinets, and office space are all costs of creating, maintaining, or transferring information.

STORAGE COSTS

Most large organizations have archives, libraries, and other storage facilities. Some even have large off-site centers for storing information. Particularly voluminous are financial records, contracts, legal records, and government-required records for chemicals, pharmaceuticals, and the like. These costs can be significant in information-driven and information-sensitive industries.

RESTATING THE PROFIT-AND-LOSS STATEMENT

After these costs are identified, the next step is to restate the profit-and-loss(P&L) statement. This restatement is intended not to replace the normal P&L, but to provide further information.

Take for example the simple P&L illustration in Table A1–1. A financial officer viewing this disclosure, assuming the accounting is correct, will feel that this P&L satisfies the investors' need for understanding the results of operations. Substantial detail exists to support these figures, but the categories as presented are generally considered self-explanatory.

Table A1–2 restates the figures for clarity of the information-work and information-technology components. With this restatement, the investment in information and information technology becomes apparent. At first, such a distinction for information expense will draw questions from management, the board of directors, and investors as to the reasons for such a distinction. In addition, the accounting community will not accept such a change without further evidence of need.

Table A1–I
Profit and Loss Statement ($000,000)

Sales	$1000
Cost of Sales	350
Gross Margin	$ 650
Expenses	
Sales and Marketing	250
Research and Development	70
General and Administrative	100
Total expenses	$ 420
Operating profit	$ 230

TABLE A1–2
Profit and Loss Statement ($000,000)

	Information Expense	Other	Total
Sales			$1000
Cost of Sales			350
Gross margin			650
Expenses			
Sales and Marketing	$200	$50	250
Research and Development	25	45	70
General and Administrative	100		100
Total expenses	$325	$95	420
Operating profit			$230

RESTATING THE BALANCE SHEET

Now that we've restated the income statement, let's complete the set of financial reports with an example of a balance sheet. Table Al–3 presents such an example.

Now the board has two perspectives. The company has spent $325 million on information in the past year. There is no asset value for this expense. So information expense must be a cost of doing business on a current basis—$325 million is 175% of retained earnings. This expenditure needs more explanation.

Let's take the example one step further. Say, upon further analysis, we find that 70 percent of the information expenses were for creating information. We further determine that it would take our current staff five years to recreate the existing information base (e.g., to achieve a steady state where additions to the information base equal deletions). In other words, it would take five years for the amount being invested in information at the current rate to reach a point at which each additional year's effort is one of maintaining a relatively fixed amount of data.[1]

Based on the five-year steady-state finding, we could then calculate the total information investment by multiplying one year's investment by five years. Thus, we would have the figures shown in Table A1–4. This means that the information investment expressed on a capitalized basis represents a figure two and one half times larger than the shareholders' equity.

TABLE AI–3
Balance Sheet ($000,000)

Assets		Liabilities	
Cash	$ 10	Accounts Payable	$175
Accounts Receivable	150	Notes Payable	50
Inventory	200	Loans	250
Plant and Equipment	500		
Other	50	Total Liabilities	$475
Total Assets	$910	*Shareholders' equity*	
		Paid-in capital	250
		Retained earnings	185
		Total Equity	$435
		Total Liabilities and Equity	$910

TABLE A1–4
Total Information Investment to Achieve Steady State

$325,000,000	One year's investment
x 70%	The amount of effort to create new information
$227,500,000	The net information investment
x 5	The number of years to achieve steady state
$1,137,500,000	The capitalized information investment

The questions that need to be answered then are

What is the point of steady state for the information investment in this company? For the industry?

What percent of sales is spent on information in this company? For this industry?

What is the return on investment for the information investment for this company? For this industry?

What is the relationship between the information-technology investment and the calculated information investment for this company? For this industry?

Some of the answers will shock management. It is not reasonable to expect that companies will report the results externally. At the very least, they should be reported on an internal basis.

External reporting could start with footnotes to the financial statements. An analysis of the profit-and-loss statement expenses should be included. Then a statement on the steady state of the company and industry should be made. Reasonable estimates of the capitalized value of the information investment would follow. All of these figures should be compared to industry norms. Comments from management should be included.

In the final analysis, the job begins and ends with a company's internal accountants working together with senior management and the board of directors. It's their task to inform management and the board about the results of operations and the state of finances. Accountants who don't analyze the information investment in today's information economy aren't doing their jobs.

ACCOUNTING FOR INFORMATION WORK

The classification of data, information, or knowledge as assets implies there is a method for determining their cost, value, and useful life. To distribute processing and other I/S costs to the users of I/S services, the data-processing accounting community has developed many methodologies, techniques, and DP cost-accounting software packages. These have resulted in complicated and confusing reports of DP standard costs and charge-back rates that have little bearing on the real nature of the information and technology investment today.

The business community must recognize information, not the data-processing hardware and software used to make it available, as its major resource. With this recognition, we can calculate the true costs of information, including the investment in information systems as well as in information. This calculation would include, as a minimum,

1. *Creation costs.* These are labor costs as well as that portion of information systsems used in the process. The labor element is considerable, especially in enterprises involved in financial services, banking, insurance, communications, utilities, transportation, and consumer marketing.
2. *Maintenance costs.* These include the updating and purging costs of information.
3. *Production costs.* These include information systems costs, labor costs, and communications expenses. These expenses are necessary to make the information available when, where, and how it is needed to benefit the enterprise.

Accountants originally developed costing procedures to account for variable material, labor, and overhead costs on a unit-of-manufacture basis. In the factory, material is neither ordered nor used unless there are units to produce. If the material is on hand, but it is not needed for production, it is inventoried as an asset.

Likewise, labor is not used unless there are units to produce. A lack of sales results in immediate layoffs to avoid unnecessary labor expenses. In the worst case, some units are produced and inventoried. Thus, accountants carry the labor expense in the inventory asset with the goods produced.

FIXED VERSUS VARIABLE COSTS

Systems professionals are very different from factory labor, which means there are few truly variable costs in the information systems environment. Systems professionals are in high demand, so a layoff would mean permanent employment loss for the enterprise. Therefore, information systems organizations try to keep people on the payroll in both good times and bad.

Other variable costs, such as removable-storage media, paper, and electricity are a small part of the total information systems cost. They are not major factors in the information investment. All the remaining systems costs are relatively fixed. These include hardware, software, development and operations staff, facilities, and management. Furthermore, some of these fixed costs have historically grown at an annual rate of 20 percent or more. Unfortunately, they haven't decreased at the same rate.

Along with the growth in information systems investment, other information investments are increasing at an accelerated rate. These are because of the productivity gains resulting from increased systems availability and accessibility. A good example is the emerging concept of the information center with its professional and executive work stations.

EXECUTIVE ACCEPTANCE

Executive acceptance of the growth rate of the information investment will only come from a clear valuation process. The valuation process relates the investment made in the information asset to expected financial return. Future financial statements will show the results as increases in revenue or decreases in expense that result in incremental profit. This valuation process will yield a calculable return on investment (ROI).

The next logical step is the capitalization and amortization of information costs over a time commensurate with their benefit or useful life. These costs can be reported in the enterprise's financial statements as any other asset is reported. The audit criteria for this asset would be similar to those used for accounts receivable: be sure its costs are accurate and confirm its connection to future cash flows.

If an item is to be reported as an asset, it must have a useful life. The cost of the investment must match the generation of future cash flows. For asset accounting, a simple accounting entry capitalizes the investment costs. This amount is then amortized over an appropriate period.

An example is the acquisition of a central processing unit (CPU) for information systems. We might, for example, amortize it over a four-year period. Some assets, such as buildings, are amortized over a much longer period. The capitalized value of the asset includes periodic improvements or additions, with a commensurate amortization schedule.

With information, the initial useful life estimate may be three or four years. We can extend the information asset's useful life with added information and maintenance.

The audit criteria are simple

1. Is the information accurate and not available to outsiders?
2. Does it relate to the generation of future cash flows?

For example, computerizing information obtained from the Bureau of the Census is simply automating public information. This information would have little asset value since it is not the exclusive property of the organization. An investment in automating census data might have value if, by automating, time to access the data can be saved. The judgement of value is then limited to future savings of labor costs.

However, by analyzing the information and adding other data, this information might become unique and usable for generating future cash flow. The audit must determine whether this is the case. The audit might include some statistical sampling to evaluate the accuracy of the data as well as its availability from some public or commercial source.

HARDWARE AND SOFTWARE COSTS

As information technology advances, hardware and software have a shortened life cycle. We might consider hardware, with its especially volatile life cycle, a throwaway asset, similar to an automobile. After the hardware has served its useful life, predictable from an obsolescence curve, its only residual value is as scrap. IBM converts its lease base to cash as it approaches the end of its technological life. When IBM makes a unit of hardware financially attractive to purchase, it's a good bet that they will soon announce new technology.

CHARACTERIZING INFORMATION-TECHNOLOGY ACTIVITIES

The characteristic behavior of each area of information-technology activity is unique. In order to measure, control, and plan the results of each activity area, uniform metrics are vital to assure information-management success. Table A1–5 offers some guidelines. The metrics shown describe the salient behavioral characteristics for each information-activity area.

All of these measures relate to time, space, and volume. The characteristics are very similar to those of a utility. The management processes are also similar. The critical nature of information flow comes from processing a given volume or transferring in a given time. Peak volume periods become a key management issue. In some cases, the metric is the same. For example, we use bytes and time to measure activity in more than one activity area.

Since each area is unique, the metrics have different connotations depending on the activity area being measured. *Time* for processing does not produce the same function as does *time* for transfer. Therefore, we can't combine the measures in different areas into total time without reference as to the kind of time (e.g., processing or transfer).[2]

STORAGE COSTS

Information storage costs include the type of media used, such as paper, magnetic tape, or disk. They should also be described according to the space occupied. The metrics of bytes and space are both quantity measures. A list of information-storage costs should include all the information systsems resources needed to get information in and out of storage.

TABLE A1–5
Information Resource Characteristics

Metric	Storage	Processing	Transfer
Basic	Space	Time	Time/Distance
Alternate	Bytes	Bytes	Bytes/Distance
Other	Media/System	Peak/Time	Peak/Time

MANAGING THE INFORMATION ASSET

Our economy sorely needs productivity gains. An understanding of information's nature and costs for each area of business activity will be the first step. Organizations with this understanding and discipline will be the corporate winners in the information economy.

Once there is a focus on information, the management processes of implementing, measuring, controlling, and planning can begin. If an organization wishes to survive in the information age, it must first have an overall organizational and strategic plan for the creating, automating, storing, and securing of information. With this plan, information managers are able to plan the information systems resource and to optimize the investment in the information asset.

One of the major planning problems in large organizations revolves around the size of the facility to house information systems. An embarrassing but familiar phenomenon is the situation in which the space requirements exceed the physical capacity of a new data center. What was adequate space a few years ago is now far too small. This phenomenon also occurs in the office. Automated office systems now require vastly larger work areas per office employee.

With the increased availability of local processing (office automation), the appetite for information will also increase. Information bases will be located in various parts of the organization as well as centrally. As a result, information transfer between the central facility and remote locations and between remote locations themselves will demand more and more of the information manager's time. This function, at present, is delegated to a network or communications department at a low level in the organization. In some cases, this function has even been found buried in the personnel department.

The job of making the information asset available represents a crucial area of information-management responsibility, a responsibility that will require significant funding in the future. The information-transfer function should be of direct concern to the chief information executive. It will involve important organizational decisions regarding the investment in telecommunications equipment and service.Many organizations have bought their own satellite systems to provide the speed and capacity needed to optimize the value of the information investment. By doing this, they have met their organizational goals for productivity and return on investment.

REEXAMINING INFORMATION-TECHNOLOGY ACTIVITIES

As previously stated, the cost of information systems is a significant investment in and of itself. Nevertheless, it is only part of a much larger corporate investment in the information asset. The information investment, because of its size, needs special consideration. Key to realizing value are the information-coordination and information management functions under the aegis of the chief information executive. They include

Storage of the information asset.
Information processing.
Information transfer.

Business units have an increasing desire for quick and easy access to information as well as for local control over manipulating information. It is becoming increasingly important to process information locally. On the other hand, large transaction-driven systems will, because of their massive size, achieve economies of scale only at a centralized source. Thus, the relative costs of centralized and decentralized storage and processing are important to know.

I/S executives need a clear understanding of economies-of-scale potential. With such an understanding, the I/S executive can determine where the corporation will benefit from large, centralized mainframes. These will handle large storage and database management systems. Decentralized processing and centralized information storage will result in a central facility larger than that of centralized processing.

Economies of scale are changing rapidly as more and more power is available on the desktop or on departmental minicomputers. Decentralizing storage and processing brings into play another set of issues: accessibility, security, and control of the information asset.

With either centralized or decentralized processing, we must apply sound economic and financial analyses. It's the chief information executive's responsibility to determine which alternatives optimize the long-term value of the information asset. These analyses will consider such costs as

- Information security and control.
- Measurement and planning.

- Documentation and training.
- Systems integration and communications compatibility.
- Information stability and redundancy.
- Maintenance of central database integrity: documenting files, management reporting, and controlling updates and changes.

Whether a database is centralized or decentralized, information transfer is a major information cost. Even though technology such as optical disks may reduce the unit costs, the volume is increasing at a geometric rate. This one area is potentially the greatest obstacle to realizing full value from the information asset.

ENDNOTES

1. For example, when a company starts, it has no customers, no prospects, and no data on either. The company starts from the first day to accumulate information about the market, its prospects, and its customers. This base of data grows at a very rapid rate in the beginning. It then slows as the company achieves its basic needs in terms of a working information base. This point at which the accumulation slows down to a replenishment basis is the point at which the information base is at steady state.
2. The confusion that will occur from adding like but unique elements can be illustrated by the labor required to construct a building. In order to construct a building, there must be an architect, electricians, carpenters, brick layers, metal workers, and so on. We measure the efforts of all these people in time (hours, people years, etc.). The simple statement that a building will require 1,000 people years of construction time is meaningless for planning. We must specify the types of unique resources individually: electrician people years, brick layer people years, architect people years, and so on.

APPENDIX 2

INFORMATION RESOURCE MANAGEMENT STRATEGIC PLANNING AT THE WORLD BANK

---

by Mel Ray[1]

BACKGROUND

The Nature of World Bank Work

Since its initial involvement in financing reconstruction in the industrialized countries following World War II, the World Bank has largely focused its attention and efforts on accelerating the development of its lesser developed member countries. This it has sought to do through an array of instruments, the most important of which are lending, economic and sector analysis, policy advice, aid coordination, technical assistance, training via the activities of the Economic Development Institute, development research, and constituency building. These instruments need little explanation except perhaps "constituency building," which may be defined as efforts by the Bank to create a favorable climate for, and supportive attitudes toward, achieving its mission of promoting the development of its member countries.

The Bank produces a complex line of products and services, fundamentally intellectual in nature, and ranging from continuing research programs to financial and technical assistance. These products are created by workers who use information as their raw material. Accordingly, the Bank is a significant collector, consumer, and producer of information, the management of which is central to the institution's effectiveness. The Bank's product mix has varied considerably over the years in response to changing circumstances, changes in perceived needs of its members, and improved understanding of the development process. Such changes, together with large increases in the volume and complexity of its activities and products over the past 20 years or so, have resulted in a continuing and hugely expanding need for information, both externally and internally derived—a need that underscores the importance of efficiently managing the information resources.

From the standpoint of internal requirements, the Bank's growth in terms of staff numbers, facilities, services, and volume of operations has generated needs for management information systems to facilitate planning, programming, budgeting, monitoring, evaluation, and control-processes increasingly recognized as critically needing improvement. Enhancing staff productivity by improved information handling, processing, and delivery requires regular and specialized attention. The changing mix of the Bank's products and the increasing complexity of projects have added further to the difficulties of information collection, interpretation, generation, and dissemination, and maintenance and operation of the systems that are in place for these purposes.

The Need for Change in the Information Environment

None of the changes referred to earlier has occurred overnight. As the Bank has grown in size and in complexity of its operations, its managers and staff have been forced to react quickly to the changing information-related demands placed upon them. Their reactions were generally, and quite naturally, designed to resolve problems in their particular areas of responsibility. Thus, local databases were created or expanded to meet perceived local needs. These actions were facilitated, particularly in the late 1970's, by the evolution of relatively inexpensive technology amenable to use by novices. Consequently, throughout the Bank, rapid and largely uncontrolled growth has occurred in acquiring and using data and word processing systems.

Excluding the very real question of cost effectiveness, several major implications arise from this mushrooming and loosely controlled growth. The first is that many existing databases contain duplicative or inconsistent data. The second is that there is no clear and comprehensive picture as to exactly what data is held within the institution. Third, there exists a proliferation of different types of computer hardware, software, and programming tools from a range of manufacturers and suppliers that are, to a greater or lesser extent, incompatible with each other. These phenomena are far from unique to the Bank. However, they are potentially more serious to the Bank than to other institutions with less dependence on efficient information handling for their product and reputation.

The Move to Information Resource Management (IRM)

As noted earlier, advances in information technology have already provided, and will continue to provide, increasing opportunities to enhance the productivity of Bank staff. These advances in technology were being utilized to a considerable extent throughout the Bank in the mid-to late 1970's, but by 1981, the magnitude of annual expenditures, and the growing investments in information technology led to recognizing and articulating the need for a more disciplined management of information (Managing Committee) agreed in November 1981 that the Bank adopt the Information Resource Management (IRM) operating concept.

The key principle underlying the IRM concept is that management of the Bank's information resources is primarily the responsibility of the user community, with policy direction and technical support provided by a central information resource management staff organization. The latter was put in place in July 1982 with the creation of the Information Resource Management Department (IRMD). The IRM concept spans all information/data activities, including office technology, multimedia electronic communications, and traditional data processing. IRMD has a finite role within this Bank-wide concept. The department operates the centralized services and provides high-tech support as needed throughout the Bank on individual project agreements.

Two other principles underlie the Bank's definition of the IRM concept. First, various types of information technology are viewed as an integrated activity, rather than as separate function. Second, effective communications between the user community and the central staff organization (IRMD) must take place on a continuing basis. IRMD has been set up to be responsive to both these principles. Further, the IRM organizational structure within the user community has been centered around the formal recognition of data administrators organizationally positioned in user areas (by vice presidency) to oversee local information projects and assure compliance with Bank-wide IRM policies.

The data administrators, joined by the central IRMD staff, are providing an ongoing forum for communications and consensus building with the creation of the Information Resource Advisory Committee (IRAC). Chaired by the Director of the Information Resource Management Department, in his capacity as Bank-wide data administrator, the Committee membership includes the data administrators and managers of Bank departments having an institutional purview. IRMD provides analytical services and coordination as needed to support the IRAC.

Certain segments of the user community have special interests, such as those using a specific type of hardware or software. These users have formed advisory groups that cut across data administration areas. The chairperson of the advisory groups may attend IRAC meetings when topics pertaining to their special interests are to be discussed. They are attuned to the specific needs and plans of the users they represent and they are a valuable resource to IRAC.

The Information Resource Management Strategic Planning Project

IRAC began functioning in October 1982. Among its first actions was consideration of a proposal for identifying a Bank-wide information resource strategy that would address the short- and long-term information needs of the institution. The proposal derived from the perception that in the Bank there had been limited recognition of information/data as a resource. Consequently, there was neither a Bank-wide management strategy nor a discernible framework for integrating information flows and office technology initiatives in a cost-effective manner.

Following review by IRAC, a formal proposal for executing an Information Resource Management Strategic Planning Project was presented in November 1982 and approved by Bank senior management, who agreed to sponsor the project. The first phase of the Strategic Planning Project began immediately. The prime objective of Phase I was to assess the capacity of installed and planned equipment required for the Bank's computing needs through FY84 while the longer-term strategic planning effort progressed. The second phase, completed in June 1983, comprised two parts: the Information Systems Planning and Office Systems Planning Studies. For each of the study teams, an appropriate cross-section of Bank staff was enlisted. Using different methods and working from different perspectives, the two teams arrived at consistent views of the institution's needs for information and for means to access and process data.

The approach of the Information Systems Planning Study was top-down, including detailed discussions with 21 senior executives of the Bank, and focusing closely on the Bank's business mission, objectives, and processes as the determinants of the information needs. The approach of the Office Systems Planning Study was bottom-up, including questionnaires completed by more than 1,200 staff at all levels, as well as selected individual interviews. The focus in this case was on how information is acquired and what generic operations are performed with it. In summary, this second phase provided the senior management a non-technical assessment of the Bank's need to collect and manage data and the need to access these data in support of the Bank's world mission.

Phase III, the highly technical step, was organized to integrate the office technology, multimedia electronic communications, and data processing requirements into a Bank-wide IRM strategy. To accomplish the Phase III objective, nine profiles were prepared by separate mini-teams of content specialists using the Phase II requirements. The nine profiles were as follows:

A conceptual information systems network profile: a conceptual view of the required institution-wide information systems to support the goals and objectives of our business. This profile includes

An assessment of the systems in operation, systems under design/development, and systems funded but not started.

Determination of the priorities for institution-wide systems.

An institutional data architecture profile: identification of the institution-wide data to be defined, cataloged, and managed.

An office systems architecture profile conceptual view of the institution-wide office systems functions required to achieve improved office productivity.

A data communications profile: identification of the data communications network(s) required to address the desired interconnectivity of information technology.

A profile of policies, procedures, and standards: identification of the policies, procedures, and standards necessary to bring the desired information resource to fruition.

A technical skills profile/scenario: identification of the skills and availability of skilled staff, plus definition of the training of present staff, to realize the desired information resource.

An information technology profile: identification of the centralization/decentralization of information technology to provide efficient and effective information services.

A facilities profile: identification of the potential demand for facilities to accommodate information technology and skilled support staff.

A financial resource profile: identification of a multi-year financial profile to address the expectations of information systems and advanced office systems.

Careful integration of these nine profiles formed the Bank's IRM strategy. For the Bank to realize the IRM strategy, some 80 major follow-on projects were defined and estimates of resource requirements given.

The IRM strategy has been widely reviewed, both inside and outside the Bank, by staff and units having special interest, by recognized industry experts, and by vendors prominent today in the Bank. A special task force of Bank financial analysts conducted an objective cost benefit analysis of two scenarios of the Bank's future: a scenario "without" the IRM strategy and a scenario "with" the IRM strategy. This team concluded that the Bank should proceed with the IRM strategy. By November 1983, IRAC considered the IRM strategy in depth and, following some refinements, endorsed the IRM strategy.

The Bank's Managing Committee then considered the IRM strategy and the impact it would have on the institution's other major resources (i.e, physical facilities, human resources, future operating and capital budgets, etc.). By late November, the Bank's Managing Committee approved the IRM strategy.

REFINEMENT OF IRM AS A RESULT OF STRATEGIC PLANNING

The IRM Strategy

The IRM strategy is articulated via seven objectives designed to bring about the information resource environment the Bank needs to support its business objectives. In the case of the Bank, the IRM objectives are:

1. To place highest priority on information quality, in order to support the credibility of the Bank's overall effectiveness.

2. To develop an institutional information architecture defined by Bank business processes and founded on shared databases.

3. To provide, at the boundary between staff and information resources in the office and elsewhere, a family of standard workstations that are ergonomically suitable and supplied to all staff according to their needs for clerical, decision-making, and computational support.

4. To interconnect information resources for widespread access to information.

5. To place the responsibility for providing an information "infrastructure" with an internal Bank information utility, which will have the necessary mechanisms to fund, acquire, and dispose of the information resources infrastructure through normal budgetary and IRM processes.

6. To distribute IRM skills among organizational units of the Bank according to their needs, and to plan and manage the acquisition and enhancement of IRM skills at the institutional level.

7. To place the responsibility for developing information applications with Bank line managers, using the information infrastructure and funding through the normal budget process.

To implement the IRM strategy, an information infrastructure must be put in place. The infrastructure is basically the "wherewithal" that users need to develop their information applications, to access institutional data, and to apply automated tools in and to their office places. That is, the infrastructure includes standard workstations, communications facilities, micro to mainframe processors, a standard data management system, selected standard analytic or other software tools, operating system software, technical documentation, and supplies.

The Information Utility

An entity named the Information Utility, functionally similar to a public service utility, is the supplier of the information infrastructure. The Information Utility makes all capital investments in infrastructure items and in turn, supplies the items to users on an appropriate chargeback basis.

The Information utility makes available central services to all Bank units, charging for some of them. It is, for example, a "shop" that performs routine data processing applications that use expensive

resources shared among multiple users. It provides technical consultants on infrastructural matters to users of information systems. It
executes projects that are institutional in nature, because such projects
by definition provide wherewithal for users to develop and manage
their information resources.

Data Administration

The IRM strategy includes a model of the institution showing which
business processes create particular data classes, and which processes
use data created by other processes. This information model has been
analyzed and arranged to create the basic building blocks of an
information architecture.

For the Bank, seven major data areas comprise its information
architecture (Figure A2–1).

An important outcome of the Strategic Planning Project has been
that data administration receives increased attention to each Managing Committee member. The institutional responsibilities are as
follows:

- To identify, define, and review information systems proposals
  within the local (vice presidential) domain.
- To coordinate the planning, creation, and use of local and
  institutional data.
- As a member of IRAC, to participate in the formulation of
  policies, procedures, and standards for data administration and
  information resource acquisition (hardware, software, services).
- To evaluate local information systems project performance and
  compliance with global policies procedures, and standards.

Each data administrator has additional local responsibilities, as
assigned and required by the local vice presidency. In summary, the
IRM strategy confirms the concept of multiple data administrators
within user organizations, as well as the need for a Bank-wide or
institutional data administrator to coordinate shared data.

Information Resource Advisory Committee

The IRM strategy recommended improvements to the IRM advisory
structure. In the case of the Bank, IRAC was improved by reconstitut-
ing the network of advisory groups into a system of subcommittees of
IRAC, which in turn would oversee some of the informal user groups.

FIGURE A2–1
The World Bank Institutional Information Architecture

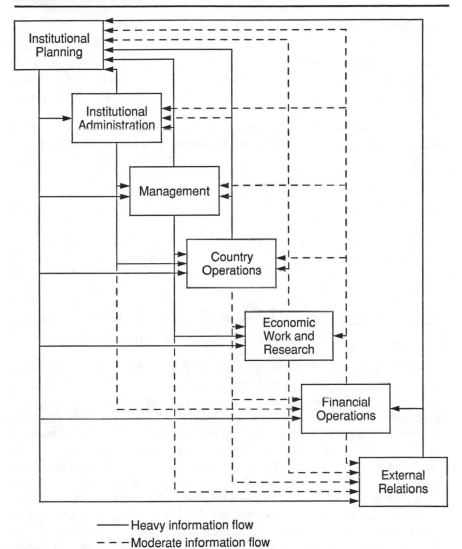

——— Heavy information flow
– – – Moderate information flow

Only when each major Bank organizational entity is uniformly represented on IRAC does the appropriate forum exist to discuss IRM issues.

Governance

The IRM strategy requires a system of governance to document the decision-making process by indicating who is involved in a decision, when, and with what authority. The governance system defines what a policy is, what a procedure is, and what a standard is.

The administrative procedures allow any staff member to propose a Bank-wide policy, procedure, or standard. The proposal is reviewed by the local data administrator. The drafting process is the responsibility of the IRMD Planning and Policy Unit. This unit acts as an agent for the originator and appoints a technical consultant to help with the drafting of the policy, procedure, or standard. The draft policy, procedure, or standard is reviewed by all concerned managers and their comments are reflected in the draft. Once a majority of the data administrators and their staff are satisfied, IRAC formally accepts the policy, procedure, or standard. Users who feel that they have valid grounds for non-compliance may go through their data administrators and apply for a waiver from the policy, procedure, or standard. This waiver process is also handled by the Planning and Policy Unit and, if routine, approved by the Director of IRMD; otherwise, requests for waivers go to IRAC for consideration.

The concept that the management of the information resource is primarily the responsibility of the user has not been meaningful in many cases, since most users feel very removed from the process of managing data. This problem was addressed by the Office Systems Planning phase of the Strategic Planning Project, which recommended that ultimately every staff member have available, through a personal workstation, at least a minimum set of office system function. The workstation will provide the common link to internal and external data resources and the tools through which staff can turn data into the value-added product called "information," the product necessary to make the decisions supporting the Bank's business functions. These workstations are to be modular in design to facilitate adding or deleting functional components as different changing work patterns dictate. The basic workstation will be intelligent: that is, it will have the capability to store and manipulate information locally with no inherent need to rely on central computing facilities, except for those functions done centrally with greater economy or timeliness.

The workstation is part of the IRM infrastructure, and just as all staff are currently provided desks and telephones, the IRM strategy states that in the future they will receive the appropriate workstation. However, initially, the workstation will have a much greater impact than the telephone, since it requires much greater support. Networks, wiring of buildings, and office furnishings are some of the physical aspects of workstation support, while staff training and education, effective work organization, and procedures are some of the human aspects of the support. Installing over 6,000 workstations and phasing out over 1,000 existing non-compatible office automation products demonstrate the need for the concept of the Information Utility in order to achieve the desired level of information technology compatibility.

INSTITUTIONAL IMPACT OF THE IRM STRATEGY

Senior Management

The IRM concept has the most apparent impact on Bank senior management. Less than six months after the IRM concept was in place, senior management approved a Strategic Planning Project and participated in the Information Systems Planning process. Soon thereafter, they were presented the results of the Information Systems Planning and Office Systems Planning Studies and then, three months later, they approved the IRM strategy.

This series of activities has required their time, increased their awareness of the problems of information management, educated them about causes and possible solutions for those problems, and raised their expectations for positive action toward solving those problems. It is clear the IRM strategy has top management attention and support.

Line Managers

During the early days of any new, organization-wide concept, it is only natural that line managers are somewhat skeptical. Many ongoing information system projects have not changed character since the announcement of the IRM concept. The role and responsibilities of the new data administrator positions across the Bank were difficult to communicate and implement; therefore, some projects for which the managers had high expectations have been held up because the data administrators have not agreed with the technical skills.

Specifications or Proposed Methods of Implementing Local Systems

The IRM strategy requires that management of the Bank's information resources is primarily the responsibility of the user community. There is mixed enthusiasm about this new responsibility during the transition to the IRM concept.

The IRM strategy provides three efforts to help user managers. First, providing each staff member with a workstation will place the tools to manage information resources in the hands of the user community. Second, a Bank-wide staff development program will educate Bank managers regarding potential uses of information technology and will teach the managers to use these tools. Third, IRM skilled staff will be available to the line managers so that managers can plan and acquire the information resources that their organization requires. These IRM professionals work in the user community as part of the user staff on a rotation basis. They have an occasional assignment in IRMD to refresh their IRM skills, and then return to a different job in the user community.

Bank Staff

Clearly, one of the main themes of the Bank's IRM strategy is to place information processing technology and ready access to data in the offices of individual bank staff. Today, staff members seem to accept information technology due to their exposure to word processing or the recent popularity of personal computers.

A major up-front IRM education initiative is required for all levels of staff. The education issues go well beyond merely acquainting staff with an understanding of technology to develop specific technical skills (e.g., word processing, programming). Bank staff are gaining an understanding of how the infusion of technology into the workplace affects people's jobs, health, and work relationships. Consequently, the success of the IRM strategy is dependent not only on how effectively the projects are implemented, but also on how well people understand their relationship to technology.

CONCLUSION

The Information Resource Management Strategic Planning Project has been one of the most pervasive intra-Bank planning efforts to date. The IRM strategy defines the institutional information resources environment the Bank needs to support its business objectives and processes, a goal to which the Bank will evolve through the 1980's and early into the next decade. To achieve this goal requires increased user participation and institutional control of the management and development of information resources, implying that managers' choices must be limited to those which are congruent with the strategy. The IRM strategy affects all segments of the institution and has major dependencies on the absorptive capacity of the Bank's human resources, physical facilities, and organizational potential. An important role for senior management is to regulate the pace and degree of change emanating from this initiative and other institutional initiatives.

The Bank made a major decision in 1981 when it adopted the IRM concept. After two years, we believe it was the correct move. We are making a few modifications to our method of implementation, but we are not changing the fundamental concept. We knew that our previous organization could not take advantage of the rapid advances in information management technology, and we think our new organization can. We did not have control of our information resources in 1981, but in 1984 we can see substantial progress toward that goal. We conclude, then, that the IRM strategy is integral to the future of the World Bank, and that the IRM concept is working.

ENDNOTE

1. This appendix was originally published by the Institute for Information Management in the *Information Executive,* volume 1, number 2 (1984). It is included in this book with the permission of Mel Ray and the Institute for Information Management. Mr. Ray was the CEO of The World Bank from 1982 to 1986. He currently is Group Sales Executive Director at the Digital Equipment Corporation.

APPENDIX 3

ABOUT THE INFORMATION GROUP

The Information Group, Inc., was founded in 1985. Since that time, it has grown from a concept on paper to an internationally recognized management consulting and education firm, and a forum for the interchange of ideas on how to apply information and information technology to achieve business success.

The firm has gained a reputation for its results-oriented assistance to senior information, financial, marketing, and operating executives. The firm's clients include executives representing such diverse industries as telecommunications and computers, chemicals and petroleum products, financial services, transportation, insurance, pharmaceuticals, distribution, manufacturing, and construction.

Geographically, the firm's principal clients span the North American continent, Europe, and Asia.

Our ongoing objective is to help prepare client firms and executives for a new business era—one in which a completely new frame of reference is essential to financial success. This new frame of mind comes from a thorough understanding of the company's stakeholders relationships and how information technology can improve them.

GLOSSARY

assumptions a set of presumed, unsubstantiated facts. Because of unexpected situations that continually arise, assumptions are often discovered to be incorrect. When assumptions are no longer valid, the plan using these assumptions may also be invalid.

asset property owned by a corporation with identifiable value.

chief information officer (CIO) the executive responsible for the functioning and security of the corporation's investment in information and information technology.

corporate imperatives actions that must be successfully completed by a corporation in order for it to meet its goals and objectives.

culture the integrated pattern of human behavior within a corporation that is based on a set of common beliefs and values. The reward systems reinforce the values.

database data in a collective and electronic form used to support the running of multiple-production computer systems.

data processing the use of computers to run production applications for the business such as general ledger, payroll, accounts payable, order entry, inventory, and customer billing and receivable systems.

driving force one of nine major strategic areas that defines the essence of a company. By selecting one overall strategic area as the driving force, a clear priority is communicated to all functional areas of the organization, which results in unity of action.

Executive Information Systems an information-based tool that allows executives to access and analyze company information for decision making.

expense a cost of business that is absorbed in the current period as contrasted with being capitalized and amortized over future periods.

frontline company employees who have direct contact with a corporation's stakeholders, especially those on the demand side.

global economy the reality that national and regional economies no longer exist as independent structures and that there is a worldwide framework of interactions and interdependencies both within and between national and regional economies.

industrial age the period of time characterized by urbanization of people, the use of semiskilled workers in large, repetitive production processes, and adversarial stakeholder roles.

information age the current period of time characterized by the conversion of physical and production work to information work, the suburbanization of people, and cooperative stakeholder roles.

information base information in electronic form for use in analysis and decision making.

information resource management the management process for managing information as an asset. This parallels the process of the treasurer's and controller's functions. Treasurers and controllers deal with money. IRM executives deal with information.

information technology uses of computers, telecommunications, and office equipment to create, store, process, and transmit data and information.

infrastructure the arrangement of plant, facilities, human organizations, distribution mechanisms, and information and telecommunications systems.

mainframe computers large computers usually used in centralized data-processing or information-base facilities.

market an organization's current and potential customers as well as its current and potential competitors.

mission the underlying task that a function is organized to fulfill. The task(s) must support the corporate driving force. They should be stated in broad terms of how the organization will fulfill the relationships defined in the organizing principle. Equivalent to the mission statement are the functional organization's purpose or charter.

organizing principle the agreement and assent to the relationship under which an organization is formed, resulting in unity of purpose. For an organization to exist, it must have agreement and assent from all the parties that will be involved in the organization. These include the investors, customers, employees, management, suppliers, regulators, and the community.

personal computers (PC's) desktop computers or workstations used by information workers to manipulate information and data. At present, PC's have limited storage capability as compared to mainframe computers.

project management a process used to coordinate and manage the undertaking of large, technically oriented construction ventures, which includes engineering, construction, cost management, quality management, scheduling completion times, delivery of the completed project, and post-delivery maintenance and repair.

productivity a measure of output divided by input. If the result is greater than one, productivity is positive. In this book, *productivity* is used to describe the increases in the ratio as a result of effective application of information technology.

return on investment (ROI) a general measure of return from a venture or investment divided by either the assets employed or equity.

reward systems the process by which people are recognized and paid for achieving the work they are assigned.

stakeholder people, groups, and other entities that have a vested interest in the success of the corporation.

strategy the science and art of directing corporate resources and relationships toward gaining a competitive advantage. Corporate resources include capital, people, and information. Relationships include the parties to an organizing principle, such as customers, suppliers, employees, investors, regulators, and the community.

telecommunications electronic means for transferring information from one point to another.

utility a service provided by a facility whose costs are borne by its users.

value added the identifiable value tied to a service or product that allows a business to charge more for its products and services than their primary purchase costs.

BIBLIOGRAPHY

Aaker, David A. *Developing Business Strategies*. New York: John Wiley & Sons, 1984.

Adams, John D. *Transforming Leadership*. Alexandria, Va.: Miles River Press, 1986.

Bender, Paul S. *Resource Management*. New York: John Wiley & Sons, 1983.

Bennis, Warren, and Burt Nanus. *Leaders: The Strategies for Taking Charge*. New York: Harper & Row 1985.

Burk, Cornelius F., and Forest W. Horton. *InfoMap*. Englewood Cliffs, N.J., 1988. Prentice-Hall.

Byars, Lloyd L. *Concepts of Strategic Management*. New York: Harper & Row, 1984.

Carlzon, Jan. *Moments of Truth*. Cambridge, Mass.: Balinger, 1987.

Capra, Fritjof. *The Turning Point*. New York: Bantam, 1983.

Deal, Terrence E., and Allan A. Kennedy. *Corporate Cultures*. Reading, Mass.: Addison-Wessley, 1981.

Drucker, Peter F. *Management*. New York: Harper & Row, 1974.

Drucker, Peter F. *Managing in Turbulent Times*. New York: Harper & Row, 1985.

_____. "Goodbye to the Old Personnel Department." *Wall Street Journal*, May 22, 1986.

Employment & Earnings, U.S. Department of Labor, Bureau of Labor Statistics, Washington, D.C. January 1989.

Gibson, Cyrus F., and Barbara Bund Jackson. *The Information Imperative*. Lexington, Mass.: Lexington Books, 1987.

Guth, William D., ed. *Handbook of Business Strategy*. Boston, Mass.: Warren, Gorham & Lamont, 1985.

_____., *Handbook of Business Strategy: 1986/1987 Yearbook*. Boston, Mass.: Warren, Gorham & Lamont, 1987.

Harvard Business Review. *Strategic Management*. New York: John Wiley & Sons, 1983.

Hawken, Paul. *The Next Economy*. New York: Holt, Rinehart, and Winston, 1983.

Hayes, Robert H., and Steven C. Wheelright. *Restoring Our Competitive Edge*. New York: John Wiley & Sons, 1984.

Hickman, Craig R., and Michael A. Silva. *Creating Excellence*. New York: The New American Library, 1984.

Imai, Masaaki. *Kaizen: The Key to Japan's Competitive Success*. New York: Random House, 1986.

Johnson, H. Thomas, and Robert S. Kaplan. *Relevance Lost: The Rise and Fall of Management Accounting*. Boston, Mass.: Harvard Business School Press, 1987.

Kilman, Ralph H. *Beyond the Quick Fix*. San Francisco, Calif.: Jossey-Bass, 1984.

Lawler III, Edward E. *Job Evaluation: A Critique*. Center for Effective Organizations, Graduate School of Business Administration, University of Southern California, Publication G85–7 (73). (1985).

Loveman, Gary W. "An Assessment of the Productivity Impact of Information Technologies." Working Paper 90s:88–054, Management in the 1990's, Massachusetts Institute of Technology, Sloan School of Management, July 1988.

Marchand, Donald A., and Forest W. Horton. *Infotrends*. New York: John Wiley & Sons, 1986.

Masuda, Yoneji. *The Information Society*. Bethesda, Md.: World Future Society, 1981.

Mendelow, Aubrey L. "Stakeholder Analysis for Strategic Planning and Implementation." In *Strategic Planning and Management Handbook*, ed. William R. King and David I. Cleland: New York. Van Nostrand Reinhold, 1983.

Musashi, Miyamoto. *A Book of Five Rings*. 1645. Woodstock, N.Y.: The Overlook Press, 1974.

Naisbitt, John. *Megatrends*. New York: Warner Books, 1982.

Naisbitt, John, and Patricia Aburdene. *Re-Inventing the Corporation*. New York Warner Books, 1985.

Naylor, Thomas N. *Strategic Planning Management*. Oxford, Ohio: Planning Executives Institute, 1980.

Nissan Motor Company. *The Dawns of Tradition*. 1983.

Ohmae, Kenichi. *The Mind of the Strategist*. New York: Penguin, 1983.

Ouchi, William. *Theory Z*. Reading, Mass.: Addison-Wessley, 1981.

Parker, Marilyn M., and Robert J. Benson. *Information Economics: Linking Business Performance to Information Technology*. Englewood Cliffs, N.J.: Prentice-Hall, 1988

Perspectives on Information Management. New York: John Wiley & sons, 1982. Compiled and edited by Jack B. Rochester, Senior Editor, *Computerworld.*

Peters, Thomas J. *Thriving on Chaos.* New York: Alfred A. Knopf, 1987.

Peters, Thomas J., and Nancy Austin. *A Passion for Excellence.* New York: Warner Books, 1985.

Peters, Thomas J., and Robert H. Waterman. *In Search of Excellence.* New York: Harper & Row, 1982.

Pfeiffer, John E., *The Emergence of Society: a Prehistory of the Establishment.* New York: McGraw-Hill Book Company, 1977.

Porter, Michael E. *Competitive Strategy.* New York: The Free Press, 1980.

————. *Competitive Advantage.* New York: The Free Press, 1985.

————. "From Competitive Advantage to Corporate Strategy." *Harvard Business Review,* May–June 1987, Vol. 65, No. 3, pp. 43–59.

Rabin, Jack, and Edward M. Jackowski, eds. *Handbook of Information Resource Management.* New York: Marcel Dekker, 1988.

Rappaport, Alfred. *Creating Shareholder Value: The New Standard for Business Performance.* New York: The Free Press, 1986.

Ries, Al, and Jack Trout. *Positioning: The Battle for Your Mind.* New York: Warner Books, 1986.

Rockart, John. "Chief Executives Define Their Own Data Needs." *Harvard Business Review,* March–April 1979, 57, No. 2, pp. 81–93.

Rogers, Everett M. *Diffusion of Innovations.* 3d ed. New York: The Free Press, 1983.

Schein, Edgar H. *Organizational Culture and Leadership.* San Francisco, Calif.: Jossey-Bass, 1985.

Schumacher, E. F. *Small is Beautiful.* New York: Harper & Row, 1973.

Smith, Adam, *The Wealth of Nations.* New York: Penguin Books, (1982). First published 1776.

Strassmann, Paul A. *Information Payoff.* New York: The Free Press, 1985.

Sun Tzu. *The Art of War.* Ca. 500 B.C. ed. James Clavell. New York: Delacorte Press, 1983.

Terplan, Kornel. *Communication Networks Management.* Englewood Cliffs, N.J.: Prentice-Hall, 1987.

Tichy, Noel M., and Mary Anne Devanna. *The Transformational Leader.* New York: John Wiley & Sons, 1986.

Tregoe, Benjamin B., and John W. Zimmerman. *Top Management Strategy: What It Is and How to Make It Work.* New York: Simon & Schuster, 1980.

Waterman, Robert H. *The Renewal Factor.* New York: Bantam Books, 1987.

Wilcock, Kenneth D. *The Corporate Tribe.* New York: Warner Books, 1984.

INDEX